ACKNOWLEDGEMENTS

No endeavor as involved as publishing a book can be accomplished without the help of many people, and this is certainly true in the case of this volume. Since the editor cannot individually thank the many persons whose combined efforts produced this volume, he extends boundless thanks to all contributors, especially the teachers of Georgia history who participated in the summer seminars funded by the Georgia Endowment for the Humanities. As with most successful ventures, however, there are some individuals who deserve special mention. Among those, one of the most deserving is Dr. Ronald Benson, Executive Director of the Georgia Endowment for the Humanities, who was the driving force behind the GEH summer seminars and the guiding force behind the completion of this book. I would also like to express my gratitude to the Board of Directors of the Georgia Endowment for the Humanities, the directors of the three summer seminars, the scholars who contributed to the volume and the contributing editors: Dr. Charles Stephen Gurr, Gainesville Junior College; Dr. John Lupold, Columbus College; and Dr. Walter Fraser, Jr., Georgia Southern College.

I owe a particular debt of gratitude to those who did the typing of correspondence and manuscripts necessary to complete this publication. For their invaluable assistance, I extend a special thanks to my two secretaries, Mrs. Bennatta Caldwell and Ms. Jessie Daniels. Finally, I want to thank my wife, Flo, and my two sons, Deron and Toussaint, who had to endure the time that I spent away from them while seeing this volume into print.

J.L.H.

CONTENTS

PART I
SECONDARY SOURCES
FOR
TEACHING GEORGIA HISTORY

INTRODUCTION

R. FRANK SAUNDERS, JR.

Because the present is either so enriched or burdened by the past, Georgians are supposed to be keenly conscious of their history. Whether one chooses to accept or reject this premise, an impressive number of native Georgians have made significant contributions to the historiography of their state, region and nation. An honor roll of distinguished historians in this century might include, among others, the names of W.W. Abbott, John W. Blassingame, Dewey W. Grantham, Jr., Fletcher M. Green, Cecelia Kenyon, Ulrich B. Phillips, David M. Potter and Ann F. Scott. And if interest and number of publications are reliable indicators, then Georgia history apparently has become a reputable field of inquiry, for members of the Northeastern historical establisment no longer view it as a provincial wasteland in American historiography. The twin iniquities of slavery and secession, once considered anathema, now appear to enhance the mystique of Georgia history.

To attempt a general survey of Georgia historiography over the past 250 years is beyond the scope of this brief essay. Readers interested in the state of the art should consult the standard bibliographic guides, e.g., Ray Rowland and James Dorsey, compilers, *A Bibliography of the Writings on Georgia History* (1978) and John E. Simpson, compiler, *Georgia History: A Bibliography* (1976). A cursory review of the writings in Georgia history, however, will reveal that scholarship has been influenced by both the external pressures of contemporary events and the tensions within the historical profession, including changing frames of reference and new methodological approaches. This essay proposes to sketch the broad contours of this legacy by focusing on the contributions of a few historians whose works have expanded our knowledge of Georgia history and raised the standards of the craft; and without presuming to chart new directions for future scholars, it ventures a few suggestions for those who teach and write Georgia history.

Although some would contend that state and local history antedates national history, our state's history, like that of other states, was the product of the new nationalism that swept the country following the War of 1812. In some respects, the nineteenth century was the golden age of state history, and only since the national bicentennial celebration has it enjoyed greater popularity. During the first half of the last century, newly organized historical societies and subscription agents promoted state histories such as those compiled by Henry Howe and John W. Barber. J.B. Lippincott Company tried to capitalize on this interest by publishing cabinet histories of several states. Hugh McCall, a native North Carolinian, was the first to attempt a general history of Georgia. His two-volume *History of Georgia*, published in 1811 and 1816, covered events from the founding of the colony to the end of the Revolution. Since documentary sources were scarce, McCall relied on the memories of Revolutionary War veterans. Even though his work is flawed by inaccuracies, it is still a prized item of Georgiana.[1]

In 1839, some fifteen years after McCall's death, the Georgia Historical Society was founded in Savannah by Israel K. Tefft, Richard D. Arnold and William B. Stevens to "collect, preserve and diffuse information in relation to the history of the state of Georgia in all its various departments, and American history generally, and to create an historical library for the use of its members and others."[2] John M. Berrien was elected first president and William B. Stevens, first recording secretary. Stevens, a native of Maine, came to Georgia in the early 1830's and became interested in medicine. He studied locally, then at the Medical College of South Carolina and finished at Dartmouth in 1837. In 1841, he was commissioned by the Society to write a history of the state, a task that was made easier when the state officials had Georgia's colonial records in London copied for Stevens' use. His two-volume work, *A History of Georgia from Its First Discovery by Europeans to the Adoption of the Present Constitution in MDCCXCVIII* (1847 and 1859), was a scholarly study of the first sixty-five years of Georgia history. Subsequently, Stevens gave up his medical practice in Savannah and was ordained to the Episcopal priesthood. While serving as a missionary in Athens, he was elected to a professorship at the University of Georgia, but he left the state in 1848 to accept clerical duties in Philadelphia where he served until his death in 1887.[3]

Bacon's *History* remained the major study of Georgia history until after the Civil War. In 1883, Charles Colcock Jones, Jr., son of the Presbyterian clergyman Charles Colcock and Mary Jones of Liberty County, whose family letters have been published in Robert M. Myers' award-winning book, *The Children of Pride*, authored his two-volume *History of Georgia* that covers the aboriginal and colonial epochs through the American Revolution. Jones, a lawyer by profession, published more than eighty titles in Georgia history, many of which were based on original sources and carefully documented. George Bancroft, the most honored historian of the age, acclaimed Jones' *History* the best state history that he had ever read and referred to its author as the "Macaulay of the South." Two of his other major writings are *Antiquities of the Southern Indians* (1873) and *Negro Myths on the Georgia Coast Told in the Vernacular* (1888). Judged by modern standards, Jones' works appear hastily written, partisan and nostalgic; however, a fair evaluation requires an acknowledgement that Jones was not a professionally trained historian. Rather, history was his avocation. Several of his works, however, continue to have scholarly merit.[4]

Allen D. Candler, a contemporary of Jones, deserves inclusion as the first official compiler of state records. Although he is perhaps best remembered as a state legislator, congressman and two-term governor, Candler (the "one-eyed plow-boy of Pigeon Roost," Lumpkin County) coedited with William A. Evans *Georgia, Comprising Sketches of Counties, Towns, Events, Institutions, and Persons, Arranged in Cyclopedic Form in Three Volumes* (1906). By the time of his death in 1910, he had supervised the publication of twenty-one volumes of *The Colonial Records of Georgia* (1904-1910), three volumes of *The Revolutionary Records* (1908) and five of *The Confederate Records* (1909-1911).[5] In 1907-1908 Lucian L. Knight,

Associate Editor of the *Atlanta Georgian*, published his first major historical work, *Reminiscences of Famous Georgians.* Over the next several years, as compiler of state records, he was responsible for the printing of four volumes of *The Colonial Records of Georgia*, a two-volume work, *Georgia's Landmarks, Memorials, and Legends* (1913-1914) and six volumes of *A Standard History of Georgia and Georgians* (1917-1919). Knight won legislative approval to establish an official department of archives and history in 1918 and served as the first director of the agency until 1925.[6]

Undisputedly, Ellis Merton Coulter (1890-1981), a native North Carolinian who spent sixty-two years teaching and writing about his adopted state, is the "Dean of Georgia Historiography." He served as editor of the *Georgia Historical Quarterly* for fifty years, was the author of twenty-two books, co-author of four others, editor or coeditor of eleven more and author of 118 scholarly articles, not to mention numerous book reviews and articles that appeared in newspapers and encyclopedias. In 1933, he published *A Short History of Georgia* which was the standard history of the state and college textbook for the succeeding forty years. Among Coulter's books are ten biographies, including *William G. Brownlow; Fighting Parson of the Southern Highlands, James Monroe Smith; Georgia Planter* and *Thomas Spalding of Sapelo.* Perhaps his most popular book is *College Life in the Old South*, a thinly disguised history of the University of Georgia in the nineteenth century. In addition to his contributions to Georgia history, Coulter, a founder of the Southern Historical Association in 1934, was one of the foremost authorities on the South; he was coeditor of the prestigious *History of the South* series to which he contributed two volumes.[7]

Over the past three decades James C. Bonner and Kenneth Coleman have made major contributions to the writing of Georgia history. Bonner, a native of Heard County, was an authority on Georgia agriculture. From 1944 until his retirement in 1969, he was a professor of history at Georgia College. In addition to *A History of Georgia Agriculture 1732-1860*, he wrote *Studies in Georgia History and Government, Georgia's Last Frontier, The Development of Carroll County* and *Milledgeville, Georgia's Antebellum Capital.* His high school textbook, *The Georgia Story* (1958, 1961), remains the best of its kind. Bonner also wrote more than thirty scholarly articles and numerous reviews for journals and contributed eleven articles to *Encyclopedia Britannica,* including the section on Georgia. A gentleman and a scholar, Bonner continued to write in spite of failing health until his death in 1984.[8]

Kenneth Coleman, now retired after more than twenty years in the history department at the University of Georgia, is Georgia's most respected living historian. He is the author of seven books, including *The American Revolution in Georgia, Confederate Athens* and the special bicentennial volume, *Colonial Georgia: A History.* He is editor of three volumes in *The Colonial Records of Georgia* and coeditor of the *Dictionary of Georgia Biography.* Likewise, he has written more than a dozen scholarly articles and over seventy-five reviews.[9]

Obviously, there are numerous others, both amateurs and professionals, whose works have enriched the fabric of Georgia history. Some readers will likely question why certain writers were included and others excluded. Why not Robert Preston Brooks, Ulrich B. Phillips, Amanda Johnson or some of the productive contemporary historians? No attempt, however, has been made to include even the major studies devoted to the various periods, topics and personalities in Georgia history. Thus, with apologies to all who were slighted, let us turn to a few of the needs in Georgia historiography addressed by a select group of scholars and teachers who participated in the summer institutes on Georgia history held at Columbus College, Georgia Southern College and Georgia Southwestern College during the summer of 1983.

Georgia history has long been taught and written chronologically, with major emphasis given to political, constitutional and economic developments. Often it has been a story that focused on the lives of elites who controlled the power structure and dictated the norms of the dominant culture. The nondominant and inarticulate groups — sharecroppers, lintheads, women and blacks — were written off as either inaccessible or unimportant. The essays selected for this volume, however, present a broader characterization of the past by focusing on the social and cultural life of all Georgians, elites and common folk. They extend the relevant range of historical causation to include some of the tenets of the "new social history" and the quantitative revolution without abandoning the framework of traditional history. The reciprocal interchange between elitists and client groups is a unifying theme in the essays. How did the lives of black and white common folk who picked the cotton, sawed the timber, dipped the tar and washed the clothes interact with the lives of planters, merchants, industrialists and politicos?

Kenneth Coleman's keynote essay portrays colonial Georgia as a land of opportunity, an open class system for free whites who had ability, a willingness to work and a little luck. Although only a few families such as the Houstons, Habershams and Joneses rose to the top socially and economically, most whites who remained in the colony made moderate gains. Professors Roger Branch and Richard Persico continue the study of class, caste and conflict beyond the colonial era in the present. Multiple images of stratification emerge both in Indian-white relations until the removal of the Georgia tribes and between whites and blacks under slavery and Jim Crowism.

Developing a sense of place as the dominant theme in Georgia literature, Hollis Cate provides an overview of the literary works of Georgia authors. The homespun humor of Augustus Baldwin Longstreet, the poetry of Sydney Lanier, the gothic short stories of Flannery O'Connor, the Pulitzer award-winning novels of Caroline Miller and Margaret Mitchell as well as those by Erskine Caldwell and Carson McCullers draw upon folk culture and history, the enduring struggle for survival and love of the land. In a related genre, Delma Presley discusses Georgia folklore, the natural language of the people. Presley reminds us that folklore, considered by many a dying idiom in the wake of mass culture and technological change, contains much for teachers and scholars to study, and he calls upon them to preserve the old sayings, place names, games, recipes, crafts, architecture, home remedies, stories, songs and music that have been passed from one generation to the next. He concludes his paper with an interesting discussion of how the "Georgia cracker" got his name.

Wayne Flynt's essay on the Southern Baptists in Georgia sketches the general patterns of Baptist life during the formative years. A major influence in shaping the course of the denomination, the Georgia tradition emanated from Augusta and Atlanta. Jesse Mercer, William B. Johnson, Henry H. Tucker, and I.T. Tichenor, personalities seldom encountered by laymen, each represented a major source of Southern Baptist thought. Flynt concludes that the Georgia heritage reaches far beyond the boundaries of the state; its legacy helped form the largest Protestant denomination in America and launch it on a course of religious moderation.

The recreational activities and pastimes of Georgia common folk are at best given summary treatment in most studies on Georgia history. Charlton Moseley returns to the simpler lifestyles of the colonial and frontier periods and describes the ball games, music and dances of the Georgia Indians; the barn-raising, shucking bees and quilting parties enjoyed by the poor folk and yeomanry; and the recreational activities of the slave quarters. He is most graphic in portraying the activities of frontier whites who engaged in "gouging matches" and enjoyed gander pullings.

Gilbert Fite, author of the scholarly new monograph *Cotton Fields No More*, examines the changes that occurred in Georgia agriculture during the decades from 1865 to the present. In many ways a microcosm of Southern agriculture, Georgia agriculture was beset by woes caused by too many marginal farmers, a one-crop system, overproduction of cotton, a vicious system of credit and backward technology. In the mid-1930's, however, a virtual agricultural revolution based on mechanization, diversification and scientific practices changed the old system drastically. Fite not only analyzes the problems of Georgia agriculture; he explains better than anyone else why the old patterns persisted so long. Many of the former sharecroppers who were driven from the land during the postwar decades found employment in textile mills. Leslie Hough discusses the ill-fated struggle of some workers to improve their wages and working conditions through unionism, concluding that Georgia workers generally had little interest in unionism. When they did attempt to organize, their efforts were thwarted by violence, hostile employers and politicians, racism, division within their own ranks and an antagonistic press.

A. Elizabeth Taylor and Charlotte Ford remind us anew that we should not forget the Georgia ladies. Taylor's essay recounts the frustrations of Georgia women in their heroic struggle to win the vote. Beginning in the late nineteenth century, Augusta Howard organized the Georgia Woman Suffrage Association, an affiliate of the National American Woman Suffrage Association. Even though the Georgia association never had a large membership, it kept woman suffrage before the Georgia voters for several decades. Each year from 1914 to 1917, the Georgia legislature rejected a resolution to enfranchise women; the Anthony Amendment was also turned down in 1919 and 1920. Even though the Nineteenth Amendment

8

was proclaimed part of the national constitution in 1921, Georgia did not officially adopt it until 1970. Ford's essay, the product of several years of research on Georgia women, provides a needed bibliographical guide along with several biographical sketches of Georgia women who dared to challenge stereotypical roles defined by gender. Any student of women's history will find Ford's essay useful.

These essays are dedicated to the teachers and students of Georgia history in whose hands our future lies. It is our sincere wish that these resources will in some way enrich, and perhaps improve, the learning experiences of those Georgians who would know more about their heritage.

NOTES

[1] For discussion of Georgia historians of nineteenth century, see Ellis Merton Coulter, "The Early Historians of Georgia," *Georgia Historical Quarterly*, 31 (September, 1947), 191-94. Anthony R. Dees, "Hugh McCall" in Kenneth Coleman and Charles S. Gurr, eds., *Dictionary of Georgia Biography* (Athens: University of Georgia Press, 1983), 2:650; hereafter cited *DGB*.

[2] Albert S. Britt, Jr., *Overture to the Future at the Georgia Historical Society* (Savannah: Georgia Historical Society, 1974), p. 1. The Society is among the oldest in the South. Virginia preceded in the establishment of a state historical society in 1831. South Carolina founded a state society in 1855. The *Georgia Historical Quarterly* was started in 1917.

[3] Ellis Merton Coulter, "William Bacon Stevens: Physician, Historian, Teacher, Preacher," *Georgia Review*, 2 (1948), 221-34; Steve Gurr, "William Bacon Stevens," *DGB*, 2:932-33.

[4] James C. Bonner, "Charles Colcock Jones: The Macaulay of the South," *Georgia Historical Quarterly*, 27 (December, 1943), 324-38; Michael M. Cass, "Charles Colcock Jones, Jr.," *DGB*, 1:546-47.

[5] Theodore H. Jack, "The Preservation of Georgia History," *North Carolina Historical Review*, 9 (July, 1927), 239-251; Elizabeth H. Marshall, "Allen Daniel Candler," *DGB*, 1:162-63.

[6] Paul Ellington, "Lucian Lamar Knight," *DGB*, 2:583-84.

[7]Michael V. Woodward, "The Publications of Ellis Merton Coulter to 1 July 1977," *Georgia Historical Quarterly*, 61 (Fall, 1977), 268-78; and "Ellis Merton Coulter: The Late Dean of Georgia Historians," *Atlanta Historical Journal*, 27 (Summer, 1983), 55-70; Albert B. Saye, "A Tribute to Ellis Merton Coulter," *Georgia Historical Quarterly*, 55 (Fall, 1981), 183-88; Valerie G. Lerda, "Ellis Merton Coulter: A Personal Tribute," *Georgia Historical Quarterly*, 55 (Winter, 1981), 307-15. Phinizy Spalding, "Ellis Merton Coulter," *Georgia Historical Quarterly*, 65 (Spring, 1981).

[8]William I. Hair, "James C. Bonner, Obituary," *Georgia Historical Quarterly*, 68 (Spring, 1984), 145. "Noted Milledgeville Historian Dies at 79," *The Union-Recorder*, January 24, 1984.

[9]Phinizy Spalding, "Introduction," *Georgia Historical Quarterly*, 60 (Fall, 1976), 205-10; Royce C. McCrary, "The Publications of Kenneth Coleman to 1 September 1976," *Georgia Historical Quarterly*, 60 (Fall, 1976), 282-86.

ELITES AND COMMON FOLK
IN COLONIAL GEORGIA

KENNETH COLEMAN

There is an old saying that the eighteenth century was a century of aristocracy, the nineteenth century a century of the middle class, and the twentieth century a century of the common man. As this saying implies, people in the eighteenth century generally took class structure for granted and endeavored to serve "in that station to which God has called them," as the Book of Common Prayer phrased it, unless they were able to rise to a higher station.

This essay focuses, however, on the European part of Georgia's population, and since there is some question that the term aristocracy applies to an area so recently settled by Europeans, the terms lower class, middle class and upper class are used for Colonial Georgia. The American Indians were usually considered outside the colony's society, and Negro slaves were the lowest class in Georgia, most of them coming directly from Africa. This discussion of class structure in Georgia, therefore, is from the eighteenth century Georgia viewpoint, not that of the older and more affluent colonies nor of Europe.

Georgia was planned as a colony to help unfortunate common folk, but the Georgia Trustees never envisioned a colony in which the colonists would not be common people. In this regard, the Trustees never got beyond their concept at the founding of the colony. The unfortunate poor originally brought to Georgia on charity (at the Trustees' expense) were not the lowest class in the English society of the day. Few, if any, of them were common laborers from either the countryside or cities. Most of them were lower middle-class, small artisans or shopkeepers who had experienced economic misfortune and were to be given a new chance in Georgia. As the Trustees expressed it, they would take "such as were in decayed Circumstances, and thereby disabled from following any Business in England; ...."[1] The people to be received would be "of reputable families and of liberal or at least, easy education; some undone by guardians, some by law suits, some by

11

accidents in commerce, some by stocks and bubbles, and some by suretyship .... These are the people that may relieve themselves and strengthen Georgia by resorting thither, and Great Britain by their departure."[2]

Among the passengers on the *Ann* who settled Savannah in February, 1733, there were only two who could be called upper class: James Edward Oglethorpe and the Reverend Henry Herbert. Herbert, the volunteer minister to Georgia, was the son of an English lord and remained in Georgia only briefly, dying at sea on June 15, 1733 on his return to England because of illness.[3] Oglethorpe was the son of Sir Theophilus Oglethorpe, knighted by James II in 1685 and definitely English upper class. James Edward always showed his upper class status by dominating everything in Georgia that he wanted to during the first ten years of the colony's life, a good part of which he spent in Georgia.[4]

The only titled nobleman to come to Colonial Georgia as a resident was Sir Francis Bathurst, a baronet who arrived on December 28, 1734 and who died on December 19, 1736, having already lost two wives and one daughter in Georgia. Sir Francis was an impecunious gentleman who came with money borrowed from his brother, Lord Bathurst, and who had little success in regaining his fortune in Georgia, as his servants either died or ran away before they could be of much use to him.[5]

Georgia's other titled nobleman during the Trustee Period was Patrick Houstoun, who came to Georgia in 1734 before he inherited his title. He was one of seven Lowland Scottish gentlemen who arrived by 1737, the group consisting of Patrick Tailfer, Hugh and William Sterling, Andrew Grant, Hugh Anderson, David Douglass and Houstoun. They all brought indentured servants with them and were given gentlemen's grants on the Ogeechee River. It was from this group that the leaders of those opponents to Trustee policy, known as malcontents, came. Most of them left during the malcontent troubles led by Tailfer, but Houstoun remained in Georgia for the rest of his life.[6] More about Houstoun and his family will be presented later.

Among the 114 passengers who came on the *Ann*, the following occupations or skills were set down in the passenger list: silkman, potashmaker, trader of goods, calender and carpenter, 9 servants, 2 peruke makers, callicoe printer, merchant, taylor, clothworker, miller and baker, writer, surgeon, gardner, turner (woodworker), understands framing, 2 carpenters and joyners, upholsterer, basketmaker, cyder trade and understands writing and accounts, carpenter, understands flax and hemp, sawyer, heelmaker and understands carpenter's work, husbandman, cordwainer, reduced military officer, stockingmaker and can draw and reel silk, apothecary, understands vines, flax and hemp dresser, mercer (dealer in textiles), smith, sawyer, vinter, wheelright, silk throwster and bred at sea.[7] These occupations represented a good cross section of later arrivals as well. Many of the occupations, however, would not be needed soon in Georgia, for the great majority of the early settlers were supposed to make their living by farming their fifty-acre land grants.

The original settlers were English, and the English continued to arrive throughout the Trustee Period as charity colonists and people who paid their own way. Records of the first decade of Georgia's settlers are preserved in *A List of the Early Settlers of Georgia* (Athens, 1949),[8] and the list shows between 1700 and 1850 charity colonists, of whom slightly over 1000 were English. There were 92 known Jews, over 100 Lowland Scots, several hundred Highland Scots and less than 300 Germans. Slightly over 1000 colonists (almost entirely English and scots) are known to have come at their own expense — obviously they were better off economically than those who came on charity.[9] From the beginning, there was some exchange of settlers — both ways — between Georgia and South Carolina, but by 1738 the Trustees had generally stopped sending charity colonists, as many of the original ones had not succeeded. Thereafter, the Trustees sent over indentured servants who were sold to the colonists or worked on Trustee projects in Georgia.[10]

The original groups, which contained a substantial number of rural people, were the Highland Scots (farmers and farm laborers) and Salzburgers (many of whom were peasants). Initially, the Salzburgers seem to have made the most satisfactory farmers, probably because they were used to this type of work in Europe. There were a few Highland Scots listed as gentlemen, but most of them were servants — undoubtedly agricultural workers. The Mackays and McIntoshs were the leaders and the highest ranked of the Highland Scots.[11]

The highest class in Trustee Georgia tended to be political leaders and clergymen. Other than Oglethorpe, the next most important political leader was William Stephens who came as

"Secretary for the Affairs of the Trust within the Province of Georgia" from 1737 to 1750 and who was President of Georgia, 1741-1750. Stephens' father, Sir William Stephens, was the Lieutenant Governor of the Isle of Wight. Young Stephens received a degree from King's College, Cambridge, and from 1702 to 1722 was a member of the House of Commons. He was unsuccessful in business undertakings, and by the 1720's, was badly in debt and had lost his seat in Parliament. However, he was definitely upper-class in England and in Georgia.[12]

Interestingly, the highest ranked person and undisputed leader among the Salzburgers was not a Salzburger. He was the Reverend John Martin Bolzius, the pastor who only met his parishioners when they were on their way to Georgia and became the dominant secular and religious leader among the Salzburgers. He arrived in Georgia in March, 1734 and died at Ebenezer in November, 1765, long after the Salzburgers had succeeded in their new environment.[13]

Two other ministers in Colonial Georgia were important upper-class leaders. Bartholomew Zouberbuhler, a Swiss, was the Anglican rector of Christ Church Parish (Savannah), 1746-1766. Anglicanism prospered under him as under no other clergyman in Colonial Georgia. He was a respected leader and clergyman who was a very successful planter and who left funds in his will to employ a catechist to instruct Negro slaves in Georgia in the Christian religion.[14]

John Joachim Zubley, also Swiss, lived and worked in Georgia and South Carolina from 1745 to 1758 when he moved to Savannah permanently. As minister of the Independent Meetinghouse (now Independent Presbyterian Church), he led his congregation well and became the guardian of dissenters in Georgia. Both Zouberbuhler and Zubley preached in English, German and French as the need arose. A man of considerable intellectual ability, Zubley probably had the largest library in Colonial Georgia. He was a planter of considerable wealth, and he became a Whig leader in the pre-Revolutionary decade (1765-1775), serving in both the Provincial Congress in Georgia and the Continental Congress in Philadelphia. He favored colonial rights within the empire but opposed independence. Hence, his property was confiscated and he was banished from Georgia. He came back to Georgia in 1779 after the British return, and he died in Savannah in 1781, still praying for his king (George III) and his country (America).[15]

The majority of the settlers arriving in the Trustee Period were lower middle-class artisans. Some of these succeeded as farmers, but in England their class looked down on agricultural labor and laborers. Perhaps this may explain why they often did not succeed as farmers in Georgia and why a number of them abandoned their farm lots for some type of work in Savannah or left the colony.

Most of the people who came as indentured servants — the lowest class in the colony originally — we know less about. Their occupations were generally not given in the *List of Early Settlers*, and many disappeared from the records after their arrival in Georgia was noted. Many of them ran away, probably to South Carolina or some other colony, and thus disappeared from the Georgia records. Most of these were undoubtedly of the laboring class in Europe rather than lower middle class. Although some of them show up in the land records of the Trustee and the Royal Periods, proving their success in Georgia, many disappeared without a trace.

Most of the early settlers in Georgia hoped to improve their lot, but often they did not succeed. It was soon discovered that many who had been useless in England were equally useless in Georgia. Even for more industrious people, the difficulties of a new colony were considerable. Lands had to be cleared and cultivated, and this frequently required more capital, strength and know-how than the ordinary settlers possessed. Nobody realized at first how difficult it was to carve farms from the wilderness which would support their owners, especially since the farm lots were assigned on contiguous lands as a part of Oglethorpe's military plan. Much land on coastal Georgia did not lend itself easily, if at all, to profitable cultivation.[16]

Skidaway Island, one of the outsettlements to guard all possible approaches to Savannah, illustrates the difficulties of early settlers very well. In January of 1734, Skidaway was settled by five families and six single men who were supposed to clear land to farm, support themselves and guard the river at the northern end of the island from a guardhouse where a boat with sail and oars was stationed in case of alarm. In January, 1735, Thomas Mouse, a clogmaker who had been in the colony a year and who had a wife named Lucy and five daughters, reported to Oglethorpe that a good beginning had been made there in clearing land and farming. But by 1740, the island was abandoned by all of its settlers, some of whom had died and others of whom had gone to Savannah or elsewhere because they could not support themselves on Skidaway. As William Ewen wrote to the Trustees in December, 1740, "I have now: almost broak my Constitution; with hard working and hard Liveing and could not see any prospect; of any return of my Labour; now I am Obliged to leave my Settlement (tho, much against my Inclination) and Skidaway; without Inhabitants." He went to Savannah where Lucy acted as a midwife and took in sewing. Thomas was employed at Bethesda; and two of their children, Mary and Lucy, were admitted there, providing evidence that their parents could not support them. Thomas died August 17, 1742, but Lucy apparently lived a considerable time longer — just how long the records do not indicate, but probably into the 1760's.[17]

The 1730's and 1740's were hard years for most settlers in Georgia. By the 1750's, however, things were beginning to change. Many had died or left, but most of those who remained had learned what it took to get along in the colony. The Spanish danger, so obvious in the years 1739-1744, was gone, and the Trustees had lost much of their early interest in Georgia and now ignored many of their regulations. Worthy poor people were beginning to rise in the colony, either as farmers or as town dwellers. Few were wealthy, but many lived comfortably.[18] Additionally, by the 1750's, plantations had begun to grow up in Georgia through inheritance of land, marriage, etc. Slavery helped their growth, and with such plantations came more wealth and more upper-class people. Now that the Spanish danger seemed over, a new rush to Georgia began. Most of the settlers came from the colonies to the north rather than direct from Europe as in the Trustee era. Georgia offered the best land available in the Southern Piedmont since most of that in the Carolinas was already taken up. Many of those who came to Georgia were the typical poor frontiersmen, but others were more substantial farmers, with some of them bringing a few slaves with them.[19]

Augusta, originally an Indian trading town, became more a farm supply and market town as time went on, especially after the Indian cession of 1773. Word of the proposed cession, however, got out before it was made by the Indians. In August, 1772, Acting Governor James Habersham wrote to Governor James Wright in England that many were waiting to settle on the lands once they were available, and some were already living on them with no authority. He said the intruders were people of no settled habitation who made their living by hunting and plundering the industrious settlers, "and are by no means the sort of People that should settle those lands .... You will easily distinguish, that the people I refer to are really what you and I understand by Crackers."[20]

By the 1770's, the great majority of free white people in Georgia were lower middle-class farmers. With ability and a willingness to work, almost any Georgian could improve his condition, considering the good land available. Thus, the Trustees' idea of a colony for the poor and unfortunate had long since been supplanted by a colony in which most people hoped to improve their status and were hard at work on it. A number of people who had come to Trustee Georgia had risen by and during the Royal Period to become leaders in the colony — clearly upper class.

Good illustrations of early arrivals who founded families of importance in Georgia are Noble Jones (who came on the *Ann* with Oglethorpe), Patrick Houstoun (one of the Lowland Scots who came in 1734) and James Habersham (who came in 1738 with George Whitefield). Studies of these men and their families have been made, and it is fairly easy to document what they did. Consider, for example, the case studies of how several of them rose socially and economically in Colonial Georgia.

Noble and Sarah Jones were both 32 when they came on the *Ann* with the original settlers.[21] In the *List of Early Settlers*, Jones is called a carpenter, but master builder would have been a more descriptive term for what he did in Georgia. He also had medical training — type and amount unknown — and practiced medicine in Georgia, beginning during the great illness in the summer of 1733. He was one of the most versatile early settlers and certainly one of the better qualified for life in the new colony. The Jones family, lower middle-class in England, brought a ten-year old son, Noble Wimberly, and a three-year old daughter, Mary, and two indentured servants.

In 1736, Jones got 500 acres of the Isle of Hope, the begining of his Wormsloe estate — a part of which is still owned by his descendants and represents the longest history of land ownership in Georgia. In all, he acquired over 5,500 acres and five town lots during his forty-two year life in Georgia.

Jones was also the first surveyor for the colony in the 1730's, although there was a great deal of objections to his slowness in surveying land.[22] He was the architect or consultant for several public works in Georgia and was probably the best qualified man for this task in the colony. In 1732, he was appointed a conservator of the peace and in 1735 a constable. In 1736, he was made an officer to enforce the rum act, an agent to regulate Indian trade, attorney to Tomo-Chi-Chi and his people, a forest ranger, surveyor and register of grants; and in 1739, he was the Commander of Jones Fort, erected on the Isle of Hope at Skidaway Narrows on his Wormsloe property.

Obviously, this was too much for one man to do, so in October, 1738 Jones was relieved as constable and as surveyor. In the 1740 expedition against St. Augustine, Jones was a lieutenant in the South Carolina regiment. About January, 1741, he set up Fort Wimberly on his Wormsloe property at Skidaway Narrows to replace the earlier Jones Fort, and a scout boat and some twelve men were stationed there under his command. Jones frequently carried dispatches between Savannah and Frederica in his scout boat. During the Spanish invasion of St. Simons Island in 1742, Jones commanded a detachment of rangers, and the next year when Oglethorpe made his final invasion of Florida, he was a captain.

Jones was made an assistant (a member of the governing board of Georgia) by the Trustees in November, 1750. To the Trustees, this was Jones' most important job and showed that he was moving up in their eyes. In 1751, the Trustees appointed him register to make a general survey of conditions in the colony. In the same year, he was made senior captain of the militia and commanded the Savannah forces when Thomas and Mary Bosomworth led a group of Indians to Savannah and thoroughly frightened the town.

With the beginning of the Royal government in Georgia, Jones and the other assistants were appointed to the governor's council, a position Jones retained until his death except for his suspension by Governor Reynolds in December, 1756 and his reinstatement in July, 1759. Jones was also a justice in the court of oyer and terminer and general goal delivery and the provincial treasurer under the Royal government. Still, he was concerned with the erection of public buildings, was involved in the many reconstructions and repairs of the Tybee lighthouse and was one of the surveyors of highways. Jones died November 2, 1775, presumably the last surviving head of a family in Georgia that came on the *Ann*, and he was buried at Wormsloe. His remains have been moved twice since and now rest in Bonaventure Cemetery outside Savannah.

Noble Wimberly Jones was a boy of ten when he came to Georgia with his parents and sisters on the *Ann*. He grew up in Savannah and at Wormsloe. Most or all of his education seems to have come from his father from whom he said he learned English, Latin and medicine. He was a cadet in Oglethorpe's regiment at the age of sixteen during the War of Jenkins' Ear, in 1751 an ensign in the militia and in 1757 was appointed to supervise the construction of log forts near Augusta. Noble Wimberly and his father practiced medicine together during the years 1748-56, and after 1756, Noble W. practiced alone.

Noble W. was elected to the first Commons House of Assembly in Georgia in 1755 and remained a member of that body for the twenty years of its existence until revolt broke out in 1775. He was frequently elected speaker and was the center of a controversy between the Commons House and both Governor Wright and Acting Governor Habersham over their veto of him as speaker in the early 1770's. He was a leader in pre-Revolutionary Whig activities, a member of the Provincial Congress, the Continental Congress and speaker of the Assembly under the state constitution of 1777.

Noble Jones was out of Georgia from late 1778 until late 1782 because of the military situation. A part of that time he was a British prisoner of war, but after living and practicing medicine in Charleston from 1783 until 1788, he returned to Savannah where he lived and practiced medicine for the rest of his life. In 1804, he was one of the petitioners to the Georgia legislature to incorporate the Georgia Medical Society. It was chartered on December 12, 1804, and Jones was elected its first president.

Jones was also a member and president of the Union Society in Savannah. He was on the committee to meet President George Washington on his visit to Savannah in 1791, the same year that Jones refused a judgeship in the Inferior Court of Chatham County when he was elected to it by the Assembly. His last public office was presiding over the state constitutional convention of 1795. Jones died on January 9, 1805 in Savannah at the age of 82.

George Jones, the only child of Noble Wimberly to survive him, practiced medicine in Savannah and occupied political and civic positions until his death in 1838. Jones' descendants continued to be important in Savannah during most of the nineteenth and twentieth centuries and are still there today. Some of them are still named Jones, but one branch of the family changed its name to DeRenne, and through marriage, that branch of the family in Savannah today is named Barrow. In the late nineteenth and twentieth century, the DeRennes were important in collecting books on Georgia's history, publishing historical books and promoting the study of Georgia history through contributions to the University of Georgia and to the Georgia Historical Society.

The founder of the second family, Patrick Houstoun,[23] was born of an old Scottish family in or near Glasgow in 1698 and was the grandson of a baronet. He attended Glasgow University but did not graduate, and at the age of 36, he was a merchant before he came to Georgia in 1734 with several of the Lowland Scots gentlemen. From 1743 and probably earlier, Houstoun was an officer in Oglethorpe's regiment, and he participated in the St. Augustine expedition. In 1736, he moved to his 500 acre grant between the Vernon and Little Ogeechee Rivers, which was soon developed into a plantation named Rosdue and was much nearer to Savannah than his original grant on the Ogeechee River. He represented the Vernonburg District in the Trustee Assembly in 1751 and assumed increasing political duties thereafter. His second cousin, the current baronet, died in Scotland on July 27, 1751, and Houstoun succeeded to the title but remained in Georgia.

When the Royal government was created in 1754, Sir Patrick was appointed a member of the governor's council and Register of Grants and Receiver of Quit Rents. He acquired more land during the Royal Period and generally seems to have prospered. He died on February 5, 1762 and was buried in Savannah.

He was succeeded in his title by his oldest son, Patrick, born in Georgia in 1742. This Patrick had been sent to Glasgow to school by age twelve and remained there several years. After his father's death, however, he succeeded to the offices as Register of Grants and Receiver of Quit Rents, but not to the seat on the council. He served in the Commons House of Assembly during the periods 1764-1768, 1769-70 and 1772-73, and he was appointed to the governor's council in 1775. Equivocable in his position when the Revolutionary troubles began in Georgia, he was on the restored colonial government's act disqualifying Georgians for political service in May, 1780, but in 1781 his petition for restoration to good standing was granted. In 1782, he was on the state act of confiscation and banishment but upon petition was removed. Two years later he went to England and died in Bath the next year. Clearly, he was uncomfortable with the Revolutionary troubles, did not want to have to take sides and contributed little to either side.

Sir George Houstoun, who succeeded to his unmarried brother's title in 1785, was born in Georgia in 1744 and was an established merchant in Savannah when the Revolutionary troubles broke out. He was a Whig and a member of the Council of Safety and Provincial Congress, but he remained in Savannah during the British occupation (1779-1782). He was a lukewarm Whig who had his property confiscated by the state in 1782. Upon petition, he was removed from the pains of confiscation and banishment just three months after the act was passed. After the war, he closed his mercantile house in Savannah and supported himself from several plantations. He held several local political offices, including vestryman of Christ Church and master of Solomon's Masonic Lodge in Savannah. He died in Savannah June 9, 1795 at age fifty.

Another Houstoun brother, John, born about 1746-48, read law in Charles Town and became a lawyer in Savannah. He worked closely with Noble Wimberly Jones and others in the Revolutionary troubles of the 1770's. He was a member of the Council of Safety, the Provincial Congresses and the Continental Congress. In January, 1778, he became the second governor of the State of Georgia. During his governorship occurred the unsuccessful expedition against St. Augustine in which the governor contributed to the confused command structure which certainly aided in the failure. He returned to assembly service in 1782 and again served as governor in 1784. He was elected chief justice of Georgia in February, 1786 but declined the office. He was one of the Georgia commissioners to settle the boundary dispute with South Carolina which resulted in the Treaty of Beaufort between the two states in 1787. His application to President Washington for a federal judgeship was not granted, but he did become the first mayor of Savannah in 1790 and later a superior court judge. He died at his White Bluff Plantation in July of 1796.

Two other Houstoun brothers achieved some importance and show the family's leadership position in Georgia. James Houstoun was a Revolutionary surgeon and served in the state legislature from 1784-86. His brother William, the youngest child of Sir Patrick and Lady Priscilla Houstoun, went to London in June, 1776, where he studied law at the Inner Temple,

21

and he returned to Georgia, probably in 1781, too late to take any real part in the War for Independence. In August, 1782, his petition to the state assembly to practice law in Georgia was granted, and the same year in December, he was elected to the Georgia legislature. One month after the assembly met, it elected Houstoun a member of the Continental Congress, a clear indication of his good standing with the legislators. He was one of the Georgia delegates to the United States Constitutional Convention of 1787. In 1788, he married Mary Bayard of New York and thereafter lived in New York.

The Houstouns are a good example of a family which produced several leaders from its second generation. The fact that this generation was almost always selected for positions of leadership in Georgia shows the family's status and popularity in the colony/state — a sign of a true upper-class family then.

The founder of the third family in Georgia was James Habersham.[24] He was born in June, 1715 in the village of Beverly in Yorkshire of parents of ordinary means. His father was a dyer and innkeeper, lower middle-class. His mother died in 1722 and soon thereafter his father apprenticed James to his Uncle Joseph, a London merchant. By 1736, James was in charge of two sugar-refining houses in London. He became interested in the religious awakening of the 1730's, and in August, 1736, he first heard George Whitefield preach. Soon they were close companions, and Habersham decided that he should renounce his future in London and accompany Whitefield to Georgia, trusting in God to make his life for him. He and Whitefield sailed for Georgia on February 2, 1738.

Upon arrival, Habersham opened a school for some thirty to forty children in Savannah, and he conducted the school as well as religious services when Whitefield was not in Savannah, which was fairly frequent. In 1740 Bethesda, Whitefield's orphanage and school, of which Habersham was temporal superintendent, moved out of Savannah a few miles, and Habersham married sixteen-year old Mary Bolton from Philadelphia, a member of the Bethesda family. By 1743, Habersham began buying goods for Bethesda in Charles Town and sold some to people in Savannah who desired them. Gradually, he became a merchant in partnership with Francis Harris, who had been a clerk in the now-closed Trustees Store; however, Habersham still kept a watchful eye on Bethesda after he moved back to Savannah for business reasons. Harris and Habersham became the Trustees' fiscal agent in Georgia to handle the sola bills (a special Trustee form of money), and this undoubtedly helped their mercantile business. In 1746, Habersham went to England to make contracts for trade, and in 1749, a shipload of goods direct from London arrived for the firm which, in turn, loaded the vessel in Savannah with Georgia produce for the return trip. As an indication of their growing prosperity, Harris and Habersham built the first dock in Savannah in 1749, and in 1754, they began direct West Indian trade.

In July, 1749, Habersham was made an assistant, a member of the Trustee-appointed governing board. In 1750-51, he was asked by the Trustees to work with Pickering Robinson to help the silk industry in Georgia, and in 1754, he was appointed to the original Royal Council and became its secretary. In 1759, Habersham had a country seat, Silk Hope, on the Little Ogeechee River not far from Savannah where he employed an Englishman to develop his garden. By 1764, however, he had turned over most of his mercantile business to Joseph Clay, a nephew from England, and his sons, and he was devoting his time mainly to planting, government duties and Bethesda. He now owned over 6,000 acres and nearly 200 slaves. He sent his oldest son, Joseph, to England for school and a merchant apprenticeship in 1768, but Joseph was back in Savannah in 1771. From July, 1771 to February, 1773, Habersham as senior councillor was acting governor during Governor Wright's leave in England.

Having been born and reared in England and having many personal and business contacts there, Habersham remained loyal to Britain when the Revolutionary troubles came. His own success in Georgia probably aided this viewpoint. He died in Brunswick, New Jersey on August 28, 1775 while traveling to New York for his health. His body was returned to Savannah for burial.

Habersham's three sons, Joseph, James and John, were all Whigs of the more conservative Savannah faction when the choice of sides had to be made. They were merchants and planters and occupied political and military offices during and after the War for Independence. Joseph was the highest Whig leader in the family. He led in pre-Revolutionary activities 1774-76, was a colonel in the Continental Army and was U.S. Postmaster General 1795-1801.

The other titled nobleman in Colonial Georgia — the fourth — received his title because of his work and leadership in

Georgia. He was Governor James Wright,[25] who came in 1760 and left in 1782, serving the longest tenure of any Georgia governor before or since. Wright came from an old upper-class Yorkshire family. His grandfather, Sir Robert Wright (d. 1689) was Lord Chief Justice of England in the seventeenth century; and his father, also named Robert, was Chief Justice of South Carolina, 1731-39. James was born in London in 1716 before his father came to South Carolina, and he entered Gray's Inn, one of the London law schools, in August, 1741 and was called to the bar. In South Carolina, he practiced law, engaged in planting and held various minor offices before he became Attorney General (1742-57). He was South Carolina's agent in London, 1757-70 and was appointed Lieutenant Governor of Georgia in 1760 and Governor in 1762.

In Georgia, Wright was a popular governor and the colony prospered under his leadership. He came to Georgia just before the Spanish had to give up Florida to Britain and the French to give up Louisiana. With these two dangerous neighbors gone, Georgia could expand as never before. The Creek Indians could no longer play one European power against another to their own advantage and now had to agree with the English to get the desired trade. The results in Georgia were the 1763 and 1773 Indian land cessions which immediately made land available to new white settlers. While there were frontier ne'er-do-wells among the new settlers, most of the settlers were hard-working small farmers, some with a few slaves, and the kind of settlers Wright tried to encourage.

Wright also prospered personally in Georgia. By 1775, he owned eleven plantations totalling 25,578 acres and worked 523 slaves. He shipped two to three thousand barrels of rice a year and was one of the wealthiest Georgians. Wright was governor during Georgia's most rapid growth period to date, and he did all he could to help this growth. While he was on leave in England, he was made a baronet on December 5, 1772 and returned to Georgia the next year as Sir James.

For most of the decade of 1765-75, Wright opposed Revolutionary activities in Georgia with considerable success, but by 1774, he was no longer able to uphold the King's position nor to prevent open revolt by late 1775. Ironically, Wright had been so successful in aiding Georgia's growth and prosperity that his efforts had made the colony strong enough to rebel in 1775.

Although Wright was an enlightened conservative who

thoroughly believed in the class structure of the eighteenth century, he wished for more tone in Georgia's society but was willing to wait and work for it. He undoubtedly achieved more wealth and position in Georgia than would have been possible in South Carolina or England.

Nobody in Georgia in the 1760's or 1770's would have doubted that the Joneses, the Houstouns, the Habershams and James Wright were upper-class. Their families led the colony politically, economically and socially, and all family members were aware of their status. They were in basic agreement about the type of world they wanted and the type of Georgia they wanted to lead. They were leaders and upper-class in the best sense of the word — people who worked for the public good and who made contributions to the welfare and betterment of the colony. Few would have argued with the idea that Georgia was better off because of their presence, except when the Revolutionary troubles came.

While they all came from good backgrounds in Britain, there seems little doubt but that they rose faster and further in Georgia than would have been possible in England. In a new society, it is possible to rise easier as the places at the top are not already occupied by people of longstanding tenure. The top places were available to people with ability who were willing to work, and in America, the ease of landownership — the traditional prerequisite of any upper class — made economic and social status easier to attain. This undoubtedly helped psychologically as did the fact that the founders of these families (except Wright) had all surmounted difficult times in their early years in Georgia and continually improved their status thereafter. Georgia was good to them, but they had ability and worked to achieve their success.

The Royal Period brought greater population, around 40,000 total by 1776, and few records for historians to use. While land-granting records are fairly complete and say a good bit about economic status, there are some wills and inventories that say more.[26] Basically, the same classes continued to come to Georgia in the Royal Period as under the Trustees, only more came from America. Proportionally, there were fewer indentured servants as the number of Negro slaves increased dramatically. With land easier to get — tied to the number of servants or slaves one owned — it was possible to build up plantations quicker, and by 1775, most of the rice lands as far south as the Altamaha had been granted. There were still many more small farmers, especially in the upcountry where plantations, worked with slave labor, were just beginning to develop by 1775. Governor Wright, always a conservative force in land granting, opposed large grants to spectators preferring smaller grants which would be farmed by the grantees. By 1776, most white Georgians were still small farmers of the lower middle class, with a few artisans in the towns. No figures on the landless poor are available, but they could hardly have been a large group in Georgia. For those who wanted to work it, land was too easy to get.

While upper-class people are the easiest to study because they leave the most records, they were a small minority of Colonial Georgians. In the Trustee Period, as we have already seen, there were the lower middle-class and the indentured servants (lowest class) who made up most of Georgia's small population. By 1750, many of these had died or left Georgia, but for those who remained, upward mobility was usually taking place. No study of those who came as indentured servants has been made, but it would undoubtedly show upward movement on the part of most of them who remained in Georgia. There are probably enough records to do something with this class. Someone should try it.

Eighteenth-century Georgia, like all new English colonies in America, was a land of opportunity for many of its settlers. For those with ability and willingness to work, those with a moderate amount of luck and those who did not experience major misfortunes, there was a good chance to rise both economically and socially. A few perhaps went from the lowest to the highest level in the forty-two years of Colonial Georgia, but most went only part of the way. Most free whites who came to Georgia did so because they hoped to improve their status, the main reason for migrations then and today. While economic and social improvement for many continued in the nineteenth and twentieth centuries, some, of course, went down the scale instead.

Today, it is still possible to go both ways in Georgia.

NOTES

[1]Francis Moore, *A Voyage to Georgia Begun in the Year 1735* (London, 1744); reprinted in *Collections,* Ga. Hist. Soc. 1 (1840), 83 and *Our First Visit in America* (Savannah, 1974), 85.

[2][James Oglethorpe], *A New and Accurate Account of the Provinces of South Carolina and Georgia* (London, 1733); reprinted in *Collections,* Ga. Hist. Soc., 1:56 and *The Most Delightful Country of the Universe* (Savannah, 1972), 130.

[3]On Herbert see Sarah B. Gober Temple and Kenneth Coleman, *Georgia Journeys* (Athens, 1961), 3, 8, 22; Kenneth Coleman, *Colonial Georgia: A History* (New York, 1976), 22-23, 33, 146-148; Reba Carolyn Strickland, *Religion and the State in Georgia in the Eighteenth Century* (New York, 1939), 84.

[4]On Oglethorpe's background see Amos Aschbach Ettinger, *James Edward Oglethorpe: Imperial Idealist* (Oxford, 1936). On his position in Georgia see Ettinger; Phinizy Spalding, *Oglethorpe in America* (Chicago, 1977); Leslie F. Church, *Oglethorpe: A Study in Philanthropy in England and Georgia* (London, 1932); and any history of Colonial Georgia.

[5]On Bathurst see Temple and Coleman, *Georgia Journeys,* 172-73, 270; Allen D. Candler et al., eds., *The Colonial Records of the State of Georgia* (Atlanta and Athens, 1904--), vols. 20-23.

[6]On the Lowland Scots see Temple and Coleman, *Georgia Journeys,* 43, 103, 111, 164-65, 167-68; Patrick Tailfer and others, *A True and Historical Narrative of the Colony of Georgia,* edited by Clarence L. Ver Steeg (Athens, 1960), especially the Introduction; *The Clamorous Malcontents* (Savannah, 1973).

[7]E. Merton Coulter, ed., "A List of the First Shipload of Georgia Settlers," *Ga. Hist. Q.,* 31:282-88.

[8]Edited by E. Merton Coulter and Albert B. Saye.

[9]*Ibid.,* Introduction

[10]*Ibid., passim;* Coleman, *Colonial Georgia,* 137-38.

[11]Coulter and Saye, *List of Early Settlers, passim;* Temple and Coleman, *Georgia Journeys,* 56-62; Coleman, *Colonial Georgia,* 118-20; P.A. Strobel, *The Salzburgers and Their Descendants* (Baltimore, 1855; Athens, 1954).

[12]Temple and Coleman, *Georgia Journeys, passim;* E. Merton Coulter, *The Journal of William Stephens 1741-1743* and *1743-1745* (Athens, 1958 and 1959), especially the Introduction.

[13]On Bolzius see Salzburger references in Note 11 above; and Samuel Urlsperger, ed., *Detailed Reports on the Salzburger Emigrants Who Settled in America*..., edited by George Fenwick Jones and others (8 vols. to date. Athens, 1968-85).

[14]Coleman, *Colonial Georgia*, 152-53, 158, 232-34; Harold E. Davis, *The Fledgling Province: Social and Cultural Life in Colonial Georgia, 1733-1776* (Chapel Hill, 1976); Strickland, *Religion and the State in Georgia.*

[15]Works cited in Note 14 above; Randall M. Miller, ed., *"A Warm and Zealous Spirit"* (Macon, Ga., 1982); Kenneth Coleman, *The American Revolution in Georgia, 1763-1789* (Athens, 1958).

[16]Temple and Coleman, *Georgia Journeys, passim.*

[17]*Ibid.*, 50-56, 182, 221, 263, 284.

[18]Coleman, *Colonial Georgia, passim.*

[19]*Ibid.;*Milton L. Ready, *The Castle Builders: Georgia's Economy Under the Trustees, 1732-1754* (New York, 1978), Chapts, 5 and 6.

[20]Habersham to Wright, *Collections*, Ga. Hist. Soc., 6:204.

[21]The main source for the treatment of Jones and his descendants is E. Merton Coulter, *Wormsloe: Two Centuries of a Georgia Family* (Athens, 1955); see also William M. Kelso, *Captain Jones' Wormsloe* (Athens, 1979).

[22]Temple and Coleman, *Georgia Journeys*, 269-78.

[23]The material on the Houstouns comes mainly from Edith Duncan Johnston, *The Houstouns of Georgia* (Athens, 1950).

[24]The study of the Habershams is W. Calvin Smith, "Georgia Gentlemen: The Habershams of Eighteenth Century Savannah," Ph.D. dissertation, Univ. of N.C., 1971.

[25]On Wright see Kenneth Coleman, "James Wright" in *Georgians in Profile: Historical Essays in Honor of Ellis Merton Coulter* (Athens, 1958); Coleman, *Colonial Georgia;* Coleman, *The American Revolution in Georgia;* W.W. Abbot, *The Royal Governors of Georgia* (Chapel Hill, 1959).

[26]Land records are in *Colonial Records of Georgia*, vols. 7-12 and in *English Crown Grants* (10 vols. Atlanta, 1972-75). For wills see *Abstract of Colonial Wills of the State of Georgia, 1733-1777* (Atlanta, 1962).

CLASS, CASTE AND CONFLICT IN GEORGIA, 1733-1983

ROGER G. BRANCH, SR.

AND

V. RICHARD PERSICO, JR.

The very mention of social class as applied to Georgia evokes vivid — and varied — images. There is the picture of an ostentatiously rich planter and his bevy of milk-faced, hooped-skirted ladies, all of whom are maintained in opulence by scores of happy, contented slaves that "sho'ly lub dey massa." This is the "Gone With the Wind" image. Another, the Erskine Caldwell portrait of Georgians in *Tobacco Road* and *God's Little Acre*, depicts ignorance, sloth, poverty, meanness of spirit and plain stupidity. Then there's the picture of noble Chief Tomochichi welcoming Oglethorpe and his band of settlers and helping them to settle into their new home. He was rewarded with a round trip excursion to England to see the king, along with an entourage of kith, kin and loyal supporters. In spite of that peaceful picture, there was in fact constant conflict with Indians who were driven from the land completely in little more than a century.

To the public understanding, Georgia, like the South in general, appears in many guises, most of them mythical. As George Brown Tindall notes:

> *The South, then, has been a seedbed for a proliferation of paradoxical myths, all of which have some basis in empirical fact and all of which doubtlessly have, or have had, their true believers. The result has been, in David Potter's words, that the South has become an enigma, 'a kind of Sphinx on the American land.'*[1]

It is our task to examine the multiple images of stratification in an effort to make this Sphinx give up some of its secrets. It will be shown that these images are like the mental pictures of the elephant generated by the seven blind princes of Serendip, i.e., "though all were partly in the right, all were in the wrong." The task of painting a broader, more accurate picture, however, requires the laying of some conceptual foundations. Class and caste are two different, major forms of social stratification, while conflict is a fundamental social process seen in interpersonal or intercollectivity relationships in which one party seeks to compel, constrain, restrain or subjugate another. Stratification, by its very nature, tends to arouse conflict.

A social class is "a set of people with similar socio -economic status — similar amounts of property, prestige and power,"[2] and a class system is made up of a number of these arranged in a ranked order or hierarchy. According to Max Weber, economic variables such as income or wealth are joined by social esteem or honor and by power variables in determining one's social class.[3] Generally, therefore, those who share a set of common economic life chances, such as similar occupation, form a class whether they are conscious of shared membership or not.

A caste system is also composed of a hierarchically arranged set of social categories. Caste membership is hereditary and permanent. One's caste membership is fixed at the moment of conception and never changes; there is no individual social mobility; and marriage is within caste. Occupation is also largely determined since each caste performs a certain set of occupations and only those. Intercaste relationships are carefully limited by rules which are supported by social, political and religious sanctions. While a full-blown caste system has existed only in traditional India,[4] attenuated caste systems have been found in many places.

It was the anthropologist W. Lloyd Warner who first made the case that a dual stratification evolved in the South after the Civil War.[5] He called it caste and class with a class system for whites and another for blacks, but with caste-like relationships between whites and blacks. His idea was explored, expanded and tested in field research reported by his students, Davis, Gardner and Gardner in 1941 and by Dollard in 1937.[6] It could be argued further, however, that the conceptual roots and part of the structure of this caste system derived from slavery and that black-white relations even before the Civil War were partially couched in a caste frame of reference. Moreover, some aspects of white-Indian relations fit a caste model fairly well, suggesting a consideration of how Indians fared at the hands of a white upper caste in early Georgia.

RED AND WHITE

Prior to the European invasion of the New World, the Indians living in the southeastern portion of what was to become the United States possessed the most sophisticated culture of any Native Americans north of the civilizations of Central Mexico. Although not everywhere the same in all particulars, to a large degree the Southeastern Indians shared the basic elements of their lifeways. They lived in towns situated along rivers where the soil was good for growing crops. In their towns, they erected earthen mounds as platforms for temples, council houses and the houses of their chiefs, whose role was both religious and political. Kinship formed the basis of their social system; it not only structured their family life and child rearing practices, but also their economics, politics, law and ceremonial life. The influences of their culture were felt by peoples as far north as Ohio and Michigan and as far west as Oklahoma and Nebraska.

The lands which were to become Georgia were within the heartland of this vigorous cultural tradition. Yet, within three hundred years of the first European explorations in the Southeast, Indian culture was destroyed. The surviving Indians had their lands appropriated and were forced to migrate elsewhere amid great suffering and death. By the end of 1839, no Indians remained in Georgia.

The Indians of Georgia and the other southeastern states, however, are not well-known today among the people who displaced them. Most modern Americans, Southerners included, are far better acquainted with the Indians of the Plains or the Southwest. The reasons for this lack of knowledge are several. The major problem is that the culture of Southeastern Indians was so different from that of the Europeans that the explorers, settlers and colonial officials who came into contact with them in large measure failed to understand them. By the time Euro-American scholars, historians and anthropologists realized that the native cultures of the continent were worth studying, the culture of the Southeastern Indians had been terribly disrupted and radically changed.[7] This lack of understanding was unfortunate. Besides being worthwhile to know about in their own right, the Southeastern Indians were an important element of the natural, economic and political milieu of the European settlers. They exerted a profound influence on the early history of Georgia, the South and the United States in general. Thus, it is useful to examine briefly some of their

31

key cultural institutions before reviewing relationships between Indians and whites in Georgia.

Indian Culture In Georgia

Prior to the arrival of large numbers of Europeans in the Southeast, the Indians of Georgia were organized into a number of chiefdoms.[8] For the most part, the chiefdoms did not correspond to the later tribal groupings of the 17th and 18th centuries. Most of the tribes seem to have formed later, after the breakdown of the chiefdoms. The chiefdom is a type of political organization intermediate between the tribe and the state. Tribes are politically and economically decentralized and equalitarian. States are highly centralized and socially stratified. In chiefdoms, everyone has equal access to economic resources, as in tribes; but some people have more prestige and power than others because of inheritance, as in states. Political power is somewhat centralized in the hands of the chief and other members of the chiefly lineage. They form a government which coordinates the activities of a number of communities and supports a slight degree of economic specialization.[9]

The source of chiefly power among the Southeastern Indians was as much religious as it was political or economic. The chief and his kinsmen commanded respect and power because they were closely linked to the gods, especially the sun which was the principal deity. Unlike tribal headmen, chiefs could give orders and expect to have them carried out, but unlike leaders in a state system, they could not use coercive force to control those who disobeyed. Southeastern chiefs relied instead on supernatural sanctions.

The town in which the chief dwelt was the political and ceremonial center of the chiefdom. Here, the people of the other towns in the chiefdom would gather on important occasions. The chief was assisted in governing by a number of priests and war leaders, many of whom were members of his own clan. Of equal importance to these, however, was a council drawn from the elders of the other clans. Indeed, all of the old, distinguished men, and in some cases women as well, played important roles in political and religious affairs.[10] The elders knew well the minds of their kinsmen. They carried their sentiments to the chief and his assistants and made the chief's wishes known to the people. Most of the discussion, maneuver and compromise that typify political activity took place informally. When a council meeting was held, the participants already knew one another's positions and often had already reached an agreement. All adults in the chiefdom could address meetings of the council to express their opinions. The role of the chief in these meetings was to maintain ritual purity and guide the discussion toward a consensus.[11]

Under the impact of epidemic diseases, depopulation and the invasion of alien people with incomprehensible customs and deadly new weapons, almost all of the Southeastern Indian chiefdoms broke down into tribes. Diseases brought from the Old World were a key factor in this breakdown. The Indians, isolated from Old World diseases for over 12,000 years, had no natural immunities. Measles, malaria, yellow fever and smallpox decimated Indian populations. In the Southeast, smallpox seems to have been the most devastating.[12] Added to the effects of depopulation on the social system was the impact of the epidemics on the religious authority of the chiefs. The Southeastern Indians saw disease as supernatural punishment. The chiefs' inability to contain the new diseases called into question their relationships with the gods and diminished their authority. Thus, the upper stratum of the Indian societies disintegrated, leaving the local communities more or less socially intact.[13]

The remaining autonomous towns allied themselves with one another, forming loose confederations. Tribes such as the Creeks, Yamasees and Cherokees were formed in this manner. There was no centralized leadership with the power to coordinate the actions of different towns. All decisions were made by consensus. The headmen led by example and persuasion, and any town, clan or individual not agreeing with the decision of the majority was not bound by it. No one could compel compliance. Most Europeans never understood the nature of the Indians' political system. Throughout the colonial period, the Europeans acted as if the various tribes were states. They called tribal headmen kings and seem to have thought of them in much the same way as they thought of European kings and nobles. When the Indian leaders did not act as kings, giving commands and enforcing compliance among their people, the Europeans declared them to be treacherous. However, no Indian leader in the Southeast had such power.[14]

Kinship was the main organizing principle of all social relations among the Indians of Georgia and throughout the Southeast. It was a model for thinking about relationships between individuals, families, towns, tribes and even between spirits and deities.[15] Kinship was matrilineal, meaning kinsmen traced their linkages to one another only on their mother's side of the family and only through women. This system produced a very different set of kinsmen with very different social characteristics than the bilateral kinship system typical of Europeans. Without discussing the details of matrilineality, it is sufficient to say that the Europeans who dealt with Indians were seldom aware of the importance of kinship to the Indians' way of thinking and almost never understood the particular features of their kinship system. Instead, they assumed that the Indians' view of kinship was the same as their own, contributing to their mutual difficulties. "Great White Father," for example, would have meant very different things to the bilateral Europeans and to the matrilineal Creeks and Cherokees.

The various tribes were organized into a greater or lesser number of matrilineal clans. These were kinship groups, the members of which claimed common descent through women from some distant ancestor. Some tribes, such as the Cherokee, had only a few clans, seven in this case. Others had many more, with the Creeks recognizing around forty.[16] These were sizable tribes; and although clan members could not trace their actual genealogical links to one another, except in the case of very close relatives, they treated one another as if they were family. Men of the same clan who were about the same age addressed and treated one another as brothers. Marriage between a man and a woman of the same clan was considered incestuous.

Clan membership gave the individual all of his human rights. A person without a clan was a nonentity; he had no access to economic resources, no legal standing, no political significance. He could be killed with impunity. Clan membership, in a real sense, gave meaning to a person's life.[17] The clans also provided the means of mobilizing the tribe, for a man living in one town could call upon the members of his clan in other towns for aid or support. These people, in turn, could call upon their in-laws and friends in their own towns. In this way, a large portion of a tribe could be mobilized. In effect, clans provided a basis for association and cooperation which extended across the boundaries of autonomous towns.[18]

Within each clan were several lineages consisting of smaller descent groups, members of which could trace their actual linkages to one another. They provided the individual's primary source of economic, legal, social and psychological security. Lineage members lived in the same area, owned valuable property in common and cooperated routinely in political and legal activity.[19] If a person was a victim of crime, he called upon his lineage mates for justice. The lineage was central in arranging and confirming the marriages of its members. Relationships between lineage members were close and provided the model for all other social relationships. A town headman, for example, was supposed to act like an elder brother to his people.[20]

The family of the Southeastern Indians was very different from the typical European family. Because descent was matrilineal and legal rights and obligations were defined in terms of kinship, fathers had no authority over their children. The responsibility for proper care and upbringing of children fell to their nearest matrilineal kinsmen, their mother and mother's brother. Boys looked to their mother's brother for instruction in the skills of manhood, aid in times of difficulty and support in their undertakings. They inherited property, titles and social prerogatives from him. Girls looked to their mother for these things. The role of father was more like that of a favorite uncle in Euro-American families. A man worked to support his family, but the lands he helped to cultivate belonged to his wife and her lineage. His sister and her husband cultivated the lands in which he held a proprietary interest. Brothers and sisters, therefore, were particularly close, even as adults. They shared a common responsibility for the same set of children and a common interest in the management of lineage property.[21]

The economy of Indians of this region before the period of European colonization was based on a combination of horticulture, gathering and hunting. The family was the primary unit of economic production, and food was the primary product. Horticulture, the cultivation of crops with hand tools, was the mainstay of their livelihood. The chief crops were beans, squash, pumpkins, sunflowers and several varieties of corn. They located their main garden plots along the banks of rivers and streams where the soil was richest and thus took longer to exhaust than higher forest soil. Women had the primary responsibility for cultivating the crops although men did some work in the fields. The women also gathered a wide variety of roots, nuts, berries and fruits from the forest to sup-

35

plement the cultivated crops.

For their meat supply, the Indians depended on wild game. They had no domesticated animals except for the dog. The white-tailed deer was the most important source of meat, but numerous other species of mammals, birds and fish were also taken. Hunting and fishing were the work of the men. Game was plentiful, and the Indians enjoyed a good diet.[22]

Family members also made most of the other things that they needed. The women made pottery, wove baskets, tanned hides and processed food. The men built and maintained structures, cleared land, made tools and concerned themselves with ceremony, politics and warfare. Before the opening of trade with the Europeans, there was little need for economic exchange. Some exchange, of course, did take place, for the Indians engaged in gift-giving and provided goods and services to the chief for redistribution. However, this was of only limited economic significance. For the most part, each family produced for itself all of the goods and services it needed.

With the opening of trade with the Europeans, the economy of the Indians changed. English and French traders offered the Indians things they could not make for themselves in exchange for deer skins. The Indians began to hunt deer in much greater numbers so that they could exchange their skins for things such as brass pots, iron tools, cloth, glass beads and firearms. Gradually, European manufactured goods replaced native crafts. As this happened, the Indians became increasingly dependent on the Europeans for goods. One consequence of this was the depletion of the deer population. A more critical consequence was that it gave the Europeans a degree of control over them. Gifts of goods or threats of embargoes were effective in obtaining concessions from the Indians.[23]

INDIANS AND WHITES IN GEORGIA

By the time of the founding of Georgia in 1733, British policy towards the Indians in the Southeast was well-established. The British were locked in a struggle with the French and Spanish for control of the region. All three powers attempted to form alliances with the large tribes, both to protect themselves and to gain advantages over their rivals.[24] Oglethorpe's meeting with Creek leaders at Coweta prior to his expedition against St. Augustine in 1740 was typical of British dealings with the Indians. He needed to insure that they would not join the Spanish and attack Savannah in his absence. He also hoped to obtain fighting men to augment his forces. Around 1,100 Creek warriors joined his expedition which included only around 900 whites.[25] The smaller tribes living near the settlements were given less attention. Militarily weak, disorganized and broken by disease and alcohol, they could do little to help or hinder the colonists.

The deer skin trade was a key element in alliance building. The colonial powers sought to make various tribes dependent on them as a source of needed goods. They could use this as a lever to manipulate their politics and obtain concessions. Traders were often government agents. At various times, the colonial powers offered their Indian allies bounties for capturing enemy agents and for enslaving or killing Indians allied to other powers. They also used trade to encourage or discourage hostilities between tribes, depending on the situation. The French and Spanish were never able to match the British in either the quantity or the quality of their trade goods. This put the French and Spanish at a disadvantage which they attempted to offset by superior diplomacy.[26]

In 1715, the British policy of manipulating the Indians through the deer skin trade, while turning a tidy profit, backfired. The Indians of Georgia had grown resentful of the sharp practices of the traders and the failure of colonial officials to give them redress. They had been cheated, robbed, enslaved, killed, drawn into conflicts caused by the Europeans and invaded. Apparently deciding that no amount of trade goods was worth this, the Creeks, the Choctaws, some of the Cherokees and a number of small tribes living along the Savannah River rose up against the Europeans in their midst. They killed several traders and attacked plantations and farms in South Carolina. Charleston quickly became a refugee center. Known as the Yamasee War after one of the small tribes that apparently touched off the fighting, this action came close to dislodging the British from the Southeast. They averted defeat at the hands of this loose alliance of Indians only by dividing them against one another. Through skillful diplomacy and large gifts, they succeeded in turning the Cherokees against the Creeks, who were never the best of friends at any time. The British were then able to make a separate peace with each of these two powerful tribes, ending the threat to the colony in 1717. The Yamasees were destroyed, the survivors ultimately fleeing to Florida to seek shelter from the Spanish. To further protect themselves, the British encouraged hostilities between the Cherokees and Creeks for several years. Following the Yamasee War, British influence among the Indians in the Southeast was greatly diminished for a time. Gradually, however, the British regained much of their former position as the French experienced similar problems of their own.[27]

The founding of Georgia created new problems for the Indians. Despite attempts by both Georgia and South Carolina to regulate trade with the Indians, unlicensed traders operating out of Augusta continued to cheat and abuse them. Criminal elements from the colonies, who robbed, beat and killed Indian and white alike, drifted to the frontier. When captured by colonial officials, they were usually punished for their crimes against the whites but seldom for their outrages against the Indians. Most disturbing, however, was the continued illegal settlement of whites on Indian lands, contrary to treaty provisions. Disappointed and disenchanted with the British, the Cherokees and Creeks turned to the French for assistance, and in 1756, the French went to war against the British. Under French urging and angry over white encroachment from Georgia and South Carolina, the Cherokees attacked the colonial frontier in 1759. The French tried to persuade the Creeks to join the fight, but with limited success because hard feelings still persisted between the Creeks and the Cherokees. The Upper Creeks attacked British trading posts in some of their towns, but most of the Creeks remained neutral. In 1760, a powerful British force from South Carolina invaded Cherokee country and forced the Indians to sue for peace.[28]

The struggle for supremacy in the Southeast between the British on the one hand and the French and Spanish on the other ended in 1763 with the close of the Seven Years War. Under the provisions of the peace treaty, France gave up all of its claims in North America and Spain withdrew south of the St. Mary's River in Florida. The British no longer needed the Indians as allies or worried about them joining their rivals. All they wanted from the Indians now was their land. Thus, a new Indian policy was pursued vigorously in Georgia. In 1763, the Creeks were forced to cede a large portion of their country which lay between the lower Savannah River and the Ogeechee. In 1771, the Creeks and the Cherokees together surrendered the remainder of their land between the Ogeechee and the Altamaha Rivers, extending northward to the headwaters of the Oconee and thence to the Savannah River. Nevertheless, despite British assurances that settlement would be restricted to the lands ceded, white encroachment continued unabated.[29]

In 1776, the Cherokees again struck back against the European invasion. The colonists responded with total warfare, burning towns, destroying crops and killing men, women and children alike. Although a faction of the Cherokees continued to struggle until 1794, most of them made peace and never again attempted armed resistence, so terrible was the destruction inflicted upon them. The Creeks largely remained neutral in the American Revolution.[30]

Following the Revolution, the Indians of Georgia, now mostly Cherokees and Creeks, attempted to accommodate themselves to the new order. The only way to survive among the whites, their leaders reasoned, was to adopt their ways, at least to some extent. In particular, both peoples attempted to build nation-states with political institutions more or less modeled after those of the United States.[31] The Cherokees were the most successful in this attempt, developing a native writing system, a national press and a constitutional form of government divided into three branches. It should be noted that these new developments, although intentionally designed to look like white institutions, had Cherokee principles underlying them. They were intended to preserve the Cherokees as a distinct social and cultural entity.[32]

The Euro-American inhabitants of Georgia, however, had no interest in having Indian neighbors. They wanted land for the development of their own economy and society. The efforts of the Cherokees and Creeks to develop social and political institutions modeled on those of the United States only served to increase the fears of Georgians that they would be unable to obtain that land. The more "civilized" the Indians became, the greater were the efforts of the whites to expel them from the state. To do this, they were willing to use any means including coercion, trickery and the flouting of their own laws and customs.[33]

On February 25, 1825, William McIntosh, a Creek leader and a mixed blood cousin of Georgia Governor George M. Troup, along with a small group of other Creek leaders, signed the Treaty of Indian Springs, ceding all remaining Creek lands in Georgia. McIntosh was reportedly given $100,000 to distribute to the other chiefs as bribes to obtain their signatures. In Creek eyes, the treaty was invalid because its signers had not been authorized by the nation to negotiate any treaty. Moreover, McIntosh's actions were illegal under Creek law and punishable by death.[34] Creek patriots killed him three months later. Because the Treaty of Indian Springs was patently illegal, the Creek leader Menewa was able to negotiate a new treaty with the federal government in 1826. President John Quincy Adams affirmed the Creeks' possession of their remaining lands. In response, Troup threatened secession from the Union, and while demanding that the Treaty of Indian Springs be enforced, he encouraged the illegal seizure of Creek land and property in an effort to force them to leave. He sent elements of the Georgia militia into the Creek country, supposedly to maintain order, but the militia perpetrated some of the worst outrages.

In December of 1831, the Creeks made a formal protest to the federal government over the actions of Georgia. By then, Andrew Jackson was president. He stated that he and his administration did not feel bound by the provisions of Adams' treaty and refused to enforce it. Under duress, the Creeks signed a new treaty in 1832. Helpless, they agreed to emigrate west to Indian Territory in five years if the federal government would provide them protection in the meantime. Little protection, however, was provided, and abuses by settlers and the Georgia militia continued to hasten them on their way. The last of the Creeks left Georgia for the Indian territory in 1837, with over one thousand of them dying during the forced migration. The Cherokees suffered a similar fate. They were moved in 1838 with a loss of some 4,000 lives.[35]

RED AND BLACK

Relations between Indians and blacks were limited. Throughout the period from 1733 to 1838, all but a tiny minority of blacks were slaves and the Indians were on the frontier. Since the planter usually arrived in the third wave of settlement after the hunter-herdsman and the mobile yeoman farmer, the Indians had often left the area before the slaves arrived. If a slave ran away into Indian territory, he stood a good chance of being killed, an excellent chance of being pressed back into slavery by Indians, some of whom were slave-owning planters, and a poor chance of being allowed to join an Indian group.

BLACK AND WHITE

On the surface, it would seem that black-white relations in Georgia at the end of the Civil War could be summed up in one word — slavery, but the reality of slavery is far too complex to be communicated accurately with one word. The practice of slavery varied widely according to region of the state, the method of organization of work, the crop being grown and the orientation of the planter and/or his overseer. Additionally, slaveholding was not evenly distributed throughout Georgia. Rather, it was concentrated in a narrow band along the Atlantic coast and up the Savannah River to the Piedmont, where it widened to become the great short staple cotton belt extending across the state and then narrowing again along the Chattahoochee River down the western boundary. Below and above this horseshoe shaped area, the practice of slavery was limited.[36] The reason for this varying concentration is that slavery was economically impractical in the northern hill country and the southern piney woods.[37] Since the types of soil and topography were not conducive to the crops that were most suitable for plantation development, these regions remained primarily the strongholds of yeoman farmers and herdsmen. While there was slavery in these areas, the average number of slaves owned was small.[38] As was the case in other Southern states, there was considerable resistance to secession by those who owned no slaves and saw themselves risking everything for a cause that did not involve their class interests and needs.

By its very nature, slavery, the holding of another human in bondage by varied forms of coercion and requiring him to work for no rewards other than the simplest necessities of life, involves conflict. However, the nature and extent of that conflict in Georgia and the South varied greatly from one place to another. In fact, the level of repression and physical punishment sometimes seems to depend upon who is telling the story. One example of differing accounts from the same site comes from the plantations of Pierce Butler on Saint Simons Island and on the Altamaha River Delta in McIntosh County. A resident of Philadelphia, Butler married the English Shakespearian actress Fanny Kemble, who visited his Georgia plantations in 1838-39 and painted a pitiful picture of inadequate food, clothing, shelter and medical care along with drudgery and degradation.[39] She admits, however, that she arrived at the plantations with a powerfully entrenched prejudice against slavery.

Kemble was a staunch abolitionist, but for reasons never reported, Pierce Butler did not inform her before their marriage that he was the largest slaveholder in Georgia, the total eventually reaching 919 by 1859.[40] She, therefore, met with a shocking surprise when she arrived at Saint Simons Island and apparently never really forgave her husband. She found nothing good about life on his Georgia plantation. Tensions between Fanny Kemble and Pierce Butler continued until their divorce in 1849. She returned to England, leaving her two daughters in their father's custody. She published her *Journal* as a propaganda piece during the Civil War to sway English sympathies and policies toward the Union and away from the Confederacy. It was not a dispassionate, objective account of plantation life.

Kemble's interpretation has been challenged by several scholars. Phillips points out numerous logical and factual inconsistencies in the *Journal*.[41] He also quotes an account written by a daughter, Frances Butler Leigh, who managed the plantation for a number of years after the Civil War, which he says "refutes her mother's argument."[42] A more telling challenge to the Kemble picture of repression and degradation has come from the research of University of Florida historical archaeologists. As a result of years of painstaking study, Fairbanks and Moore concluded that "an idea of the common field slave living in a hovel, dressing in rags and marching to an overseer's whip is as ludicrous as an idea that the planter's family lived like Rhett Butler and Scarlett O'Hara."[43] These scholars use both historical documents and archaeological evidence to support their conclusions.

Moore's excavations produced evidence that slaves on Saint Simons ate about the same things as overseers, although they did not eat as well as the plantation owners except in the case of small plantations. Fish, fowl and mammal bones reflect considerable variety in the diet, and evidence suggests that the slaves had the free time and equipment to catch fish or kill game for themselves. Although they supposedly were forbidden to have firearms, there is extensive evidence that they did in fact have guns.[44] Owners and overseers obviously closed their eyes to the putatively unbreakable rule and probably provided the guns, powder and shot as a way to supplement their own diets and those of the slaves.

Moore also discovered that some of the Butler slaves had writing instruments, another forbidden possession.[45] Bodenhamer points out that in Savannah laws to limit the public activity of slaves were routinely evaded or rarely enforced.[46]

Thus, it is obvious that the picture of universal oppression has been overdrawn. Extensive additional evidence could be cited to support that conclusion. Many, indeed most, slave owners in Georgia had five slaves or fewer.[47] In such cases, the owner and his family worked alongside slaves in the fields. While the color bar remained firmly in place, the social distance between master and slave was not great. The differences in type, quality and amount of food, clothing and shelter were modest. Neither one had much.

On those plantation where work was organized by task rather than gang labor, a fast, skillful worker could make for himself considerable free time. Certain types of work, such as the hand separation of sea island cotton from its seed, almost demanded assignment of work to individuals on a task or daily production quota basis.

The conclusion of all this is that how well or ill slaves fared and the nature of relationships between whites and blacks fit no single pattern. There is ample evidence of humane treatment and strong emotional ties. However, slavery is by nature a violation of person. Moreover, there is clear evidence of floggings and other mistreatment. The exploitation of black women by their owners, producing children who were owned by their fathers, is well-known. Phillips records a litany of sufferings, including unjust beatings and the grief of a mother whose son has been sold away to another owner.[48]

The slaves did not always placidly accept their fates. Many of them attempted to run away and a few succeeded. Some rebelled violently. Phillips quotes from a Savannah newspaper account that "six new (newly arrived from Africa) Negro fellows and four wenches killed their overseer, murdered his wife and ran amok in the neighborhood until overpowered."[49] Incidentally, their leaders were burned at the stake as punishment.

CASTE-CLASS FOUNDATIONS

The foundations for the dual systems of caste and class in the South, reported by social scientists in the late 1930's and early 1940's, were laid during the period of slavery. The caste-like character of relations between whites and black slaves was rather obvious, with caste membership being fixed at birth and not changing. Blacks were not allowed to become a part of the white world. Marriage between the two castes was strictly forbidden, although sexual intercourse between upper caste males and lower caste females was widely practiced. Children of such unions took the caste of the mother. Any sexual relations between lower caste men and upper caste women, however, were severely punished. Blacks were restricted to selected occupations, and whenever possible, whites avoided this sort of work as "nigger work."

Moreover, a rudimentary class structure was emerging among blacks. There was status differentiation among slaves, with house servants generally ranking above field hands. Another stratum, one normally of higher status than house servants, was composed of skilled artisans and craftsmen. In many cases, selected slaves served as foremen, directing the activities of field crews or other work gangs. Naturally, such trust and authority set them aside as people of higher social standing.

The "free people of color" during the era of slavery also became part of the foundation for the black class sytem after the Civil War. Treated as essentially a third caste in society, this category of people was still defined as Negro. It was formed by refugees, often wealthy, from the civil war in Saint Dominique, along with manumitted slaves and individuals who had purchased their freedom.[50] For the most part, these people had financial resources and useful skills and filled occupations needed by the dominant caste. After the Civil War, their superior education, skills and knowledge of the white world readily cast them into roles of leadership among blacks, for they found themselves now defined in the same social category with the former slaves. They helped to shape the upper stratum of an emergent black class system.

THE CLASS SYSTEM AMONG WHITES TO 1865

At the time of the Revolution, Georgia was basically on the frontier, consisting of a narrow strip of settlement along the coast and up the Savannah River to a point just above Augusta. While many of the first colonists were poor, they were not of lower class origins. Bringing with them useful skills, they usually prospered, if modestly so. They were soon joined by the Highlanders at Darien and the Salzburgers up the Savannah River, both being groups of able, industrious settlers. While a few plantations, devoted to the cultivation of rice and indigo following the model of South Carolina, developed along the coast, most of these settlers became farmers, not planters. Add the craftsmen and small businessmen of Savannah and scattered smaller towns, and the result is a largely middle-class society.

Expansion along the western boundary followed the French and Indian War, which resulted in land cessions by the Creeks, but this was soon foreclosed by the Revolution. This conflict was especially divisive in Georgia where so many people opposed the war that it often took on the character of a civil war. At various times, both loyalists to the crown and patriotic enthusiasts for independence fled Georgia to areas of greater security, depending upon the ebb and flow of the fortunes of war. At the end, only half of the population remained. After the war, however, came a period of explosive growth along an ever retreating western frontier as the Indians were pushed back by a series of land cessions culminating in final removal of both Creeks and Cherokees. The introduction of long staple cotton to the sea islands about 1790 marked the real beginning of the plantation era and the extensive practice of slavery in Georgia. Immediately thereafter, Whitney's gin for separating the fibers from the seed of short staple cotton was developed, and with it a profitable crop for the red hills of the Piedmont was born.

The pattern of settlement of the frontier has often been described, but perhaps most clearly by Owsley.[51] First came the hunters and herdsmen of cattle, hogs and sheep, often thrusting into Indian lands ahead of treaties or official sanction. They ran their livestock on public lands until farmers arrived with titles, fences and their own livestock. Then they converted to farming or more likely moved on, sometimes to new frontiers and sometimes to land undesirable for farming but valuable for grazing. Thus, when Georgia had been fully settled, the herdsmen occupied the vast piney woods of the south and the mountains of the north. If their permanent land holdings were too small to support large herds, they were usually poor because they could not profitably resort to farming their land. With adequate open land at their disposal, they continued to prosper as their type had done from the beginning of the English colonies.

With the hunger for land that was a post-Revolutionary War obsession, the farmer pressed hard upon the frontier, sending people westward across the mountains or southward past their end in Georgia. With ability and good fortune, the farmers prospered on vigorous virgin soil, and some bought slaves to expand the number of acres they could plant in cotton. Thus developed the Piedmont plantations. These small planters were johnnies-come-lately — a raw, unpolished, recent aristocracy, still more culturally akin to their backwoods cousins than the largely mythical cavalier planter.

By 1860, a complex system had emerged in Georgia. Different ways of gaining increase from the land — herding, farming, operating slave-powered plantations, large and small — created a multi-layered class structure.[52] Moreover, emergent industrialization was beginning to have its effects upon the character and structure of the stratification system. It is possible to identify and in a global fashion characterize five classes, using the classic Weberian definition cited earlier:

> **Class I.** Rich and powerful planters, successful cotton factors, owners of the largest wholesale and retain merchandizing operations.
>
> **Class II.** Medium range planters, professionals, successful businessmen, factory managers.
>
> **Class III.** Small planters, farmers, herdsmen, overseers, tradesmen, craftsmen.
>
> **Class IV.** Subsistence farmers, backwoods herdsmen, laborers (usually found in factories or other urban work).
>
> **Class V.** "Poor white trash" — In rural settings, they subsisted on hunting, gathering, limited farming, handouts and occasional agricultural day labor for farmers or planters. In towns and cities they were sporadically employed at unskilled tasks and scavenged for food and clothes.

Georgia had always had a middle class from the founding of Savannah until the Civil War, and the Class I wealthy planters were never numerous. Most Georgians in 1860 fell into Classes II-IV, with Classes II and III dominating.

What about the issue of class conflict during the period 1733-1865? Cash[53] and Owsley[54] strongly contend that there was none, citing several reasons: extensive kinship networks that cut across class lines, linking planter with small farmer; recentness of most planters' climb to high status, leaving some identification with and affection for those still in the lower classes; availability of opportunity in the form of unexploited lands, fueling continuing aspirations on the part of the less affluent to join the planter class themselves. This picture of interclass harmony, however, is almost certainly overdrawn. The social structure had too many built-in conflicts of interest to be free of tension and potential conflict. Fraser in a relevant study of 18th century South Carolina discovered sharp, sometimes deadly conflicts between officers drawn from the planter stratum and the common man conscripts who served under them during the Revolution.[55] Would similar class structures in Georgia not tend to produce similar conflicts? Georgians from the mountains and piney woods who had no vested interest in slavery, like similar people in virtually every Southern state, opposed secession. Fighting to maintain slavery in no way promoted their class interests. It was not a world free from conflict.

AFTER 1865: CASTE AND CLASS

Reconstruction turned the familiar world on its head. Under laws enforced by the Union army, the freed slaves were granted all basic civil rights, including the right to vote. They swept into elective offices, even dominating the state legislature, but unskilled in politics and often illiterate, these new politicians were used by others, both to punish the vanquished and for economic exploitation. Whites became increasingly fearful. Their resentment at losing the war, at their treatment by the Union government, at carpetbagger exploitation and at their former slaves' new status also smoldered at intense heat.

White reaction broke out, even under the watchful eye of an army of occupation as the Ku Klux Klan was born as a vehicle of intimidation and coercion. The period after Reconstruction was one of intense conflict across the South as the whites fashioned a caste system and forced blacks into servile status. Lynchings became commonplace. Regaining control of state legislatures, whites systematically enacted packages of Jim Crow laws that stripped away blacks' newly acquired civil rights, especially the right to vote.[56] Georgia was, of course, no exception, although its Jim Crow legislative package passed in 1908 was the last to be enacted by the Old South states.

An important factor in the negativism of the era was the broken economy. In the first place, the war destroyed the economic infrastructure, took the lives of many economic leaders and led to rapacious carpetbagger exploitation. Markets for Southern crops were lost, never to be regained fully during the war as England and other European nations turned to or developed alternative sources of supply. Additionally, planters were unprepared to develop a new production system to replace slavery. Donald contends that another major factor in the weak economy was diminished productivity due to the withdrawal of many black women from the work force after emancipation, reducing productive capacity by about 30 percent.[57]

Often overlooked in discussions of the post-bellum Southern economy is the fact that the marketplace was under the control of Northern economic interests. In large part, the war itself was a result of a long political struggle over which regional power center would run the country and determine economic policy. Eastern interests, particularly those from New England, were at last in the driver's seat. With that power in hand, they often treated the South like European powers treated their colonial territories, extracting its resources and exploiting the labor of the natives who toiled in poverty while the colonial power kept the profits. The price of Georgia cotton was little affected by world supply; it was determined by an Eastern economic elite, which also decided the economic fates of Midwestern farmers and New England sweatshop laborers. In the South, profit was rare no matter how well a farm was managed. Want was prevalent and the ex-slaves and other poor people suffered most, as is always the case.

The alternative to the plantation system which emerged in the South was sharecropping. There were landowners without anyone to work their fields, and there was a vast multitude of freed slaves and impoverished whites who had lost everything — workers without land, equipment, houses or food. Pledging cotton yet to be grown to banks and supply merchants, the landowners secured credit to underwrite the necessities of life for themselves and the sharecroppers who worked their land. Usually, the chief beneficiaries, other than those who controlled the cotton market, were bankers and supply merchants.

Sharecropping lent itself to abuse and all too frequently was a vicious system, little different from slavery. Sharecroppers found themselves caught up in debt peonage. Whether because of a poor crop year, low prices or fraudulent manipulation of accounts, they would find at the end of the year that their "run bills" — the debts which were charged against them for food, medicine and other necessities — were greater than their shares of the gross profits from the crops. Thus, they were still in debt and obliged to work for the same landowners the next year in an attempt to pay off the balance along with new debts accrued in securing the necessities of life on credit while the next crop was being grown. Since an entire social order rested upon the working of this system, the law and the courts vigorously supported the landowners.

Although the life of the field hand was little improved over plantation slavery, there were differences in sharecropping. Blacks were not alone in peonage, for there were more white sharecroppers than black, reflecting the impact of the Civil War on the white middle class. Moreover, the system tended to victimize both races of poor people rather equally.

There were occasional, scattered variations in this almost feudalistic world of King Cotton. Southern Georgia experienced brief periods of greater prosperity through concerted efforts in extraction of natural resources. The practice of floating timber down the Altamaha River and its tributaries for sale in Darien began during the frontier era but redoubled after the Civil War. Systematic timber cutting began late in the century with the introduction of portable steam-driven sawmills that were moved from one central location to another throughout the vast forest region on narrow-gauge railroads that were extended deep into the woodlands to transport the timber to the sawmills. Although millions of virgin pines and cypress were harvested, only the timber entrepreneurs prospered significantly. The farmers who sold the timber were poor bargainers, and the sawmill hands who harvested it had no other option other than sharecropping. So both received scant rewards for their contributions.

Practiced during colonial days on a limited scale, turpentining expanded rapidly in the 1880's. From the 1890's forward, Georgia replaced North Carolina as leader in naval stores production. Turpentine camps sprang up across the pine barrens, employing thousands under a variation of sharecropping. A few large-scale turpentine producers amassed fortunes in Southern Georgia, in most cases by exploiting the labors of black people who had little or no alternative way of making a living. Turpentining also was valuable to some family farm operations which produced a few barrels of tar as a sideline.

Transportation centers in the middle and Piedmont regions attracted gradual industrial and commercial development. Henry W. Grady's vision of the New South was founded upon industrialization, and true to that vision, evidences of urban prosperity began to appear prior to the Great Depression. In keeping with this development, foundations were laid for an industrial proletariat — occupational specialization and other elements of a modern stratification system.

However, for all of these variations, the stratification system remained remarkably stable and encompassing from 1865 to 1941. It was a dual system of caste and class with a sharp line of demarcation separating black from white and a fairly well-defined class structure for each of the two races. It should be noted, however, that a white sharecropper from near the bottom of his class system had a higher status than a black physician at the top of his class hierarchy.[58] The characteristics of a caste system fit the situation closely: caste membership set by ascription (birth), no intercaste marriage, strong social sanctions to maintain the system and ties between occupational assignment and caste membership. The only escape was to leave the South as blacks did in increasing numbers after World War I.

The boll weevil and the Great Depression began the process of a painful but liberating death to the Georgia of the Old South. Reforms initiated by the Franklin D. Roosevelt administration also helped to usher in a new social and economic order, one in which old caste and class lines could not stand if for no other reason than that they were hopelessly outmoded. However, World War II was probably the effective watershed in the destruction of the caste system and the restructuring of the class system. Millions of people were dislocated by World War II and never settled back into old ruts. Military service changed white and black Georgians alike, exposing them to new places, ways of life, skills and opportunities, as well as danger and death. Manpower shortages opened employment opportunities never before available to those who were not in military service. After the war, many were reluctant to return to old roles, particularly if it meant sharecropper poverty and subservience. G.I. Bill provisions made possible technical training, higher education, ownership of a home or business and other opportunities never before seriously envisioned by thousands of young men. The old economic, political and social order was thereby doomed.

Many blacks used their broadened knowledge and opportunities to escape the South. The trickle of migrants to Northern cities in the 20's became a stream during the Depression and a flood after World War II. However, among those who benefited from improved education and income and who remained in the South, a broad new leadership emerged to challenge the decaying caste system during the 50's and 60's.

The civil rights movement brought into the open the hidden, repressed conflict that had always been at the heart of the black-white caste structure. Blacks had been retained in an inferior status by a variety of forms of coercion, and even though they often seemed to accept this state of affairs, their resentment was profound. Conflict simply awaited an opportunity for expression. In the case of the civil rights movement, blacks took the initiative, redefining the basis and character of the conflict. They redirected it more on their own terms. On the whole, the conflict fostered by the civil rights movement was constructive in its impact upon society. It laid bare the oppressive character of the old order, and it won legal and moral victories that created a new order in black-white relations. The opening of access to the economic, educational and political spheres of society destroyed the foundations of the caste system in Georgia.

The economic changes in Georgia since World War II have been revolutionary in scope. Its industrial and commercial base has changed, broadened and deepened. It appears to be poised at the gateway to more dramatic economic development in the pattern of other "sunbelt" states. A new era of economic opportunity would further alter social stratification, fostering an open class system in which the inevitable conflicts will be mainly economic in character, freed of the burden of ascriptive designations based on race. The stratification system of Georgia's future, in contrast to its history, will be one of class without caste.

NOTES

[1]George Brown Tindall, *The Ethnic Southerners* (Baton Rouge: Louisiana State University Press, 1976), 35-36.

[2]Metta Spencer, *Foundations of Modern Sociology,* 3rd edition (Englewood Cliffs, N.J.: Prentice Hall, 1982), 240.

[3]Max Weber, "Class, Status and Power" in *Max Weber: Essays in Sociology,* ed. H.H. Gerth and C. Wright Mills (New York: Oxford University Press, 1946), 180-195.

[4]Max Weber, *The Religion of India,* trans., Don Martindale (Glencoe, Ill.: The Free Press, 1958).

[5]W. Lloyd Warner, "American Caste and Class," *American*

Journal of Sociology, 42:2 (1936), 234-237.

⁶Allison Davis, B.B. Gardner and M.R. Gardner, *Deep South* (Chicago: University of Chicago Press, 1941); John Dollard, *Caste and Class in a Southern Town* (New Haven: Yale University Press, 1937).

⁷Charles Hudson, *The Southeastern Indians* (Knoxville: University of Tennessee Press, 1977), 3-4.

⁸*Ibid.*, 202-206.

⁹Marshall D. Sahlins, "Poor Man, Rich Man, Big Man, Chief: Political Types in Melanesia and Polynesia," *Comparative Studies in Society and History*, 5 (1963), 205-303.

¹⁰Hudson, *The Southeastern Indians*, 223-225.

¹¹Fred Gearing, *Priests and Warriors: Social Structures for Cherokee Politics in the 18th Century*. American Anthropological Association Memoir 93 (Washington, D.C., 1962), 3, 42.

¹²Hudson, *The Southeastern Indians*, 105.

¹³*Ibid.*, 205-206.

¹⁴Gearing, *Priest and Warriors*, 38; V. Richard Persico, "Early Nineteenth Century Cherokee Political Organization" in *The Cherokee Indian Nation: A Troubled History*, ed. Duane King (Knoxville: University of Tennessee Press, 1979), 95-98; John P. Reid, *A Law of Blood: The Primitive Law of the Cherokee Nation* (New York: New York University Press), 63-64.

¹⁵Hudson, *The Southeastern Indians*, 184-185.

¹⁶William H. Gilbert, *The Eastern Cherokees*, Bureau of American Ethnology Bulletin, no. 133 (Washington, D.C., 1943), 203-209; John R. Swanton, *The Indians of the Southeastern United States*, Bureau of American Ethnology Bulletin, no. 137 (Washington, D.C., 1946), 654-660.

¹⁷Reid, *A Law of Blood*, 37-48.

¹⁸Gearing, *Priests and Warriors*, 21-24; Elman R. Service, *Primitive Social Organization: An Evolutionary Perspective* (New York: Random House, 1962), 112-113.

¹⁹Hudson, *The Southeastern Indians*, 189.

²⁰Gearing, *Priests and Warriors*. 73-76; Reid, *A Law of*

Blood, 39-40.

[21]Gilbert, *The Eastern Cherokees,* 245-253; Hudson, *The Southeastern Indians,* 187.

[22]Hudson, *The Southeastern Indians,* 272-299.

[23]*Ibid.,* 435-437.

[24]Charles Hudson, "Why the Southeastern Indians Slaughtered Deer" in *Indians, Animals and the Fur Trade: A Critique of Keepers of the Game,* ed. Shepard Krech (Athens: Univ. of Georgia Press, 1981), 169-170; Verner W. Crane, *The Southern Frontier 1670-1732* (Ann Arbor: Univ. of Michigan Press, 1929), 206-234.

[25]Harold H. Martin, *Georgia: A Bicentennial History* (New York: W.W. Norton, 1977), 28-29.

[26]Gearing, *Priests and Warriors,* 85-88; Hudson, "Why the Southeastern Indians Slaughtered Deer," 162-163, 166-168.

[27]Hudson, *The Southeastern Indians,* 438-440.

[28]R.S. Cotterill, *The Southern Indians: The Story of the Civilized Tribes Before Removal* (Norman: Univ. of Oklahoma Press, 1954), 29-32; David H. Corkran, *The Creek Frontier, 1540-1783* (Norman: Univ. of Oklahoma Press, 1967).

[29]Cotterill, *The Southern Indians,* 32-36.

[30]Ibid., 37-42; Corkran, *The Creek Frontier,* 298-299; James H. O'Donnell, *Southeastern Indians in the American Revolution* (Knoxville: Univ. of Tennessee Press, 1973).

[31]Hudson, *The Southeastern Indians,* 449-451.

[32]Persico, "Early Nineteenth Century Cherokee Political Organization," 92, 99-108.

[33]Cotterill, *The Southern Indians,* 215-222.

[34]Jesse Burt and Robert Ferguson, *Indians of the Southeast: Then and Now* (Nashville: Abingdon Press, 1973), 173-179.

[35]Hudson, *The Southeastern Indians,* 454, 457-461, 462-464.

[36]Frank I. Owsley, *Plain Folk of the Old South* (Baton Rouge: Louisiana State Univ. Press, 1949, reprinted by Quadrangle Books, 1965), 150-181.

[37]*Ibid.,* 34-35.

[38]*Ibid.,* 156-157.

[39]Fanny A. Kemble, *Journal of a Residence on a Georgia Plantation in 1838-39*, ed. John A Scott (New York: Alfred A. Knopf, 1961).

[40]Sue Mullins Moore, "The Antebellum Barrier Island Plantation: In Search of an Archaeological Pattern," unpublished doctoral dissertation, the University of Florida, Gainesville, 1981, 1983.

[41]Ulrich B. Phillips, *Life and Labor in the Old South* (Boston: Little, Brown and Company, 1929), 261-269.

[42]*Ibid.*, 267.

[43]Charles H. Fairbanks and Sue Mullins Moore, "How Did Slaves Live?" *Early Man*, 2:2 (1980), 6.

[44]Moore, "The Antebellum Barrier Island Plantation," 221; Fairbanks and Moore, "How Did Slaves Live?", 3.

[45]Moore, "The Antebellum Barrier Island Plantation."

[46]David J. Bodenhamer, "Law and Disorder in the Old South: The Situation in Georgia, 1830-1860," *From the Old South to the New*, ed. Walter J. Fraser, Jr. and Winfred B. Moore, Jr. (Westport, Conn.: Greenwood Press, 1981), 109-119.

[47]Owsley, *Plain Folk of the Old South*, 157-181.

[48]Phillips, *Life and Labor in the Old South*. 208-213.

[49]*Ibid.*, 194.

[50]Ira Berlin, "The Structure of the Free Negro Caste in the Antebellum United States," *The Southern Common People*, ed. Edward Magdol and Jon L. Wakelyn (Westport, Conn.: Greenwood Press, 1980), 109-115.

[51]Owsley, *Plain Folk of the Old South*, 23-77.

[52]W.J. Cash, *The Mind of the South* (New York: Alfred A. Knopf, Vintage Books, 1941 and 1969), 22-29; Phillips, *Life and Labor in the Old South*, 340-366; Owsley, *Plain Folk of the Old South*, 1-90.

[53]Cash, *The Mind of the South*, 36-37.

[54]Owsley, *Plain Folk of the Old South*, 133-134.

[55]Walter J. Fraser, Jr. "Reflections of 'Democracy' in Revolutionary South Carolina?: The Composition of Military Organizations and the Attitudes and Relationships of the Of-

ficers and Men," *The Southern Common People*, ed. Edward Magdol and Jon L. Wakelyn (Westport, Conn.: Greenwood Press, 1980), 11-20.

[56]David H. Donald, "A Generation of Defeat," *From the Old South to the New*, ed. Walter J. Fraser, Jr. and Winfred B. Moore, Jr. (Westport, Conn.: Greenwood Press, 1981), 3-20.

[57]*Ibid.*, 15.

[58]Davis, Gardner and Gardner, *Deep South;* Dollard, *Caste and Class in a Southern Town.*

Lost But Found:
Georgia Women

CHARLOTTE A. FORD

Generally, American history has been defined in masculine terms such as politics, government, military, banking, exploration — areas in which women were rarely involved. Those few women included in the history books were there because their activities fell within the men's value systems. The Revolutionary heroine Nancy Hart, for example, is depicted as masculinized, shrewish and coarse, not as courageous, intelligent and determined. Historians, therefore, concluded that women played no important role in the decision-making process. Growing out of the turmoil of the 1960's, however, the new interest in women marked a change from the traditional male orientation of American history. Thus, it has been only within the last two or three decades that women's history has become a recognized field.

Women have fared no better in Georgia history, for historians of the state have largely ignored them. A two-volume work published in 1895 included three women out of about one thousand persons, with each woman being identified through her father or husband. E. Merton Coulter, author of the longtime standard work on Georgia history, listed twenty-six women in a thirty-four page index in the 1960 edition. In a new history of Georgia, women fare slightly better with thirty-one entries in the ten-page index. The recently published *Dictionary of Georgia Biography* includes ninety-two women in the more than one thousand entries.[1]

A major difficulty in learning about Georgia women, therefore, is the dearth of information about them. Biographies of men have paid scant attention to female relatives, and there are few biographies of women. It becomes necessary in the quest for Georgia women, then, to search these books as well as public and private records — diaries, letters, journals. At present, several Georgians are working to increase public awareness of the contributions made by women, but there is no general history as yet. Because most textbooks do not include a great deal of material about women, the teacher of Georgia history must add this information. To assist teachers in finding information on women, this article will present first some of the sources, and second, some of the women.[2]

In order to interpret the information to students, teachers also need to be familiar with the broad range of the women's movement and the theories of women's history. Some students of the movement credit Betty Friedan with the opening salvo in contemporary feminism. In her classic critique of the social role of the housewife, Friedan analyzed popular magazines, advertising, modern education and Freudian psychology. Kate Millett, another early feminist, emphasized the powerlessness of women and showed the sexism in society by using selected quotations from prominent writers. The battle cry of Shulamith Firestone is the call for revolution. Asserting that women can and must offset the sexual imbalance of power, she demanded that women be freed from the tyranny of reproductive biology, childbearing and economic dependence.[3]

Genealogy is another way women have been studied. Advocates of this method point out that since women's experiences have been largely domestic, the family defines the woman. Opponents of this method maintain that family history obscures women's experiences since women have been the passive variables in the study of how men established the family.

Writers also disagree over the interpretation of women's place in an era. Was the colonial period a golden age for women or an age of dependence and submission? Joan Hoff Wilson and Mary Ryan believe that colonial women, though economically dependent on males, actually had a high status in that agrarian world. The housewife's daily contribution to survival gave her self-respect, some equality with her spouse and a sense of self-worth and significance in the larger society. These authors consider the debasement of women's value a corollary of industrialization.[4] Historians Mary Beth Norton, Linda Kerber and Nancy Cott view colonial women as living in a non-egalitarian world with little sense of their own importance and with low self-esteem. They believe that the rise of industrialism and post-Revolutionary nationalism elevated women's status.[5]

Our textbooks, however, generally ignore women living on the frontier and those working in factories. Authors write about males in the westward movement but neglect the women who made the trek at the insistence of the men in the family. The work of Joanna Stratton emphasizes these pioneer women. In similar fashion, female slaves receive scant attention except in studies of slave families. Since relatively few women worked outside the home until the twentieth century, they have been easy to forget. Recently, Barbara M. Wertheimer published a study of working women, and as more material on pioneers, slaves and working women becomes available, these situations should change.[6]

The usual view is that women were not part of the political process because they did not vote. Although denied the franchise, women had some influence on the political scene through their involvement in various reform movements and charitable activities which did not violate society's conventions. While these volunteer and church-related groups provided a "cause" for women, they also proved to be training grounds for future leaders. One reform movement that went beyond acceptable limits was that of the feminists. Georgia women as a rule, however, did not support the feminists of the Seneca Falls Convention in 1848. In ante-bellum Georgia, most women lived in traditional roles which they described in their letters and journals.[7]

A number of books by women describing the ante-bellum and war years appeared many years after the events. Emily P. Burke's *Pleasure and Pain, Reminiscences of Georgia in the 1840's* first appeared in 1850 and was reprinted by the Beehive Press of Savannah in 1978. Both Margaret Mitchell and Mark Twain borrowed scenes from Mary A.H. Gay's *Life in Dixie During the War, 1863-1865,* published by the Atlanta Constitution Job Office in 1897.[8] The Washington, Georgia teacher-novelist-botanist, Eliza Frances Andrews, kept a journal for 1864-1865, when she was twenty-four years old, and after revising the manuscript in 1908, published it as *The War Time Journal of a Georgia Girl, 1864-1865.* Among other diaries and journals published are those of Dolly Sumner Lunt Burge, Anna W. Habersham and Josephine Habersham Clay.[9]

During the late nineteenth and early twentieth centuries, the lives of many women changed. More professions were open to them and more jobs became available, but the struggle for women's rights continued. Aileen S. Kraditor points out the many issues confronted by the suffragists; Anne Firor Scott recounts the struggle for the franchise; and Eleanor Flexner writes about women's movements. Women active in the reform movements of the period are described in books by David Pivar, Karen Blair and Jacquelyn D. Hall.[10] An overview of the issues in the Progressive Era is found in Peter G. Filene's work, which also deals with the revival of feminism in the 1960's. He finds post-World War II antifeminism rooted in the hostility to working women in the Depression. Much of the research in the modern period has been on the white middle-class women, but authors Ann Moody and Maxine Hong Kingston focus on minorities.[11]

The teacher of Georgia history, if resourceful, can find materials to supplement the general historical overview and to learn about women — what they did and what they thought. Women who wrote journals, diaries and letters provide insight into their life experiences, but since not all women were literate, the number is limited. Newspapers, both past and present, are useful for articles about women and news about their activities. Students can also learn from the artworks of the period. Formal portraits and paintings, folk arts and crafts teach about people, as do the literature and music of the time. A wealth of information can be found in the legal documents — wills, household inventories, court records, tax digests, land transfers, deed records. Additionally, articles in publications like *The Georgia Historical Quarterly, The Atlanta Historical Journal, The Georgia Review* and some popular magazines often include material about women. The information about women in Georgia may have to be accumulated little by little, but it can be found. While an examination of the position of women in Georgia reveals that most were engaged in the traditional woman's work in the home, the domestic scene, there are some women who did other things.

On the Atlantic crossing aboard the *Anne,* the women, according to one male writer, made stockings and caps and mended clothes. One, Mrs. Warren, gave birth to a child, although the physician on board made no record of the event. He did, however, note a few weeks later that Mr. Oglethorpe presented a dolphin he caught to "some Bigbellyd Woman in the ship." Another time Oglethorpe ordered that every woman receive a glass of wine, and when he was preparing to settle Frederica, he told the men to talk over the move with their wives. The women elected to go — we do not know whether voluntarily or under coercion. From these few incidents, one may conclude that early Georgia women fulfilled their domestic and maternal roles, while at the same time, their spirit of adventure and courage shows in their daring to come to the New World, and then, in daring to leave the relative security of Savannah for a less settled area.[11]

One woman who is not ignored in the Georgia books is Coosaponakeesa, daughter of an Indian mother and an English father, and married to a Carolina trader, then a soldier and finally a clergyman. Mary Musgrove Matthews Bosomworth, fluent in both the Creek language and English, was a diplomat whose skills Oglethorpe utilized. Why else would he have agreed to pay her an annual stipend of 100 pounds, the same salary paid the civil administrators, and why else would he have taken a diamond ring off his finger to give her? An entrepreneur who owned 6,200 acres of land, Mary provided food and warriors when needed. When she could not collect on Oglethorpe's promises, Mary challenged the Trustees who had her arrested. She was described as an "insignificant squaw and a lyar," but she had the last word when Governor Henry Ellis presented her with 2,100 pounds and St. Catherine's Island in 1760.[13]

That Mary Musgrove owned land sets her apart from the majority of Georgia women. It was not easy for women to own land because the Trustees, claiming military necessity, entailed property to men, implying that women owning land would reduce military strength. In due time this restriction was eliminated, and between 1755 and 1775, at least 164 women received about 6,700 acres of land under the headright system which gave the head of a family 100 acres plus 50 acres for each dependent. The majority of these grants went to either widows or spinsters so that they would be able to support themselves and not be a burden to the colony.[14] One group which included women threatened to leave Georgia over the land issue. The "Red String Conspiracy," so-called because the plotters wore a red string around their wrists, originated at the home of widow Elizabeth Browning according to storekeeper Thomas Causton. These plotters threatened to leave the colony "upon pretence, that they have no title to show for their lands," Causton explained.[15]

Widows were somewhat better off than wives in the colonial era because they could work outside the home. Their work, however, was usually related to the domestic sphere, or they continued the business of their husband. Widow Martha Bamford notified Savannahians in 1768 that she would "carry on the business as usual and ladies and gentlemen may be dressed; tates and wigs made." Mrs. Mary Hughes announced that she proposed to "carry on a millinery business and had imported a new assortment of millinery, laces, French trimmings and earrings of pearl and garnet." Other jobs advertised by women included their services as hair dresser, washer of lace and silk stockings, bakers and seamstress for women and children.[16]

Women also operated boarding houses, coffee houses and taverns. After her husband's death in 1775, Lucy Tondee continued to operate Peter Tondee's tavern, meeting place for Patriots. Not all of these women, however, were as successful as Abigail Minis who owned a tavern before the Revolution. She also held 3,000 acres of land and was wealthy enough to furnish provisions for the colonials. Lucretia Triboudet suffered a break-in and robbers took a variety of goods, including 18 boys' hats, ivory and horn combs, paper money, a wooden bowl full of eggs and silver shoe buckles. Mary Hepburn advertised the opening of a coffee house where "Gentlemen may breakfast on the same footing as in London," but four months later she closed the business. Perhaps her failure was due to the absence of enough men interested in a London breakfast, or to her admission that she was a novice in the business.[17]

The misadventures of Mary Simons show another side of what happened to women in Georgia. Oglethorpe "gave" Mary, who came to Georgia with Mrs. Magdalene Papott, to Arthur Ogle Edgcomb. After being sold twice, she was either sold or hired out to Paul Cheeswright as a servant. Reports reached Thomas Causton, the storekeeper, that Mary was being misused, and on investigating he found Mary and four men in one room. Mary was placed in the service of John Fallowfield, who was "Marryed to a Carefull woman." An account to Oglethorpe reported that the midwife feared that Mary was pregnant but added that "If any in ye Town can Brek her from her ill habbit they (the Fallowfields) will."[18] Poor Alice Riley came to Georgia from Ireland as an indentured servant. She and Richard White worked for William Wise, a farmer, under unpleasant conditions. They fell in love, but as indentures could not marry, they decided to murder Wise by drowning him. White was hanged, and Alice was hanged six weeks after the birth of her son who soon died.[19] This is the first record of a woman criminal who was put to death in Georgia.

Since the opportunities for an education were limited in colonial Georgia, teaching the children was usually the responsibility of the mother. However, if a family lived in Savannah, the girls could attend Elizabeth Bedon's school as boarders or day scholars. There they would learn reading, writing, arithmetic and needlework. At Edward Langworthy's school, young ladies could receive private instruction in English grammar and writing. For his male students, Langworthy offered Latin, Greek writing, arithmetic, reading and pronunciation.[20]

During the Revolution, Georgia women, like those in other parts of the country, did everything that was expected of them. Some were like Nancy Hart who was a spy and combatant. She once held six Tories at bay in her log cabin until her husband and his patriot friends arrived. They wanted to shoot the Tories, but she insisted that they be hanged. While the story cannot be documented, the *Atlanta Constitution* reported in an article in 1912 that railroad workers excavating in the vicinity of the Hart cabin uncovered a shallow grave that contained six male skeletons.[21] There were also women like Hannah Clarke, wife of General Elijah Clarke, the hero of Hornet's Nest, the Wilkes County backcountry. When her husband was wounded, Hannah went to camp to care for him and usually ended up pregnant. She celebrated the victory at Yorktown by giving birth to twins.[22] Probably most women were like Susannah Fort, wife of Arthur Fort, who lived on the Georgia frontier in Wilkes County. Once when Arthur slipped home to visit his family, Tory marauders surprised him and threatened to kill him. Tiny Susannah Fort threw herself in front of her six-foot tall husband, and the intruders spared Fort's life because of the "little woman."[23]

After the war, the thoughts and interests of women turned back to the traditional model. Even so, there were women who represent a less conventional role. Catherine Greene, widow to General Nathanael Greene, lived at Mulberry Grove near Savannah, which she managed with the assistance of an overseer. Eli Whitney was at Mulberry Grove when he designed a machine to separate cotton seeds from the fibers. Whitney had some difficulty in finding a way to pull the lint off the rollers, and Catherine Greene is credited with suggesting that a brush would solve the problem. The invention of the cotton gin in 1793 made cotton king in the South before the Civil War. Caty's second marriage was to Phineas Miller who became Whitney's partner in building the gins.[24]

The first woman newspaper editor in Georgia was Sarah Porter Hillhouse who had moved with her husband to Washington, Wilkes County sometime prior to 1787. David Hillhouse opened a general store, purchased a plantation and the *Washington Gazette* in 1801. After her husband's death in 1803, Sarah Hillhouse operated the newspaper, the store and the plantation. Under her direction, the printing business expanded to include the reports of the state legislature and local lottery tickets. She probably published the paper for about ten years before relinquishing the control to her son.[25] During this time John H. Barclay, a local merchant, was found shot to death. The merchant's beautiful young wife, Polly, alleged to be in love with another man, was arrested. Two men charged with her were released, but she was found guilty and sentenced to be hanged. The hanging took place on May 30, 1806, even though she pled with the sheriff not "to hang so beautiful a woman." An unsubstantiated account claims that the sheriff fixed the noose so that it would not cause instant death and that she was cut down, revived by a doctor and lived to be an old woman, free because the state's sentence had been carried out.[26]

Women were not encouraged to show any interest in scientific fields, but plants were accepted by society as an area in which women could dabble. One who did not dabble was Anna Rosina Gambold, a Moravian missionary to the Cherokees in North Georgia from 1805 until her death in 1821. She established a botanical garden at the mission, including medicinal herbs, and compiled a list of the plants grown in the vicinity. The list was published in *The American Journal of Science* in 1818. Another pioneer, Charlotte Scarborough Taylor of Savannah, was Georgia's first woman entomologist. Born into a wealthy family and educated in New York, she became at twenty-three the reluctant bride of James Taylor, a Scottish immigrant and partner in a cotton factoring firm. Her husband went bankrupt and financial pressures may have led to her writing career. Between 1859 and 1864, she published eighteen signed articles in *Harper's New Monthly Magazine*. She wrote about spiders, gnats, flies, fleas, moths, grasshoppers and silk worms and illustrated the articles with incredibly detailed drawings. Although she had completed twenty years of research before she began writing, her work failed to attract the attention of the scientific world, possibly because it was published in popular magazines.[27]

While there were some women who stepped outside the domestic sphere in the ante-bellum period in Georgia, generally they left economic and political affairs to men. Employment outside the home occurred before marriage or in widowhood for most working women, except for slave women. Reform movements, charitable activities or church-related groups, however, provided outside interests which were sanctioned by society and proved to be training grounds for future leaders. As the wives of planters and yeoman farmers, politicians and professional men, women learned to manage farms and to sell produce, even if it were chicken and egg money. They gained knowledge which would be put to use during the Civil War.

The eruption of the war allowed women to participate in various activities from nursing and teaching to fighting and operating plants. For this period, there are numerous diaries and journals (see notes 8 and 9). While the major portion of the published works are by white women, there are some detailing the lives of black women. Susie King Taylor, in her autobiography written after the war, described conditions of her people during slavery and Reconstruction. She learned to read and write, became a teacher, a domestic and a social worker.[28] Matilda Beasley, a free black who lived in Savannah before the war, conducted a clandestine school for black children. Her husband was a free man mulatto in the slave trade who, during Reconstruction, had a great deal of money. After the war, Matilda Beasley studied with the Franciscan nuns and gave the Roman Catholic Church the property that she inherited from her husband. The church sent her to England for her novitiate, and Mother Beasley, the first black nun in Georgia, established an orphanage for black children in Savannah before her death in 1903.[29]

Teaching continued to be an approved job for women, but not all the teachers were native Georgians. The letters of a New York woman, Amelia Akehurst Lines, describe her experiences in different towns in Georgia. Hers was not a very exciting life, but perhaps that is the kind of experience most teachers had.[30] After the war, Northern teachers came to educate blacks. Eliza Ann Ward, a forty-two year old spinster from Massachusetts, arrived in Savannah in 1867 to teach at Beach Institute and stayed five years in Georgia. Ward is typical of the teachers who came South, although she remained longer than most did. She left no memoirs, but the records of the American Missionary Association contain the account of her years in Georgia.[31]

Georgia has the distinction of being the first state to charter a college for women. In 1821, a proposal for a state-supported college for women failed, and it was not until 1836 that the legislature chartered the Georgia Female College in Macon. Catherine Brewer received the first degree in 1840, but when the Methodist Conference acquired control of the school two years later, the name was changed to Wesleyan Female College.[32] A widely known school for women, founded in 1889 as the Decatur Female Institute, was renamed Agnes Scott College the next year when George W. Scott donated money to build a permanent home for the school. From the beginning, Agnes Scott upheld the traditional role for women, but the course of study undermined the difference between the sexes as the women pursued an academic course modeled after that of schools for men. Agnes Scott students were encouraged to take their intellectual abilities seriously, while the liberal curriculum quietly weakened prejudices against the socially active woman.[33]

Perhaps the best-known woman associated with a Georgia school is Martha Berry. The Berry family lived at "Oak Hill" near Rome in Floyd County. After the Civil War, Martha Berry began a Sunday School for mountain children which later became a boarding school for boys. A work-study program enabled any student to work his way through school. The enrollment grew and Martha Berry appealed to philanthropists Henry Ford and Andrew Carnegie for aid. In 1909, a girls' division opened, followed by a junior college and in 1932 by a senior college. Miss Berry guided the schools until her death in 1942. In 1980, Berry College named its second woman president, Dr. Gloria Shatto, who had been the first woman academic administrator at Georgia Tech as Associate Dean of the College of Management before moving to Berry.[34]

There are other women educators who deserve mention. One woman who worked to give black children the same opportunities that white children had was Lucy Craft Laney. Born in Macon in 1854 into a family who had purchased freedom, the child learned to read from her mother. She also had access to the library of her mother's former owner. At age 15, she completed high school and entered the first class of Atlanta University, graduating in 1873. Lucy Laney taught in the public schools of Macon, Milledgeville, Savannah and Augusta, where she opened a school in 1883 with the mission to improve the quality of life for black citizens. She initiated the first kindergarten in Augusta, established the first training school for nurses and conducted teacher-training institutes throughout the area.[35]

A prominent educator in Athens was Miss Mildred Rutherford, Principal of Lucy Cobb Institute from 1880-1928. Hundreds of women came under Miss Rutherford's influence, both academically and morally.[36] Atlanta chose a woman, Dr. Ira Jarrell, as superintendent of the public school system in 1944. She was not only the first woman to hold that job, but she was also the only woman in the United States to head a major school system. Under her leadership, the system made many advances, including establishing equal pay rates for black and white teachers, opening a kindergarten and being the first school system in the United States to operate educational radio and television. Marie Sewell Kinnard, a nationally recognized authority in teaching the deaf for forty years (1920-60), taught at the Cave Springs School for the Deaf. Celeste Parrish came to Georgia Normal School in 1900 to supervise teacher-training and introduced progressive education to Georgia. She later became supervisor of rural education in North Georgia, the first woman to hold such a post.[37]

In the twentieth century women moved into scientific areas, although their training was still limited. Eliza Frances Andrews, Washington diarist and novelist, was also a self-taught botanist who wrote two textbooks for high schools. She wanted to make plants exciting for students and to encourage them to conserve wild plants. The proceeds from her texts, *Botany All the Year Around* and *A Practical Course in Botany*, she left to Rome, Georgia to provide for a park.[38] There are several Georgia women who are in the forefront of the conservation movement at present, including Marie Mellinger who works with children and senior citizens; Barbara Blum who was President Jimmy Carter's Deputy Administrator of the United States Environment Agency; Eleanor Torrey West of Ossabaw who has written a child's book about the island and film scripts about the coast; Jane Yarn who has been especially interested in the coastal marshes; Virginia Callaway who supervised construction of Callaway Gardens; and the late Mary Hambridge who set up a nature center in Rabun County.[39]

The medical field has opened for women in this century. Dr. Evangeline Thomas Papageorge, the first woman to teach at the Emory Medical School, was appointed in 1929 to instruct medical students in biochemistry. She was also the first woman to hold any high administrative post at Emory, retiring in 1975 as Executive Dean of the Medical School.[40] Not until 1946 did a woman, Winton Elizabeth Gambrell, receive her M.D. degree from Emory. Already known for her research on malaria, tuberculosis and brucellosis, Gambrell had earned her doctorate from the University of Chicago and was the recipient of numerous grants and awards while teaching at Emory. Upon completing her degree and internship, she elected to set up private practice, but still continued her affiliation with Emory.[41]

Although Emory did not open its medical school to women before World War II, the first woman doctor graduated from the Medical College of Georgia twenty-two years earlier in 1924. For about ten years, however, only one woman graduated annually. The third graduate was Leila Daughtry Denmark, who received her degree in 1928, interned at the newly opened Henrietta Egleston Hospital for Children in Atlanta and has been associated with the hospital since that time. Dr. Denmark, born in 1898, continues her private practice and her work at the Central Presbyterian Church Baby Clinic.[42] An Atlanta obstetrician, Dr. Luella Klein, took office in May, 1984 as the first woman president of the 3,500-member American College of Obstetricians and Gynecologists. She is Deputy Director of the Obstetrical Service at Grady Memorial Hospital.[43]

The business world has attracted a number of Georgia women entrepreneurs, estimated at 13, 549 in 1977. According to 1980 Internal Revenue Services figures for Georgia, women-owned proprietorships accounted for 20.5 percent of all such businesses in the state, but only 5.5 percent of the receipts. Most of these businesses employ from 1 to 5 persons, and nearly half are in service areas such as health care, house cleaning and office services. Another one-third is in wholesale-retail trade. There is growing evidence of improvement in these figures, and there are some success stories about women in non-traditional businesses. In Clarkesville, Joyce Eddy, faced with having to support herself and two sons, bought 20,000 old wooden spools from a textile mill in 1973. She and her brother made these into towel racks, candlestick holders and chandeliers, and her $400 investment has grown into the multi-million dollar Habersham Plantation furniture business. In

1984, Eddy was named Georgia Small Business Person of the Year.[44]

Another successful businesswoman is Margaret Lupo, owner of Mary Mac's Restaurant in Atlanta. In her family the women worked — her grandmother ran a plantation near Jonesboro and her mother was a school dietician. Since buying the restaurant in 1962, Lupo has expanded it from 75 to 250 seats and serves an average of 2,000 meals daily. When she needed money to buy the building in which her restaurant is located, the banks turned her down because of her sex. As a result of this experience, she became aware of the need for a support group of women with similar business problems, and she was one of the founders of the Commerce Club in Atlanta.[45]

The story of Carolyn Stradley is literally one of rags to riches. She is the principal owner of C & S Paving, a company that is making big money doing small jobs in a field that has traditionally been for men only. Born into poverty in the North Georgia mountains, she lived in a two-room house where water was drawn from a spring. Her mother died when she was eleven, and her father abandoned her and her fifteen-year old brother. Carolyn Stradley remained in the hills, scrounged for food and worked for neighbors to save money to go to Atlanta where her brother then lived. In Atlanta, she worked in a fast food place and attended high school, marrying a machine operator while she was in the eleventh grade. Eventually, she worked for a construction firm that encouraged her to attend Georgia Tech where she earned a degree in construction engineering. After her husband died, she went into business in 1979, and within five years, the company was solvent. *U.S. News & World Report* picked Stradley as one of eight women considered most likely to succeed in business. In 1982, the Georgia Small Business Council nominated her as Small Business Person of the Year, and *The Woman's Advocate* selected her as one of three role models for America's women, along with astronaut Sally Ride and TV producer Pat Macmillan.[46]

The clothing business attracts women owners also. Shirley Miller, whose husband is Lieutenant Governor Zell Miller, had a store in North Georgia before opening a dress shop in Norcross, an Atlanta suburb. She has also been co-publisher of a weekly county newspaper, a banker and a member of the President's Committee on Mental Retardation.[47] Two other women who hold responsible positions in large business operations are Anne Cox Chambers and Dean Day Smith. Chambers is chairman of the board of Cox Enterprises, a $2 billion media empire according to a *Wall Street Journal* estimate. A former director of Bank South Corporation, she was the first woman director of the Atlanta Chamber of Commerce and the only woman on the Coca Cola Company board. Additionally, she served as Ambassador to Belgium under President Carter. Deen Day Smith was chairman of the board of the multi-million dollar real estate holding company that controlled the Days Inn motel chain. When the business began operating from the Day home, she was secretary; then she became vice-president. In 1984, the chain of 322 motels with 44,000 rooms was sold.

The story of McKaysville Industries is an ongoing story of a small group of women who established a sewing cooperative in 1968. McKaysville, population about 1,600, is located on the Georgia-Tennessee line. When the recession of the late 1970's hit, demand for dresses and blouses fell, and the cooperative had to let some of the 35 women go. Though the women wanted to continue working without pay, the National Labor Relations Board would not agree. The business was dissolved in 1981; but in January, 1984, Bernice Ratcliff, who had been president of the cooperative, and her daughter opened Blue Ridge Textiles. Employing four women who worked for McKaysville Industries, they make table cloths and napkins and aprons for industrial use.[48] In a different kind of business venture, Frankie Jennings of Atlanta, sometimes called "the black Mary Kay," began a cosmetic company in 1976 which seven years later had sales in excess of $1 million. Frankie Jennings Cosmetics, Inc. employs about 300 sales people nationwide. Like Atlanta, most communities have women entrepreneurs whose story can add local interest to the classroom.

The number of Georgia women writers includes some well-known authors as well as lesser ones. One of the first successful writers was Augusta Jane Evans Wilson, who was born in Columbus in 1835 and earned over $100,000 in royalties during her lifetime. Her best selling novel, *St. Elmo,* was published in 1866. The heroines of Wilson's novels gave up fame and fortune for the love of a good man and a home, but the author was a role model who had both home and husband.[49] Although Augusta Jane Evans moved away from Columbus when she was a child, another woman began to write after moving to Columbus. Caroline Lee Hentz, born in Massachusetts, published her first novel in 1850 in order to support her family. She wrote in defense of the Southern way of life.[50]

Corra Mae White Harris (1869-1935) published her first article in a magazine outside the South in 1899. For the next ten years, she continued to write articles, stories and book reviews for the *Independent;* then she turned to writing novels. The first of her fourteen books was *A Circuit Rider's Wife,* which was based on her experiences in the first year of her marriage to Methodist minister Lundy Harris. Although critics do not consider her work of the highest quality, she was very popular and successful during her productive years.[51] Virtually unknown today is the work of Sarah Barnwell Elliott, born in Montpelier, Georgia in 1848. Her father became the first Protestant Episcopal bishop in Georgia and played a major role in the organization of the University of the South at Sewannee, Tennessee where she studied. She is thought to be the first female student to attend special summer classes at Johns Hopkins University in 1886. In 1891, *Scribner's Magazine* published her serial about "Jerry," a "poor white" Tennessee boy, that scholars claim whetted the interests of Americans in the mountaineers of the South. A feminist, Elliott was the first president of the Tennessee Equal Suffrage Association, and in 1912, she organized the meeting that was the turning point of the suffrage movement in the state.[52]

When Lula Carson Smith McCullers was twenty-three years old, she became an instant celebrity with the publication of her novel, *The Heart Is a Lonely Hunter,* in 1940. Beset by poor health, she continued to produce stories, verse, novels and children's verse until her death in 1967. The major themes in her work are loneliness, the need for communication and the search for identity.[53] For forty years, Lillian Eugenia Smith advocated human rights through her writing and lecturing. Her first novel, *Strange Fruit,* an indictment of the South's tradition, was a best-seller and *Killers of the Dream,* her second novel published in 1949, analyzed the Southern mind and morals. Lillian Smith wrote about racial prejudice and injustice in a time when many white Southerners would not face the issues.[54] Another celebrity, one of America's foremost short story writers, was Mary Flannery O'Connor of Milledgeville. She was a Catholic writer in the Bible Belt South who wrote about Protestants and the South. In her short lifetime, thirty-nine years, she published two novels and a collection of short stories, and two more collections appeared posthumously.[55]

The three Georgia women who have received Pulitzer Prizes are Caroline Miller, Margaret Mitchell and Alice Walker. Miller's novel, *Lamb in His Bosom*, won the prize in 1933. Set in the backwoods area around Waycross where her family had lived, the novel depicts the lives of Georgia frontiersmen before the Civil War.[56] The second Pulitzer, won in 1937, also had a Civil War setting. *Gone With the Wind*, the only book Margaret Mitchell wrote, has been translated into twenty-seven languages, and worldwide sales exceed thirty million.[57] Alice Walker, a native of Eatonton who now lives in San Francisco, received the Pulitzer in 1983 for *The Color Purple*, becoming the only black woman to win the Pulitzer for fiction.[58] Incidentally, the first Pulitzer to come to Georgia was shared by a couple, Julia and Julian Harris. In 1926, the *Columbus Enquirer-Sun* received the award for Meritorious Public Service for the couple's energetic fight against the Ku Klux Klan and the enactment of the law barring the teaching of evolution in Georgia. Local blacks, recognizing the couple's efforts, presented them a silver loving cup in appreciation.[58]

Georgia women write many different kinds of books today. For example, among the mystery writers are Wylly Folk St. John, the author of nine books, and Celestine Sibley. Two Brunswick residents — Beth Bland Engel and Doris Buchanan Smith — write children's books. Wickie Chambers and Spring Asher co-author non-fiction books for children and produce TV shows for them. Three of Joyce Rockwood's four books concern Indian lore and lifestyle. After working fifteen years as a clerk in an Augusta store, Louise Shivers has just published her first novel, which was nominated for several prizes. Franckina Glass' *Marvin and Tige* was made into a movie that was filmed in Atlanta. Rosemary Daniell, who lives in Savannah, combines both feminism and feminity in her autobiographical poetry and books. Cynthia Simmons, Bonnie Pike and Pearl Cleage are playwrights. These are a few of the many women writers.[59]

Women have also been involved in handwork as an art form for a long time. They stitched pictures, memorials, samplers and made quilts and clothes, but the Georgia women who may have been painters are hidden from us. The name of Louisa Catherine Stroebel is mentioned simply as a miniaturist in the early 19th century. Lucy Stanton, a miniaturist who studied in

Paris before she settled in Athens in 1906, painted men, women, children, blacks, mountain people and still lifes. Thirty-five of her miniatures are in a collection at Emory University. In addition to painting, Stanton was active in the woman suffrage movement and the Georgia Peace Society.[60] Some of the other women artists working in Georgia today include Shirley Fox, Ouida Canaday, Sloan Borochoff, Amelia Kames, Emi Macmiller and Gail Corcoran. In the Savannah area, the watercolors of Myrtle Jones were recognized nationally, and Leonora Quarterman's sketches of the historic district are well-known.

There is a number of women folk artists who are active in Georgia. Mattie Lou O'Kelley, born in Banks County in 1908, began painting when she was about sixty years old. The warmth of her approach, her stunning colors and her stylized symmetry have found admirers who pay up to $8,000 for her work. She has published two books, *A Winter Place* (1982) and *From the Hills of Georgia: An Autobiography in Pictures* (1983). A Newnan housewife, Jeanette Dingler, began painting fruit and flower still lifes in 1963. Once she retired from school teaching in 1968, Rosa Campbell had time to take a correspondence course in art. At the request of a patron, she once painted a picture of a man behind a mule, making the plowman white and incensing her patron who demanded that she paint him black. Campbell, however, refused, saying both races plowed. Nellie Mae Rowe, a blacksmith's daughter, expressed her life in colors and symbols. One of her paintings is of a yellow woman with dark blue hair holding a flower behind her head, and on her right are a blue tree with red flowers and a pair of yellow songbirds. Linda Anderson translates her visions of Georgia cock fights, funerals and mountain life onto canvas. This folk artist's paintings now sell for as much as $5,000.

Georgia's vocal artists range from opera to soul. Two divas who have sung at the Metropolitan Opera House are Mattiwilda Dobbs, an Atlanta native who made her debut there in 1958, and Jessye Norman, an Augustan, who has just returned from a successful European career to sing at the Met. Bessie Jones and the Sea Island Singers are known nationally for their slave songs and games. For thirty years, Atlanta-born Gladys Knight and some of her relatives have been singing as a group known as Gladys Knight and the Pips. In a related field, Dorothy Alexander has been a force behind the growth of modern dance and ballet in Atlanta. She began a city-wide school dance program in 1927, and two years later, started the Dorothy Alexander Concert Group. These are some of the women who are known in the world of the arts, but there are many others who have local and regional recognition.

Various reform movements have also attracted women, Georgia women being no exception. Kate Waller Barrett, who moved to Atlanta in 1886 when her husband became dean of St. Luke's Cathedral, was interested in and concerned for unwed mothers. Her interests led to local homes for these women before she decided to become a doctor in order to do more for them. The Florence Crittenton Homes for unwed mothers grew out of her interest in returning these women to society.[61] Nellie Peters Black was also interested in sick people, an interest which resulted from her visits with her mother to Civil War hospitals. She organized one of the first charity hospitals in Atlanta, and it later merged with Grady Hospital. A religious leader, she was also an organizer of the Georgia Federation of Women's Clubs, an advocate of compulsory attendance laws for school children, a supporter of medical examinations for children and a promoter of experimentation and education for agricultural improvements. She has been acclaimed as one of the two hundred persons who contributed most to Atlanta.[62] A second woman who made a significant contribution to Atlanta's art community was Harriet Wilson High. She grew up in a home where she learned to love art, music and learning. In 1884, she married Joseph Madison High who was a very successful businessman. After his death, Harriet took over the business responsibilities, became involved in philanthrophy and supported patriotic groups. She donated her home to the Art Association and added more property for future expansion. The High Museum building was razed in 1963, but the property is still used for art.[63]

Women organized missionary societies for relief and benevolent work. Laura Askew Haygood founded the Trinity House Mission Society in Atlanta in 1882. The society operated an industrial school to teach poor and unemployed women to sew, a school for poor children and a Sunday School for workers. After two years, Haygood accepted a call to do missionary work in China where she died in 1900.[64] Black women also organized to improve their lives. In 1908, the faculty wives and women of Spelman and Morehouse Colleges established the Atlanta Neighborhood Union, which developed

73

a wide range of social, moral and racial goals and activities. The key person in this group was Lugenia Burns Hope, wife of the president of Morehouse College. Hope worked with the Commission on Interracial Cooperation, the Association of Southern Women for the Prevention of Lynching, the NAACP and many other organizations.[65] A nationally known black woman leader today is Coretta Scott King who continues her husband's work at the Martin Luther King Jr. Center in Atlanta.

The main focus in the writings of Mary Clare DeGraffenreid was the economic and social problems of women and children. Born in Macon and a graduate of Wesleyan at age sixteen in 1865, she moved to Washington, D.C. to teach in 1876. Ten years later, she took a job with the Patent Office and soon became one of the first women to investigate labor conditions. A writer and lecturer before her death in 1921, she published almost thirty articles on labor issues facing an industrializing America. DeGraffenreid also wrote about housing and working conditions, wages and hours and living costs and called for stricter laws to regulate child labor, for compulsory education, factory inspection laws and industrial safety.[66]

Other Georgia women were involved in the suffrage struggle. Augusta Howard organized the first suffrage society in Georgia in 1890 in Columbus with her four sisters and mother as members. After affiliating with the National American Woman Suffrage Association, the group began to distribute literature and grew within three years to about twenty members. In 1894, Howard addressed a subcommittee of the United States House of Representatives Judiciary Committee in behalf of women's suffrage. She invited the national association to hold its convention in Atlanta, which it did in 1895. After a few years, she ceased to be active though her interest in the struggle for the franchise continued.[67]

A number of women combined their interest in voting with social concerns. Jessie Daniel Ames became active in the suffrage movement in Texas as a result of discrimination she faced in business. Realizing that the problems of women and blacks were interrelated, in 1922 she began to work with the Commission on Interracial Cooperation and became director of the women's programs for the CIC in 1928. She moved to Georgia, and in 1930, organized the Association of Southern Women for the Prevention of Lynching. Fourteen years later, the CIC was absorbed into the Southern Regional Council.

Ames retired to North Carolina and became active in Methodist church work and voter registration.[68] Dorothy Tilly was another white Southern woman who was a civil rights leader. She was interested in religious education and was active in the Women's Missionary Society of the Methodist church, but her real concern was to improve the living conditions of Southern blacks. Tilly was one of the first Georgians to join the ASWPL with Ames. She was on the board of the Commission on Interracial Cooperation, and she was in charge of women's work for the Southern Regional Council when it absorbed the CIC. She founded the Fellowship of the Concerned under the auspices of the SRC to campaign against lynchings and to improve the quality of justice in the courts. With her death in 1960, the F of C was dissolved.[69]

While some fields were open to women, politics was a male bastion, and women who were interested in politics opened themselves for criticism until recent years. The public life of Georgia women began in the religious societies, missionary societies, temperance and other reform movements. One woman emerges in the 1820's as a political woman. Nancy Rumsey lived in Elbert County on the Georgia-South Carolina border between the Broad and Tugaloo Rivers. On court days, she could be found selling cider, ginger bread and chestnuts to the public from a traveling restaurant set up in the back of her wagon. The business was so lucrative that she amassed enough money to build a comfortable house six or eight miles on the main road from the county seat of Elberton, where she kept a country tavern. From a capitalist she became a politician. The first thing any candidate in the vicinity had to do was to subsidize her. She took tribute from all and promised favor to all. Even when the candidates knew that she accepted everyone's money, they dared not cease paying her for fear of her opposition. A local judge described the situation this way: "And so this white female levied black mail on all office-seekers in Elbert County for half a century."[70] Another politician, Rebecca Latimer Felton, earned a footnote in the history books when she became the first woman to sit in the United States Sentate in 1922. In recognition of her influence in Georgia politics, the governor appointed her to the Senate when Thomas E. Watson died. The newly elected Walter F. George delayed presenting his credentials so that the 87-year old Georgian could be sworn in as a senator for one day.[71]

In the 1930's and 1940's, women began to achieve some

recognition for their political activity. Viola Ross Napier served four years, 1923-1927, in the Georgia House and opened the way for Bessie Kempton who in 1930 was the first woman to be elected to the state legislature from Fulton County. In 1946, Helen Douglas Mankin of Atlanta defeated nineteen other candidates to become the first Georgia woman elected to the Congress. Helen Douglas' parents were both lawyers, but her mother was ineligible for the Georgia Bar. Not until 1921 was the mother admitted to the Bar, the same time Helen was admitted. Mankin served ten years in the state legislature, and her opposition to Governor Eugene Talmadge led to her defeat in the Democratic primary in the summer of 1946 when Talmadge supporters took control of the state Democratic executive committee. She did not seek political office after 1948, the year she made another unsuccessful race for the Congress.[72] State Senator Iris Blitch did not move on to the U.S. House of Representatives until 1954, after she had fought and won the battle to let Georgia women sit on juries. The issue of women jurors was talked about as early as 1937, and ten years later, it had the support of various women's groups — the League of Women Voters, Georgia Federation of Women's Clubs and Georgia Business and Professional Women's Club. After failing to pass both houses of the legislature three times, the bill was finally signed by Gov. Eugene Talmadge in 1953. Blitch served four terms in Congress before retiring from active political involvement in the state.[73]

The third woman to be elected to the state House of Representatives was Helen Williams Coxon from Ludowici. In 1932, she decided to run from Long County and mounted a door to door campaign. The next two campaigns she won without opposition. Then in 1941, Coxon won a seat in the state Senate, and in 1943, Gov. Ellis Arnall appointed her to the only seven-year term on the newly created Pardons and Parole Board. In addition to her political interest, Coxon has also owned an insurance company and a newspaper. Although she was not a native Georgian, Jeanette Rankin owned a farm near Athens which became a center for both the suffrage and the peace movements. Rankin served two terms in the United States House of Representatives from Montana, and during her terms, she voted against both World War I and II. An active feminist, Rankin was chosen by the National Organization for Women as the first member of the Susan B. Anthony Hall of Fame.[74]

Up to now there have been no women elected to the highest executive positions in the state; however, two women have run for governor. Mrs. Jessie W. Jenkins was the first woman candidate for governor in the Democratic primary in 1952. Although she came in last in a field of five, she ran as an example to other women. Grace Wilkey Thomas was a candidate for governor in 1954 and received one percent of the votes. She did slightly better in her last race for governor in 1963, raising her percentage of votes a half point.[75] Potential women candidates for governor face two serious problems: money and recognition. Former state Senator Virginia Shapard of Griffin, who lost a race for the U.S. Congress in 1976, had to work four years to pay off the $100,000 debt incurred in her campaign. State Representative Peggy Childs from Decatur emphasizes the point that women need statewide recognition in jobs such as attorney general, labor commissioner or agriculture commissioner. A vice-president and director of Ivan Allen Co. and President of United Way, Marie Dodd has never held an elective office, but she has had high visibility as chairman of the State Board of Regents which oversees the University System of Georgia. Mary Hitt, ex-mayor of Jesup and Democratic National Committeewoman, believes the votes for a woman governor are there for the asking.[76]

The few women included in this article are not all the women in Georgia who have been active in the social, religious, political or economic arenas, but they are a representative sample. While Georgia women have been active in many different fields, some of them are known to us — some are lost — and many more wait to be found.

NOTES

[1]*Memoirs of Georgia* (Atlanta: Southern Historical Association, 1895); E. Merton Coulter, *A Short History of Georgia* (Chapel Hill, N.C.: University of North Carolina Press, 1960); Kenneth Coleman, editor, *A History of Georgia* (Athens, Ga.: University of Georgia Press, 1977); Kenneth Coleman and Charles Stephen Gurr, editors, *Dictionary of Georgia Biography* (Athens, GA: University of Georgia Press, 1983), 2 vols. Hereafter cited as DGB.

[2]Suggested sources include, among others, the following: Barbara B. Reitt, editor, *Georgia Women: A Celebration* (Atlanta: The Conger Printing and Publishing Company for the Atlanta Branch, American Association of University Women, 1976); D. Dean Cantrell, *Georgia Women: Yesterday, Today and Tomorrow* (The American Association of University Women, Georgia State Division, West Georgia College, Carrollton, Georgia, 1983); Darlene R. Roth and Louise B. Shaw, *Atlanta Women: From Myth to Modern Times, A Century of Atlanta History* (Atlanta: Atlanta Historical Society, 1980); Darlene Roth and Virginia Shadron, compilers, *Women's Records: A Preliminary Guide* (Atlanta: Georgia Department of Archives and History, 1978); *Historic Georgia Mothers, 1776-1976* (Atlanta: Stein Printing Company for the Georgia Mothers Association, 1976). There are also older sources including Sarah Harriet Bush, *The Mothers of Some Distinguished Georgians of the Last Half Century* (New York: J.J. Little and Company, 1902); Annie Laura Eve Blacksheare, *Georgia Women in Georgia Development* (Athens: Women's Club Institute, 1938); James Banks Nevin, editor, *Prominent Women of Georgia* (Atlanta: The National Biographical Publishers, 1928).

[3]Betty Friedan, *The Feminine Mystique* (New York: Norton, 1974); Kate Millett, *Sexual Politics* (Garden City, N.Y.: Doubleday, 1970); Shulamith Firestone, *The Dialectic of Sex: The Case for the Feminist Revolution* (New York: Morrow, 1970).

[4]Mary Ryan, *Womanhood in America: From Colonial Times to the Present* (New York: New Viewpoints, 1975); Joan Hoff Wilson, "The Illusion of Change: Women and the American Revolution" in Alfred Young, ed., *The American Revolution: Explorations in the History of American Radicalism* (DeKalb, IL, 1976).

[5]Mary Beth Norton, *Liberty's Daughters: The Revolutionary Experience of American Women, 1759-1800* (Boston: Little, Brown and Company, 1980); Linda Kerber, *Women of the Republic: Intellect and Idealogy in Revolutionary America* (Chapel Hill, N.C.: University of North Carolina Press, 1980); Nancy F. Cott, *The Bonds of Womanhood: "Women's Sphere" in New England, 1780-1835* (New Haven, CT: Yale University Press, 1977).

[6]Joanna Stratton, *Pioneer Women: Voices from the Kansas Frontier* (New York: Simon and Schuster, 1981); Annette Kolodny, *The Land Before Her: Fantasy and Experience of the American Frontiers, 1630-1860* (Chapel Hill: University of North Carolina Press, 1984); Barbara M. Wertheimer, *We Were There: The Study of Working Women in America* (New York: Pantheon Books, 1977); John Blassingame, ed., *Slave Testimony: Two Centuries of Letters, Speeches, Interviews, and Autobiographies* (Baton Rouge, LA: Louisiana State University Press, 1977); Gerda Lerner, *Black Women in White America; A Documentary History* (New York: Pantheon Books, 1972); James Loewenberg and Ruth Bogin, eds., *Black Women in Nineteenth Century American Life* (University Park, PA: Pennsylvania State University Press, 1976).

[7]Eleanor Flexner, *Century of Struggle: The Women's Rights Movement in the United States* (Cambridge, MA: Belknap Press of Harvard University, 1975); Anne Firor Scott, *The Southern Lady: From Pedestal to Politics, 1830-1931* (Chicago: University of Chicago Press, 1970); Catherine Clinton, *The Plantation Mistress: Woman's World in the Old South* (New York: Pantheon Books, 1982).

[8]Kristina Simms, "Mark Twain and the Lady from Decatur," *The Atlanta Journal and Constitution Magazine*, November 12, 1972; Howard Pousner, "Forgotten Heroine of the Civil War," *The Atlanta Constitution*, May 13, 1982.

[9]Dolly Summer Lunt Burge, *A Woman's Wartime Journal: An Account of the Passage Over a Georgia Plantation of Sherman's Army on the March to the Sea* (Macon: The J.W. Burke Co., 1927); Anna Wylley Habersham, *Journal of Anna Wylley Habersham* (Savannah, GA: n.p., 1926); Spencer Bidwell King, Jr., editor, *Ebb Tide, As Seen Through the Diary of Josephine Habersham Clay* (Athens, GA: University of Georgia Press, 1958); James C. Bonner, editor, *The Journal of a Milledgeville Girl, 1861-1867* (Athens, GA: University of Georgia Press, 1964).

[10]Eleanor Flexner, *Century of Struggle: The Women's Rights Movement in the United States* (Cambridge, MA: Belknap Press of Harvard University, 1975); Aileen S. Kraditor, *The Ideas of the Woman Suffrage Movement, 1890-1920* (New York: Columbia University Press, 1965); Anne Firor Scott, *One Half the People: The Fight for Woman Suffrage*

(Philadelphia: J.B. Lippincott Company, 1975); David Pivar, *Purity Crusade: Sexual Morality and Sexual Control, 1868-1900* (Westport, CT: Greenwood Press, 1973); Karen Blair, *The Club Woman as Feminist: The Woman's Culture Club Movement in the United States, 1868-1914* (Westport, CT: Greenwood Press, 1973); Jacquelyn Dowd Hall, *Revolt Against Chivalry: Jessie Daniel Ames and the Women's Campaign Against Lynching* (New York: Columbia University Press, 1979).

[11]Peter G. Filene, *Him/Her/Self: Sex Roles in Modern America* (New York: Mentor, 1976); Ann Moody, *Coming of Age in Mississippi* (New York: Dial Press, 1968); Maxine Hong Kingston, *The Woman Warrior: Memoirs of a Girlhood Among Ghosts* (New York: Alfred A. Knopf, 1976).

[12]Robert G. McPherson, "The Voyage of the Anne — a Daily Record," *Georgia Historical Quarterly*, v. 44, 220-230. Hereafter cited as *GHO*. Unless otherwise stated, information about Georgia women is from the author's files.

[13]Kenneth Coleman and Milton Ready, eds., *Colonial Records of the State of Georgia: Original Papers of Governors Reynolds, Ellis, Wright, and Others, 1757-1763*. vol. 28, pt. 1 (Athens: University of Georgia Press, 1976), 256-279. Hereafter cited as *CRG*.

[14]Lee Ann Caldwell Swann, "Landgrants to Georgia Women, 1755-1775," *GHO*, v. 61, 23-24.

[15]*CRG*, v. 10, 246-247, 252, 258-259, 269-272, 286, 301.

[16]*Georgia Gazette*, March 3, 1768; October 1, 1766; January 12, April 10, May 25, 1774.

[17]*Georgia Gazette*, August 5, 12, November 25, December 2, 1767; January 19, 1764; January 10, 1765; January 7, 1767; February 22, 1765; August 5, 12 and December 2, 1767.

[18]*CRG*, v. 20, 285, 302.

[19]*CRG*, v. 20, 125-126, 183, 273.

[20]*Georgia Gazette*, August 2, 1769; October 25, 1769.

[21]Milton Ready. "Is It True What They Say About Nancy?" *The Atlanta Journal and Constitution Magazine*, October 21, 1973; Zell Miller, *Great Georgians* (Franklin Springs, GA: Advocate Press, 1983), 101-103.

[22]For information about Hannah Clarke see Louise Frederick Hays, *Hero of Hornet's Nest* (New York: Stratford House, 1946).

[23]Kate Haynes Fort, *Memoirs of the Fort and Fannin Families* (Chattanooga, TN: Press of Macgowan and Cooke Company, 1903), 8-9, 199-202.

[24]See John F. Stegman and Janet K. Stegman, *Cathy: A Biography of Catherine Littlefield Green* (Providence, RI: Rhode Island Bicentennial Foundation, 1977).

[25]Eliza A. Bowen, *The Story of Wilkes County* (Marietta, GA: Continental Books Company, 1950).

[26]Writers' Program of the Works Progress Administration, *The Story of Washington-Wilkes* (Athens: University of Georgia Press, 1941), 99. Another story of Georgia women involved in violence is the mention of a duel fought by two "ladies" in 1817 in *Pistols at Ten Paces, the Story of the Code of Honor in America* by William Oliver Stevens (Boston: Houghton Mifflin Co., 1940), 140.

[27]Kenneth Coleman and Steve Gurr, eds, *DGB*, v. 1, 963-964.

[28]Susie King Taylor, *Reminiscences of My Life in Camp* (New York: Arno Press, 1968 reprint of 1902 edition).

[29]Julia F. Smith, *Slavery and Rice Culture in Low Country Georgia, 1750-1860* (Knoxville, TN: University of Tennessee Press, 1985), 197.

[30]Thomas Dyer, ed., *To Raise Myself A Little: The Diaries and Letters of Jennie, a Georgia Teacher, 1851-1886* (Athens: University of Georgia Press, 1981).

[31]George A. Rogers and R. Frank Saunders, Jr., *Swamp Water and Wiregrass*, (Macon: Mercer University Press, 1984), 139-150; Jacqueline Jones, *Soldiers of Light and Love: Northern Teachers and Georgia Blacks, 1865-1873*, (Chapel Hill: University of North Carolina Press, 1980).

[32]Richard W. Griffin, "Wesleyan College: Its Genesis, 1835-1840 ," *GHQ*, v. 50, 54-73.

[33]Amy Friedlander, "Not a Veneer or a Sham: The Early Days at Agnes Scott," *Atlanta Historical Journal*, v. 23, 31-44. Hereafter *AHJ*.

[34]Two biographies of Martha Berry are Tracy Byers, *Martha*

Berry, The Sunday Lady of Possum Trot (New York: Putnam, 1932; Joyce Blackburn, *Martha Berry, A Biography.* (Philadelphia: Lippincott, 1968). On Gloria Shatto see Sam Heys, "Letter Brought Her Another World," *The Atlanta Constitution,* May 17, 1984.

[35]Coleman and Gurr, *DGB,* v. 2, 599-600.

[36]See Virginia Pettigrew Clare, *Thunder and Stars: The Life of Mildred Rutherford* (Oglethorpe University, GA: Oglethorpe University Press, 1941); Coleman and Gurr, *DGB,* 863-864.

[37]Reitt, *Georgia Women,* 48-49; Scott, *The Southern Lady,* mentions some of the above women and others as well.

[38]Coleman and Gurr, *DGB,* v. 1, 29-30.

[39] Joe Ledlie, "The Big Four for Environment," *The Atlanta Journal and Constitution Magazine,* February 12, 1978; Margaret Shannon, "Doing What Comes Naturally," *The Atlanta Journal and Constitution Magazine,* August 24, 1975.

[40]Reitt, *Georgia Women,* 80.

[41]Sid Howell Fleming, "Emory's First Woman Medical Graduate," *Medicine at Emory,* v. 20, 21-25.

[42]*Buckhead, Atlanta,* January 11, 1979.

[43]*Atlanta Journal-Constitution,* September 5, 1983; *The New York Times,* May 13, 1984.

[44]Barbara Laker, "She Used the Spools to Become Big Wheel," *The Atlanta Constitution,* April 12, 1984; Phil Garner, "Mrs. Eddy's Furniture Factory and How It Grew," *The Atlanta Journal and Constitution Magazine,* April 11, 1976.

[45]Harold V. Shumacher, "A 30-year Owner of Mary Mac's, She Has Achieved Stirring Success," *The Atlanta Constitution,* June 10, 1983.

[46]Steve Walburn, "Ain't Nothing Gonna Break Her Stride," *The Atlanta Weekly,* February 26, 1984; *Atlanta Constitution,* May 11, 1984.

[47]Sam Heys, "Shirley Miller," *The Atlanta Journal and Constitution,* October 23, 1983.

[48]Walter C. Jones, "A Factory the Women Won't Let Die,"

The Atlanta Weekly, October 12, 1980, 34-38. Author's interview with Ratcliff March 1, 1984.

[49]Coleman and Gurr, *DGB,* v. 2, 1073-1074.

[50]Reitt, *Georgia Women,* 66-68.

[51]Coleman and Gurr, *DGB,* v. 1, 397-398.

[52]Webb Garrison, "Sarah Elliott Redirected the Course of Southern Literature," *The Atlanta Journal and Constitution,* July 31, 1983.

[53]Coleman and Gurr, *DGB,* v. 2, 654-655; Virginia Spencer Carr, *The Lonely Heart: A Biography of Carson McCullers* (New York: Doubleday, 1976).

[54]Coleman and Gurr, *DGB,* v. 2, 903-904; Eugene Moore, "Lillian Smith Remembered," *The Atlanta Journal-Constitution,* September 29, 1968.

[55]Coleman and Gurr, *DGB,* v. 2, 757-758.

[56]Reitt, *Georgia Women,* 71.

[57]Coleman and Gurr, *DGB,* v. 2, 723-725; Anne Edwards, "Frankly, My Dear . . .," *Atlanta Weekly,* May 1, 1983.

[58]David Bradley, "Telling the Black Woman's Story," *The New York Times Magazine,* January 8, 1984, 24-37; Helen C. Smith, "Julia Harris, Husband Shared Pulitzer Prize," *The Atlanta Journal and Constitution,* February 15, 1976.

[59]Barbara B. Reitt, "Women Authors of Atlanta: A Selection of Representative Works with an Analytic Commentary," *AHJ,* v. 23, 55-70.

[60]W. Stanton Forbes, *Lucy M. Stanton, Artist* (Darien, GA: Ashantilly Press, 1975).

[61]Reitt, *Georgia Women,* 14-15.

[62]Jane Bonner Peacock, "Nellie Peters Black: Turn of the Century 'Mover and Shaker.'" *AHJ,* v. 23, 7-16.

[63]Carlyn Gaye Crannell, "The High Heritage," *AHJ,* v. 23, 71-84.

[64]Harvey K. Newman, "The Role of Women in Atlanta's Churches, 1865-1906," *AHJ,* v. 23, 17-30.

[65]Scott, *The Southern Lady,* 134-161; Coleman and Gurr, *DGB,* v. 1, 474-476.

[66]Coleman and Gurr, *DGB*, v. 1, 248-249.

[67]A. Elizabeth Taylor, "Woman Suffrage Activities in Atlanta," *AHJ*, v. 23, 45-54; Coleman and Gurr, *DGB*, v. 1, 482-483.

[68]Coleman and Gurr, *DGB*, v. 1, 22-24. See also Hall, *Revolt Against Chivalry*.

[69]Arnold Shankman, "Dorothy Tilly and the Fellowship of the Concerned" in Walter J. Fraser, Jr. and Winfred B. Moore, Jr., *From the Old South to the New: Essays on the Transitional South* (Westport, CT: Greenwood Press, 1981).

[70]Garnett Andrews, *Reminiscences of An Old Georgia Lawyer* (Atlanta: Franklin Steam Printing House, 1879), 36-38.

[71]John Erwin Talmadge, *Rebecca Latimer Felton, Nine Story Decades* (Athens: University of Georgia Press, 1960). Two works by Felton herself are *Country Life in Georgia in the Days of My Youth* (Atlanta: Index Printing Company, 1919) and *My Memoirs of Georgia Politics* (Atlanta: Index Printing Company, 1911).

[72]Lorraine Nelson Spritzer, *The Belle of Ashby Street: Helen Douglas Mankin and Georgia Politics* (Athens: University of Georgia Press, 1982).

[73]Robert Azar, "The Liberation of Georgia Women for Jury Service," *AHJ*, v. 24, 21-26.

[74]Ted C. Harris, "Jeannette Rankin in Georgia," *GHQ*, v. 58, 55-78.

[75]Robert W. Dubay, "Political Pioneers: Georgia's Gubernatorial Lady Campaigners," *AHJ*, v. 24, 21-26.

[76]Margaret Shannon, "Ms. Governor: Will It Happen in Georgia?" *Atlanta Weekly*, June 3, 1984; *The Atlanta Constitution*, June 7, 1984.

Southern Baptists In Georgia

WAYNE FLYNT

William Faulkner once told a group of students that a character in one of his novels was a "bucolic, provincial, Southern Baptist." A student asked the great novelist to explain what he meant. The religion of a Southern Baptist, Faulkner replied, was an "emotional condition that has nothing to do with God or politics or anything else." Like most generalizations, Faulkner's characterization applies to many Southern Baptists and completely distorts the religion of others. Perhaps a more accurate description, however, comes from Appalachia: the Baptist denomination is like a raft on the Clinch River; you can't control it and you can't sink it.

Since the history of Southern Baptists is long and varied, I can do little more in this essay than sketch some general patterns of Baptist life in Georgia, focusing primarily on the formative years before 1860. There are, of course, some more contemporary elements whose origins can be seen in this earlier period, and not all of them are ones which might be expected.

First, there is among Baptists an aggressively evangelistic tradition which dominates religious life in Georgia. As in most Southern states, the similar traditions of Methodists, Baptists and Presbyterians account for some ninety percent of the state church membership. In most Georgia counties, Baptists constitute by far the largest single denomination. They are no longer a poor, uneducated frontier people; indeed, the most prominent Southern Baptist in Georgia was elected President of the United States. Incidentally, Jimmy Carter's candidacy raised religious issues to a prominence matched in this century only by the Catholicism of John F. Kennedy in 1960 and Alfred E. Smith in 1928. Carter's frank admission that he was a "born again" Christian resulted in major stories about evangelicals and Baptists in *Newsweek, Time* and other journals. The resultant furor demonstrated that Baptists can be both as controversial and as simplistically stereotyped as Catholics, Mormons or Jews.

Other contemporary issues are the debate over Biblical interpretation, the denominational split between moderates and Fundamentalists, the increasing involvement of Baptists in controversial political issues and the vigorous missionary efforts of the denomination. Largely because of a long educational tradition, because Georgia Baptists have strong ties to the South Atlantic states (Virginia and the Carolinas) and because the S.B.C. Home Mission Board is located in Atlanta, Baptists in this state are among the most moderate (Fundamentalists would say "liberal") in the Southern Baptist Convention. As evidenced by periodic attacks on them by Fundamentalists, Mercer University and the Baptist state paper are among the most open and sensitive Baptist institutions. The most socially enlightened, official S.B.C. publication, *Home Missions,* is published by the Home Mission Board in Atlanta; but perhaps the single most socially engaged journal within the denomination is *Seeds,* an independent ministry of Oakhurst Baptist Church in Decatur devoted to "enabling Christians, and especially Southern Baptists, to respond to the poor, not just with charity, but with Biblical justice." Walker Knight, who served for many years as editor of *Home Missions* and is a supporter of *Seeds,* recently retired in order to edit *SBC Today,* a "national, autonomous publication of news and opinion for Southern Baptists" which has become the major voice for moderates within the denomination. Published at Decatur, Georgia, the *SBC Today* has an executive board which contains seven Georgians and one Tennesseean.[1] All of this conflicting, even mind-blowing information provides a unique vantage point for a trip back into time.

The Baptists trace their immediate roots to Reformation England and two quite different traditions. General Baptists formed their first congregation about 1612 and were so named because they believed in the doctrine of general atonement. The grace of God was offered freely to all, not to a few who were his special elect. One of their number wrote the first published plea for religious freedom in England, an attack on the religious prerogatives of the state which landed him in jail. General Baptists also favored a highly centralized church government with power delegated to a central body.

Particular Baptists founded their first congregation in 1638 and also favored religious freedom, but beyond that issue, the two groups could not agree. Particular Baptists believed in a limited or particular atonement — that Christ died only for the elect. They feared central authority and magnified the role of the local congregation. Members of both groups migrated to the South, with the Particular Baptists' influence somewhat more extensive.

Soon new conditions in America blurred these earlier distinctions. The Great Awakening of the 1740's swept across the colonies, creating new religious patterns. In New England, Shubal Stearns left the Congregational Church in 1745 to become a Baptist, thus establishing a separate congregation apart from the official state church. Harassed in the Northeast, Stearns moved his congregation to North Carolina where the members alienated many Baptists loyal to the older traditions. The Separate Baptists were known for their emotional preaching, the use of uneducated ministers, exuberant meetings and extensive use of women in services. Those who represented the earlier English elements were called Regular Baptists to distinguish them from Separate Baptists.[2]

All of these diverse elements left their marks on Baptist life. A recent study of Southern Baptists locates four major intellectual sources of the denomination, each associated with a locale. The Charleston, South Carolina tradition drew its Calvinistic Puritanism from the English Particular Baptists; and the First Baptist Church of Charleston was the first congregation in the South, and for a long time, the most influential. Believing in the importance of religious experience and the sole authority of Holy Scripture, this tradition can be characterized by the word order: order in liturgy, ministry and church governance. It was pro-education and not anti-intellectual, and from it came Baptist colleges and seminaries.

The second tradition came from the Separate Baptists and was centered in Sandy Creek, North Carolina. It was emotional, revivalistic, charismatic, independent, not much concerned with theology but obsessed with Biblical literalism. Separate Baptists opposed confessions of faith as man-made substitutions for the word of God. They were known for exaggerated localism and their commitment to personal evangelism.

Briefly omitting the third source of Southrn Baptist thought for reasons which will soon be obvious, the fourth tradition is associated with Tennessee and the Landmark Movement of J.R. Graves. Operating first from Nashville and later from Memphis, Graves took Baptist localism to an extreme. He traced Baptist roots through a "trail of blood" back to New

Testament times and believed that true Christian succession was only through Baptists. Strongly anti-ecumenical and sectarian, Landmarkers delighted in doctrinal hair-splitting and theological controversy. Glorifying the local congregation, they were suspicious of any centralizing tendencies.[3]

The third source of Baptist life is the Georgia tradition, emanating from Augusta and Atlanta, but more about this tradition later. First, let us follow the spectacular growth of this small sect as it confronted the Georgia wilderness. Although individual Baptists came to Georgia early, the first Separate Baptist congregation was not founded until the spring of 1772 when Daniel Marshal, who had been preaching in southwestern South Carolina, moved a few miles into Georgia to form a church at Kiokee. The enthusiasm of the Separate Baptists won many converts, and by 1790, the state contained 42 Baptist churches with 3,211 members.

Even more spectacular was the growth after the Cane Ridge revival which swept east from Kentucky. Sometimes called the Second Great Awakening, the religious exuberance and emotional excesses particularly benefited Methodists and Baptists between 1801 and 1814. By 1814, Georgia contained 171 Baptist churches organized into five associations (Georgia, founded in 1784; Hepzibah, 1794; Sarepta, 1799; Savannah, 1802; and Ocmulgee, 1810). The annual rate of increase, 17.72 percent, was the highest of any South Atlantic state and much higher than Georgia's population growth. Jesse Mercer, one of the most important figures in Georgia Baptist history, baptized 300 persons in a two-year period, and in 1812 alone, four associations added 3,800 members. Although the growth slowed after 1814, the annual increase still exceeded the population growth. By 1845, there were 26 associations containing 620 churches with 47,151 members. On the eve of the Civil War, the Georgia Baptists numbered 84,567.[4]

The source of this growth is complex. The uncertainties of frontier life, the proximity of death and disaster, constantly reminded one of his mortality and encouraged commitment to some force beyond himself. Baptists were also drawn from the common people, no small advantage in such raw and uncivilized circumstances. Unlike Presbyterians, Congregationalists or Episcopalians, Baptists drew their ministers from unlettered common folk. All that was necessary for ordination was a call from the Lord and a willingness to preach. The aversion of many Baptists to a paid clergy guaranteed that most ministers would be bi-vocational, earning their living the same way as did their parishioners. The democratic spirit of Baptists fit the times and the place.[5]

There were other elements as well. The missionary spirit infected Georgia Baptists and provided a remarkable unity. Three conferences held between 1801 and 1803 united the various factions in a common mission enterprise primarily aimed at slaves and Indians. The first Baptist church organized among Georgia blacks was begun in 1788. Additional impetus came from contact with the national missionary movement which was just getting underway. Luther Rice, a pioneer Baptist missionary, visited Georgia in 1813 and influenced creation of the first mission society at Savannah in December, 1813. By 1817, the first female mission society had been formed and women subsequently played the leading role in missions. Additionally, the first Baptist missionary magazine in America and the earliest religious journal of any denomination in the South was established in Georgia in 1802 by Henry Holcombe, pastor of the Savannah Church. It was entitled *The Georgia Analytical Repository*.[6]

This intense mission activity served as an internal binding for Baptists who differed on theological and ecclesiastical issues, but it also drove a wedge between them and anti-mission elements. Increasingly called Primitive or anti-mission Baptists, these brethren were most numerous in the hill country and piedmont. Strongly Calvinistic and predestinarian, they believed God would save his elect without the puny efforts of Baptists; hence, they opposed tract and mission societies and other forms of education and benevolence. Bitter feuding occurred in Georgia as in other Southern states, with the more missionary-minded associations quickly outdistancing their opponents.

Their victory was aided by a well-organized and efficient state Baptist organization. The General Baptist Association of the State of Georgia (a name happily changed in 1827 to just the Baptist Convention for the State of Georgia) was organized in June, 1822. Each association could send three to five delegates and its chief function was to encourage mission activity. Despite opposition from some anti-educational elements, the convention voted in 1831 to establish a classical and theological school for those preparing for the ministry. Mercer Institute was begun in 1833, the same year that Jesse Mercer purchased a Washington paper and moved it to

Georgia to begin *The Christian Index.*

Jesse Mercer was one of several distinguished Baptist leaders. Although well-known as a preacher, his contribution to Georgia life extended well beyond the pulpit. He was author of the articles on religious freedom in the 1798 state constitution, and using his political acumen, he blocked a move to deny preachers the right to serve in the legislature. In fact, the notion of Baptists as apolitical or even antipolitical hardly fits Georgia. Of 68 delegates to the 1798 constitutional convention, eight including Mercer were Baptists, seven of them ministers. At that time Baptists constituted only three percent of the state's population.[7]

Another prominent name finally brings us to the third of those sources of Southern Baptist thought. William Bullein Johnson came to Georgia from South Carolina in 1811 to pastor the influential Savannah Baptist Church. In 1813, he founded a foreign mission society, and in subsequent years, became one of the most articulate spokesmen for missions. Although he returned to South Carolina and was elected president of the South Carolina Baptist Convention, his most important contribution to Baptist life was made at a May, 1845 meeting in Augusta, Georgia.

By the mid-1840's, the slavery controversy dominated Southern thought, and Baptists were bound tightly to their culture. They defended slavery as fiercely as any Southerners, employing an entire battery of arguments based on the Bible, physiology and philosophy. Disagreements over slavery, however, had poisoned relations between Baptists in the South and elsewhere, focusing by 1845 on the question of whether a slaveowner should be appointed as a foreign missionary. This was the climate for a regional meeting of Baptists summoned to Augusta in 1845. W.B. Johnson, one of the ablest thinkers in the denomination, arrived at Augusta with a proposed constitution for a new convention. He wrote the address, explaining why the Southern Baptist Convention was being organized and two themes dominated his speech: sectionalism and denominationalism. The structure established at Augusta in 1845 created a new kind of denomination, one more centralized and cooperative than previous, but loosely organized Baptist forms. Delegates to the Augusta meeting formed one convention with two boards, Home and Foreign, which were accountable to the convention. The nature of the two boards, both devoted to missions, indicates what would hold the convention together: not common theology but a common commitment to the propagation of the Gospel. In fact, the delegates wrote that "We have constructed for our basis no new creed; acting in this manner upon a Baptist aversion for all creeds but the Bible."[8]

Georgia Baptists also had a role in intensifying sectionalism and denominationalism in the years after the Civil War. Henry Holcombe Tucker bore a proud name in Baptist history. From his college days in Washington, D.C., he had been fascinated with politics and often had forsaken the college campus for Congress, where he had listened to Clay, Calhoun and Webster. He later studied law and was admitted to the bar in 1846. Subsequently, he felt the "call" to preach, taught at Southern Female College (LaGrange) and at Mercer. He defended the rights of slaves to religious freedom and opposed secession, although he supported the Confederacy once it became a reality. After the Civil War, he served for twelve years as President of Mercer University, as Chancellor of the University of Georgia, and as the editor of *The Christian Index,* Georgia's Baptist paper. In these influential positions, he firmly identified Georgia Baptists with a sectional religious viewpoint. He defended a conservative social order and opposed education for blacks, Reconstruction, female equality, organized labor and large standing armies. A "soul" brother of Jesse Mercer's, he rejected the notion that preachers could not speak on political issues. Although he argued that a religious newspaper normally ought not engage in partisan politics, he conceded that such activity might be necessary to teach good citizenship.[9] In his political involvements, he might be considered a spiritual godfather both to a Georgia Baptist preacher named Martin Luther King, Jr. and to Jerry Falwell.

The final person who represents the sectionalism and denominationalism of the Georgia tradition is I.T. Tichenor. Like Tucker, Tichenor was a public man. In Alabama before the war, he had been a distinguished pastor; but when the war ended, he felt his first duty to the region was to assist its material recovery. Acting upon that belief, he launched a career as a New South industrialist with the same enthusiasm he had earlier invested in saving souls; and convinced that education was as much a key to the New South as factories, he became President of Alabama Polytechnic Institute (now Auburn University). Incidentally, he served as interim pastor of Auburn's First Baptist Church and often supplied its pulpit while he was president of A.P.I.

After rescuing a nearly defunct business and an equally desperate college, he left in 1882 to offer his recuperative skills to the crippled Baptist Home Mission Board. His first act was to move the agency from Marion, Alabama to the booming town of Atlanta. To save the board, he performed two additional acts. First, he won Southern Baptist support for the board by breaking all its ties with the Northern Board Home Missions Society, which was more influential and affluent. Although he continued to recognize separate jurisdictions to prevent overlapping efforts by Northern and Southern Baptists, the board gradually moved away from that position. In time, Southern Baptists would refuse to recognize any part of America as exclusively reserved and would send their home missionaries from "shore to shining shore." Paradoxically, the most rapid growth would occur in non-Southern territory, and the fundamentalism and lack of strong denominational ties in the so-called mission territories would contribute measurably to the late twentieth century strains in the denomination. By appealing to Southern sectionalism, Tichenor had saved his agency.

Furthermore, he persuaded Southern Baptists to work through a central mission board rather than through their powerful state conventions. By preventing the fracturing of resources, he was able to expand home mission efforts greatly in the years to come. Cooperative denominationalism came to characterize a people renowned for their stubborn independence and uncooperative spirit.[10]

Although continuity with the past is not absolute, Georgia's Baptist heritage should hold no surprises for those who observed the political sagacity of Jimmy Carter or Martin Luther King, Jr. Nor should it surprise anyone that so many current Baptist leaders in Georgia are "denominational loyalists," moderates who emphasize the common Baptist commitment to missions, while rejecting the notion that Baptists need to impose theological loyalty oaths. Their commitment to denomination outweighs loyalty to creed. Move west to Arkansas or Texas or north to Michigan or to the Pacific slopes, and it is more likely that one will find the spiritual descendants of the Tennessee Landmarkers, not the Georgia tradition.

So the Georgia heritage is far broader than events which occurred only in this state. Its legacy helped form the largest Protestant denomination in America and launch it on a course of religious moderation.

NOTES

[1]*Seeds*, II (November/December, 1979), p. 1; *SBC Today*, I (April, 1983), p. 1.

[2]William L. Lumpkin, *Baptist Foundations in the South* (Nashville: Broadman Press, 1961), pp. 147 ff.

[3]Walter B. Shurden, "The Southern Baptist Synthesis: Is it Cracking?", The 1980-81 Carver-Barnes Lectures, Southeastern Baptist Theological Seminary, Wake Forest, North Carolina, November 4-5, 1980. This lecture contains a most perceptive statement of the origins of the Southern Baptist intellectual tradition.

[4]Robert A. Baker, *The Southern Baptist Convention and Its People, 1607-1922* (Nashville: Broadman Press, 1974), pp. 85, 131, 186.

[5]Wayne Flynt, "The Impact of Social Factors on Southern Baptist Expansion, 1800-1914," *Baptist History and Heritage*, 17 (July, 1982), 20-31.

[6]Baker, *The Southern Baptist Convention and Its People*, p. 85.

[7]Spencer B. King, Jr., "Baptist Leaders in Early Georgia Politics," *The Quarterly Review*, 38 (October-November-December, 1977), 76-79.

[8]Shurden, "The Southern Baptist Synthesis: Is It Cracking?"

[9]David N. Duke, "Henry Holcombe Tucker, Outspoken Baptist Journalist," *The Quarterly Review*, 38 (October-November-December, 1977), 67-75.

[10]Shurden, "The Southern Baptist Synthesis: Is It Cracking?"

Folklore In The Cracker State

DELMA E. PRESLEY

Georgia folklore is a Charlton County farmer describing a local resident: "He's crooked enough to steal a sucking bottle from a blind orphan baby." If that is not enough: "He's mean enough to skin a flea for its hide and then swim a mile to hell for the cracklins." Georgia folklore is also this aphorism tossed lightly by the grandson of a slave: "Don't crow till you get out of the woods. Might jus' be a bear behind the last tree."

If someone wants to know the lore about our state, he does not have to enroll in a course, and he can get started without even purchasing a set of books. The only indispensable tools are two good ears. Once tuned to the local frequency, he can listen his way into the fascinating and rewarding subject that is the folklore of Georgia. Make that plural — subjects — for Georgians have more variety than a litter of spotted pups.

They speak with the nasal twang of Rabun Gap and the liquid lips of Tybee Light. They are Crackers and Geechees, Hillbillies and Swampers, City Slickers and Wiregrass Kickers. They come in the customary races, ages and sexes — the gentler of which are sometimes referred to as "peaches." They worship in traditional churches, not to mention Hardshell Primitive Baptist and the Shouting Methodist.

They live in places with famous names: Athens, Berlin, Cairo, Damascus, Egypt, Rome, Sparta, Turin and Vienna. They have incorporated their optimism in placenames like A One, Cornucopia, Eureka, Fancy Bluff, Ideal, Jolly Fashion, Prosperity, Social Circle and Zenith.

Maps, however, remind us that our early pioneers cut their teeth on tougher stuff. Like other American pioneers, those of Georgia's frontier in the nineteenth century sought opportunity. The sobering reality of the age for many, nevertheless, was misfortune. Laments still echo from dozens of placenames like Hungry Valley in Whitfield County, Hungry Creek in Carroll and Hungry Hill in Bryan. Hardscrabble, a tough-hoeing name in Fulton County, also is found in West Virginia, Indiana,

Wisconsin and California. Less common. but no less evocative are Hard Up and Hard Fortune in Baker and McDuffie Counties. In 1860, a Troublesome post office served a small number of settlers who lived to the west of the Okefenokee Swamp, and the state has at least three Troublesome Creeks.

How rough was life on the state's northeastern frontier? It takes less than a day's rough sledding to make it from Bad to Worse Creek. Then, moving westward, there is Lordamercy Cove on the way to Rough Creek and Tearbritches Creek. Listening to stories about our placenames is an education in itself. Even when counties tend to glorify their origins, the frontier character has a way of shining through. The second largest of Georgia's 159 counties is typical in this regard. Local residents take pride in explaining that their county was named in 1777 for the great English political thinker, Edmund Burke, and they point out that their county seat, Waynesboro, honors the same Revolutionary general who founded Fort Wayne, Indiana — "Mad" Anthony Wayne.

That is well and good for public relations, perhaps, but what about those individuals who transformed the wilderness into farms, homesteads, churches and schools? These were the Crackers, and their silent testimonials are places like Keysville, Bryants Grove, Storys Millpond, Palmer Branch, Doyle Grove and scores of cemeteries like Taylors, Greshams and Hughes. Some streams have mundane sounds — Rocky Creek, Dry Branch, Sandy Branch, Brushy Creek and Sweetwater. But others vividly recall rough passages for horses and wagons and people: Brier Creek must have been an onerous place, especially at the turn called Little Hell. Burke has its Gut Creek (from the English "Pinch Gut") and Boggy Gut Creek; Hell's Half Acre even now is so thickly overgrown that hunting dogs have trouble getting through. Perhaps it was a disillusioned traveller who questioned the very justice of God at Job's Branch. Consolation, however, was found at Hopeful Branch, Pleasant Grove and Thankful Church. Such also seems to be the meaning of two landing points on the Savannah River — Flowery Gap and Point Comfort.

Just as the people reveal their character through placenames, they also indicate insight through their music. Even seemingly frivolous fiddle tunes hint at some residents' earthy humor:

Jaybird died of the whoopin' cough,

95

> *Bullfrog died of the cholic.*
> *Jack came along with a fiddle on his back*
> *And asked them all to the frolic.*[1]

The square dance still perpetuates such zany lyrics. The truth about folk music, of course, is that it passes naturally from generation to generation, or at least it used to.

Earlier in this century, folk music had that unique advantage. I am speaking, of course, of an architectural anachronism known as the front porch, which alone can be credited with transmitting hundreds of songs for the seasons of our lives. Many a mother once believed it impossible to bring babies into this world without the advantages of a granny rocker on the front porch. Some still cannot get the rhythm of "Go to sleep, little baby" without that helpful squeak of the rocker after each line.

In the yard beside the porch, young ones have jumped rope to the accompaniment of absolutely clever lyrics:

> *Cinderella, dressed in yellow*
> *Went upstairs to kiss her fellow.*
> *Made a mistake, kissed a snake.*
> *How many doctors did it take?*
> *1-2-3-4-5-6-7-8-9-10*
> *Rope hit your leg, an'*
> *You're a rotten egg.*[2]

People who listen to children at play can hear folklore in the process of transmission. The following rhyme is familiar to many communities in southeastern Georgia:

> *"Mother, mother, I am ill,*
> *Send for the doctor from over the hill."*
> *In comes the doctor, in comes the nurse,*
> *In comes the lady with the alligator purse.*
> *"Measles," says the doctor, "Measles," says the nurse,*
> *"Measles," says the lady with the alligator purse.*[3]

Back to the front porch where singing was spontaneous: Grandpa could line out the do-re-mi for "Amazing Grace," with the reportoire moving gracefully from the sacred to the secular. In such a healthy climate grew many vital traditions, not the least of which was the ballad. In isolated communities of South Georgia's piney woods, for example, students have found four versions of "Barbara Allen."[4]

The front porch singers faithfully preserved folksongs many

of us have forgotten. "The Lassie Mohee" is a good example. Scholars disagree about its origin, some claiming it is a British broadside. Others guess it began in the South Seas, but in Louisiana a similar song, "The Creole Girl," is set in the swamps of Pontchartrain. It tells the story of a lost and lonely young man who is befriended by a Creole maiden. The outcome is similar to the one described in "The Lassie Mohee" as sung in the 1920's by Gerti Lou and Ruby Chesser who lived on Chessers Island in the Okefenokee Swamp. They learned it from some relatives who sang it during Civil War times. The tune is the same as "On Top of Old Smokey."

As I went out walkin' for pleasure one day
In sweet creation to while time away.
As I sat amusin' myself on the grass,
What could I see but a fair Indian lass.

She sits down beside me, an' taking my hand,
Says, 'You are a stranger an' in a strange land.
An' if you will follow, you're welcome to come
An' dwell in the cottage that I call my own.'

The sun is fast sinkin', an' o'er the deep sea,
I wandered day long with the lassie Mohee.
Together we wandered, together we roamed,
Till we came to a cottage in a cocoanut grove.

This kind of expression she made unto me:
Says, 'If you consider to stay here with me,
An' go no more roaming from o'er the deep sea,
I'll teach you the language of the lassie Mohee.'

One morning so early, one morning in May,
Unto my kind maiden, those words I did say.
'I'm going to leave you, so farewell, my dear,
My ship sails are spreaded, and for home I must sail.'

The last time I saw her, she stood on the sand,
And as my ship passed her, she waved me her hand.
Says, 'When you are landed, with the one that you love,
Think of the lassie Mohee in the cocoanut grove.'

An' when I was landed on my own native shore,
Friends an' relations aroun' me once more,
I gazed all aroun' me, no one could see
That was fit to compare with the lassie Mohee.

The girl I had trusted proved untrue to me.
I'll turn my ship backwards from o'er the deep sea.
I'll turn my ship backwards, from this I must flee,
Spend the rest of my days with the lassie Mohee.[5]

Beyond the importance of the song for students of American folk music, "Lassie Mohee" has special meaning for Georgians. One of the earliest recorded myths from the region concerns hunters who were lost in the swamp. As Bartram recorded the story, these men met "a company of beautiful women, whom they called daughters of the sun." Upon returning to civilization, the hunters repeated stories about those fascinating creatures to their countrymen, who "were enflamed with an irresistible desire to invade, and make conquest of, so charming a country."[6]

Now that the front porch has vanished, folk music has taken a beating, but it is no accident that much has survived. A few individuals heroically have acted at the right moment. In the 1920's and 1930's, Hamp Mizell farmed and ran a fishing camp in Ware County. Singlehandedly, he rescued much of South Georgia's folk music. Hamp happened to believe that some things were more important than fishing and farming: "I've stuck the plough in the field many a time and run to the house to play a tune on the fiddle when it come to me. I reckon I've wrote out a thousand ballads for people, just to keep 'em a-going. If it wasn't for me — I don't want to brag — I reckon they'd a died out."[7]

Fortunately, there have been other Hamp Mizells in Georgia who have gathered folk music. They have done their part in saving an invaluable and beautiful part of our cultural heritage. Unfortunately, Georgia has neither a state folklorist nor an archive of folklore. Our best collection is housed in the Archive of American Folksong at the Library of Congress in Washington, D.C. The Archive's Georgia file includes material recorded by John and Alan Lomax in the 1930's and by other random researchers. There are twenty file drawers of ex-slave narratives and folklore transcriptions, all by and about Georgians; some of these have not been printed and must be read on location at the Library of Congress.

So, Georgia folklore is the natural language of her people — their sayings, placenames, children's games and music. But it is more, much more. It is a hefty volume of passed-down recipes for favorite foods like cornbread, barbecue, ham and red-eye gravy, turnip greens with "pot licker," tater pie and real iced tea. It is the collected tricks of the trade of the travelling blacksmith, the handsaw carpenter and the seamstress. It is a file of the right remedies for what ails you. (To cure a child who stutters, feed him mockingbird eggs. To soothe a sore throat, use a gargle made from red oak bark.)

And what about hollering? People of the piney woods used to tell the time of day by the kind of hollering that filled the air. There was the "waking-up holler," the "going-to-work holler," the "dinner-time holler" and the "coming-home holler." Calling hogs and cows required special talents, and other occupations had their special renditions. Not many recall the famous river holler that at the turn of the century resounded along the banks of the mighty Altamaha. James Kelton Rollison, a native of Ohoopee, converted me to the river holler in 1972 when he demonstrated it and explained its significance:

> It was rather plaintive, especially at dark — you know, when you're gonna tie up [the timber raft]. I think it has the same effect on you as a bell or a gong would have on a dog .... It was saying 'goodbye' to a hard day in your own fashion. And you made everybody else a little happier. When old John Rewis would start hollerin' that river holler, everybody would shut up. If they were whisperin,' they'd shut up. And I want to tell you, it would almost make you cry. If you weren't so hard-hearted and inured to hardships and everything else, you'd cry.[8]

Georgia folklore draws strength from men and women of the workplace. It is the different ways people build chimneys, often pronounced "chimleys." There is architecture in general — from the rough and ready dog-trot cabin to the clean-cut lower Chesapeake style dwelling. Tobacco barns, meat-curing houses, syrup sheds, chicken coops and pender (peanut) stacks — these and other structures belong to our architectural lore. The collection also has room for tales by and about Atlanta's John Portman — twentieth century architect of America's urban renaissance.

"Curious Outbuildings of Georgia: the Structure and Maintenance of Rural Sanitary Disposal Units" would be a fitting title for a scholarly monograph on the venerable forerunner of the modern bathroom. Though some might turn up their noses at it, the subject deserves, well, thoughtful contemplation. I have seen makeshift one-holers perched atop the Piedmont plateau. I have marvelled at plush Victorian four-holers framed with sculptured boxwoods in Middle Georgia. A vented split-level model — the prized possession of the Russell family — still stands at the homeplace near Winder, Georgia. Thanks to this honored and loquacious family, it has become a part of our folk history.

Few pleasures surpass reading oral traditions by sure enough story tellers. The state's first and foremost folklorist, Joel Chandler Harris, published over two dozen engaging volumes, and many of them are still available. The folklore of Northeast Georgia fills seven volumes of *Foxfire*, and there are more to come. For South Georgia, I recommend with prejudice my *Okefenokee Album*, based on the notes and photographs of the late naturalist Francis Harper. Among the volumes that recapture the black heritage of coastal Georgia are Lydia Parrish's *Slave Songs of the Georgia Sea Islands* and the WPA Georgia Writers' Project, *Drums and Shadows*. County histories and old newspapers make excellent hunting grounds, and even contemporary papers can be mines. Celestine Sibley's *Atlanta Constitution* columns have focused on such germane topics as light'ood knots, log cabins and ladies' quilting bees.

But why do it? Why spend time collecting and reading the folk traditions of Georgia's people? Some say they are "into folklore" because of the "quaint and curious people who still live on the fringes of society." Such a reason demeans both the speaker and the subject, for the folklorist in this case is the elitist whose superior education allegedly qualifies him to judge "remnants of the good old days."

True folklorists — be they academic or amateur — will tell you that the people themselves carry significant traditions which are transmitted orally. Like written traditions, the oral ones are worthy of study in their own right. They are a part of our collective record of the great human journey. I could go on, but perhaps the best justification for studying folklore in general applies to Georgia as well. It was given by Harold Thompson, an English professor at Cornell University. In response to a student's impatient question, the professor summarized: "The study of folklore is an opportunity to meet your grandfather."

If the goal of education is to lead us to know ourselves, then an important path that leads to the goal might be called "Appreciating our Common Past." Georgia's rich and varied folklore helps us down the path toward self-understanding. Indeed, in some ways we can better know the character of Georgia by pursuing diligently the folk record. We can begin with what appears trivial or mundane, but if we follow the path carefully, we can discover the deeper roots of meaning.

Let us begin, for example, with Georgia's nickname, "The Cracker State." For several years official welcome centers on the state's major highways have distributed a brochure which contains a brief article entitled "How the Georgia Cracker Got His Name." The explanation has to do with the sounds of poor farmers' whips as they drove their mule wagons to Savannah markets, "in the old days." The article ends as follows: "To this day people who don't know better think all us Georgia folk are crackers."

Clearly the nickname "Cracker" has a negative overtone. As a student of this term, I have followed closely the term's history of usage. Because of the nature of my occupation, perhaps, I have been able to observe the term in a variety of political and intellectual contexts. In the spring of 1978, a writer for the *New York Times* attributed President Carter's difficulties to his Cracker status: "Carter and his pals are today's embodiment of the poor white . . . who needs to cleanse himself of his guilt and his name as a crude 'cracker' and blind bigot."[9] In response to a deluge of defensive letters from irate Georgians, the journalist acknowledged that his views on the subject had been influenced by the Southern writer and social historian, W.J. Cash. "Genesis of the Southern Cracker," a piece by Cash in the *American Mercury*, contains the following:

> *The cracker goes on steadily tumbling down into the slope of degeneracy, waxing ever more shiftless, and perforce discharging his energies . . . making him at his worst a dangerous neurotic, a hair-trigger killer, a man-burner, a pig quite capable of incest — in brief, everything that William Faulkner and Erskine Caldwell have made him out to be, and perhaps something more.*[10]

Something more indeed! That the word itself has colorful ambiguities has been noted in an article by Raven I. and Virginia McDavid. They cite several derogatory inferences by informants in North Carolina, Georgia and Florida: "rough," "riotous," "uncultured," "common" and "sorry people I don't like." However, the linguists tell about an informant in Sylvania, Georgia who took a liking to McDavid and introduced him to some local friends as "a real cracker."[11] It was intended and apparently was received as a compliment.

We can improve our understanding of this word and of the people who are associated with it — through usage and abusage — by taking a brief look at its history. We begin with the people who settled Georgia.

After the founding of Georgia in 1733, the colonial trustees developed a slow-growth policy which called for thoroughly developing the coast and gradually extending settlements into the interior.[12] This perfectly reasonable idea, however, failed to take into account the large numbers of immigrants who started pushing their way into the colony, crossing the Savannah River north of Augusta in the early 1760's. Official correspondence from the mid-1760's to the early 1780's reveals that Georgia's coastal authorities were both concerned and perplexed by the people called "Vagabonds" and "Villains."[13] Noting that many of them were among the independent North Carolina "regulators," Acting Governor James Habersham wrote Governor James Wright the following: "You will distinguish that the People I refer to are what you and I understand by Crackers."[14] Later, the provincial chief justice said that these Scotch-Irish, English and German frontiersmen from Virginia and the Carolinas were like the "Tartars of Asia," bent in this case on overrunning the orderly rice planters on the coast. He was at a loss about how to stop what he called the "increase by the accession of the Crackers from the Provinces."[15]

In colonial Georgia, the word "Cracker" apparently was an epithet the British preferred to use when describing the upcountry's new settlers. Evidence suggests that loyalists used the term consciously as it had been used as early as 1509; according to the *Oxford English Dictionary:* the "Cracker" was a "boaster," a "proud person." A British officer who led an unsuccessful assault on Georgia's upcountry wrote of his distrust of rebel prisoners because "they were mostly Crackers, whose promises are often like their boasts."[16] Another instance of this same usage in the Southern colonies is listed in *A Dictionary of Americanism.*[17] The political undertones of the word are clarified by Jamieson's etymology of the

Scottish language. Jamieson cites Hardying's "Chronicle to Henry VIII": "For the Scottes will aye be bostyn and craky-ing/Euer sekyng causes of rebellion."[18] To be sure, the American Scotch-Irish, who were Scots Lowlanders before moving to Northern Ireland, had a reputation for being what a New England loyalist called "the most God-provoking democrats this side of hell."[19]

Further insight into the British attitude toward colonial Crackers can be found in that fascinating journal of the Reverend Charles Woodmason who represented the Anglican church in South Carolina's backwoods in the 1760's. One significant revelation is that Woodmason felt sorry for the poor whites in the upcountry, and he condemned legislators in Charlestown who "look on the poor White People in a Meaner Light than their Black Slaves, and care less for them."[20] But these poor whites apparently were not among those Wood-mason labeled as "Crackers" for whom he reserved the most righteous wrath. Crackers were "Ignorant, mean, worthless, beggarly Irish Presbyterians, the Scum of the Earth, and the Refuse of Mankind." Woodmason obviously opposed their religious and political views: "Not less than 20 Itinerant Presbyterian, Baptist, and Independent Preachers traverse this Country poisoning the Minds of People — instilling Democratical and Common Wealth Principles into their minds."[21] In a burlesque sermon for delivery in what he called a "Cracker" dialect — Scots — he ridiculed the "Virginia Crackers — for they'll bluster and make a noise about a Turd — and they'll think they have a Right, because they are American born to do so as they please to any Body."[22]

At the time of the American Revolution, the Crackers of the Southern frontier were despised not for their poverty but for their politics. They were "proud," "boasting" and "democratical." So the contemporary boast about Cracker pride may well be rooted in history ("I'm a Georgia Cracker and I'm proud of it!")

If modern folklore about Crackers — like the welcome center brochures — has a negative ring, the reason has to do with a linguistic transformation in the term "Cracker." The transfor-mation took place at least before the end of the nineteenth cen-tury. Dictionaries published in American since 1900 have almost unanimously preferred definitions like these currently in print:

"*Disparaging.* one of a class of poor whites in parts of the southeastern U.S." *(Random House)*

"*POOR WHITE* — usu. used disparagingly . . . a native or resident of Georgia or Florida." (*Webster's Seventh New Collegiate*)

"A poor white person of the rural southeastern United States. Used disparagingly. *(American Heritage)*

I suggest that a transformation in the meaning of "Cracker" took place in the nineteenth century because the word was used to suit the ideological demands of two significant social movements, just as the word has been used for the same purposes in this century. Let us look briefly at how two profound social forces used "Cracker" in the antebellum era: first, the abolitionist movement and second, the planter-based aristocracy. Their ultimate social objectives were contradictory, but they used "Cracker" in precisely the same manner: as a tool of propaganda.

Some of the most influential travellers who chronicled their trips through the "slave states" were active abolitionists. Northern magazines regularly carried features about deplorable living conditions in the "real south." Also there were many episodes describing the antics of people called "Crackers" who spoke in hilariously ungrammatical English.[23] A case in point is Henry Benjamin Whipple's 1843-44 *Southern Diary*. The Episcopal clergyman from Minnesota recorded several of his favorite ethnic jokes — all at the expense of the Crackers — noting that their speech was like that of the "backwoods population of North Carolina . . . not a specimen of the English language."[24] The Reverend Whipple wrote: "I had rather be a well treated slave than one of the low and poor whites."[25]

Typically, the literary traveller depicted the Cracker as a shiftless, despicable, disease-ridden, undernourished and ignorant Anglo-Saxon. Such a deplorable fate, of course, was said to be the consequence, and a sad one at that, of slavery. Frances Anne Kemble's *Journal of a Residence on a Georgia Plantation in 1838-39* makes this point about the "cracker" or "pinelander" as does the journal of Sir Charles Lyell in the 1840's. Lyell found the "crackers" around Darien, Georgia, to be "slovenly," perhaps because they didn't have slaves to do their work for them.[26] James Sterling summarized the living conditions of the white population of northern Florida, known then and now as "Cracker country": "The white inhabitants, as of all the Slave States . . . constitute but two classes — the planters or rich class, the poor white class, variously denominated as 'crackers,' 'white trash,' 'poor whites,' 'mean whites.' This social characteristic I consider the most remarkable and important feature of Southern civilization.''[27] So the Cracker perfectly illustrated the abolitionist's point that slavery harmed members of both races. The stereotype easily replaced the colonial image of the Cracker as a "democratical," anti-establishment frontiersman.

Although their cause was opposite that of the abolitionists, the antebellum Southern humorists stereotyped the yeoman farmer. They depicted the Cracker as a bumbling rustic not yet ready for self-government. The Southern men of letters did not sympathize with the Cracker as did many Northern writers, but their one-dimensional portraits seem familiar. Augusta Baldwin Longstreet's *Georgia Scenes* is a good example. "Darby Anvil" was a blacksmith by trade, Longstreet writes, "the first man who, without any qualifications for the place, was elected to the Legislature." He was voted in by drunken and ignorant white frontiersmen — Georgia's great unwashed democracy.[28] Longstreet's humor, like his Whig editorials, was a serious and largely ineffectual attempt to impose his politics-of-privilege both upon his state and his nation. His fellow Georgians laughed with the Whigs, perhaps, but they voted overwhelmingly for such candidates as Andy Jackson and his unpredictable band of Democrats.

Among the few writers who defended the Cracker in the nineteenth century was the popular humorist of the Reconstruction Era, Charles H. Smith ("Bill Arp"). In an address to the fourth congress of the Scotch-Irish Society, Smith pointed out that the Cracker never did like the slavery system and that his defense of the Confederacy sprang from patriotism:

> What a mistake to say that these men were fighting for slavery .... When nearly the entire voting population were Democrats, Democrats because the slave owners in Southern and Middle Georgia were generally Whigs, and those backwoodsmen had no love for either the negro or his master. But they fought. They fought as did their fore-fathers who resisted a little tax on tea, though not one in a thousand drank it.[29]

A Methodist minister and Confederate veteran, George Gilman Smith wrote several biographies of people who achieved greatness — not in spite of but because of their frontier experiences. In his volume of 1888 entitled *Berry's Triumph: The Story of a Georgia Cracker,* we read: "Berry Wood would have been called a Georgia Cracker in his day, and so he was just such a Cracker as many of our grandfathers were. I have been not a little amused and somewhat vexed at what I have read and heard of the Georgia Cracker from those who never knew him; but I have solaced myself by the thought that the easiest thing to do is to ridicule people you never saw, and whom you do not like too well."[30]

The victims of stereotyping also protested in non-literary ways, and the "proud Cracker" boast of today could be a remnant of their verbal defense. Likewise, the origin of the word in popular lore — derived from the sound of mule drivers' whips — could have been an effort to ameliorate the negative social inferences.[31] In 1912, the naturalist Francis Harper found that non-slaveholding whites who had settled the secluded islands of the Okefenokee Swamp before the Civil War perpetuated a very positive definition of "Cracker." One of the old timers Harper met preferred "light 'ood knot Cracker," meaning that he was an authentic, persevering representative of the species.[32]

Today, there is a resurgence of the traditional Cracker-as-boaster motif among Georgians, even though some journalists and historians still prefer the nineteenth century stereotype. "I'm a proud Cracker" is the motto printed boldly on popular T-shirts worn on August 26, 1978 (and every last Saturday in August since) at the state's first "Cracker Day." Ironically, the event was celebrated in Savannah, Georgia on the riverfront where General James Edward Oglethorpe stood 245 years earlier as he established the colony of Georgia.

NOTES

[1]Delma E. Presley, "Francis Harper and the People of the Great Swamp" in *Okefenokee Album* by Francis Harper and Delma E. Presley (Athens, Ga., 1981), p. 4.

[2]Versions of this are fairly common in the United States. This particular version was recorded by the author on September 1, 1978 on the playground of the Marvin Pittman Laboratory

School in Statesboro, Georgia. Both black and white students of this kindergarten were familiar with the words. See also Mary and Herbert Knapp, *One Potato, Two Potato: The Folklore of American Children* (New York, 1976), p. 125.

[3]Ibid.

[4]Francis Harper (see n. 1) collected four versions in his notebooks which record natural history and folk life from 1912 through 1940 in the Okefenokee Swamp.

[5]Harper and Presley, pp. 103-04.

[6]Francis Harper, ed., *The Travels of William Bartram.* Naturalist's Edition (New Haven, 1958), pp. 17-18.

[7]Harper and Presley, p. 62.

[8]Interview with James Kelton Rollison at Hilton Head, S.C., December 12, 1972.

[9]George McMillan, "The Dixie Myth," *The Atlanta Journal and Constitution,* April 2, 1978.

[10]W.J. Cash, "Genesis of the Southern Cracker," *American Mercury,* 14 (1935), 105-08.

[11]Raven I. McDavid, Jr. and Virginia McDavid, "Cracker and Hoosier," *NAMES,* 21 (1973), 164.

[12]See Allen D. Candler, ed., *The Colonial Records of the State of Georgia,* 26 vols. (Atlanta, 1904), 14, 475-76; for Governor Wright's favored strategy of slow development of the coast, see vol. 28, pt. 2, 840-44.

[13]James Habersham, *The Letters of Hon. James Habersham, 1756-1777* in *Collections of the Georgia Historical Society,* 15 vols. (Savannah, 1904), 6, 204.

[14]*Ibid.*

[15]Anthony Stokes, *A View of the Constitution of the British Colonies in North America and the West Indies as the Time of the Civil War Broke Out on the Continent of America* (London, 1783), 140.

[16]Doyce B. Nunus, ed. "Colonel Archibald Campbell's March from Savannah to Augusta, 1779," *Georgia Historical Quarterly,* 45 (1961), 286.

[17]In 1766 Gavin Cochrane to the Earl of Dartmouth: "I

should like to explain to your Lordship what is meant by Crackers; a name they have got from being great boasters; they are a lawless set of rascalls on the frontiers of Virginia, Maryland, the Carolinas, and Georgia, who often change their places of abode." In Mitford M. Mathews, ed., *A Dictionary of Americanisms on Historical Principles*, 2 vols. (Chicago, 1951), I, 426.

[18]John Jamieson, *An Etymological Dictionary of the Scottish Language*, 2 vols. (Paisley, 1879), I, 517-18.

[19]Cited by James G. Leyburn, *The Scotch-Irish: A Social History* (Chapel Hill, 1962), 308.

[20]Charles Woodmason, *The Carolina Backcountry on the Eve of the Revolution*, ed. Richard J. Hooker (Chapel Hill, 1953), 240.

[21]*Ibid.*, 241.

[22]*Ibid.*, 154.

[23]An especially good source of writings by northern travelers is *Travels in the Old South*, ed. Eugene L. Schwaab, with Jacqueline Bull, 2 vol. (Lexington, Ky., 1973), 2, 531. See also *The Rambler in Georgia*, ed. Mills Lane (Savannah, 1973).

[24]Henry Benjamin Whipple, *Bishop Whipple's Southern Diary, 1843-1844*, ed., Lester B. Shippee (Minneapolis, 1937), 39.

[25]*Ibid.*, 74-75.

[26]Sir Charles Lyell, *A Second Visit to the United States of North America*, 2 vols. (New York, 1849) I, 243-44.

[27]Cited by A.N.J. Den Hollander, "The Tradition of Poor Whites" in *Culture in the South*, ed. W.T. Couch (Chapel Hill, 1935), 417.

[28]Augustus Baldwin Longstreet, *Georgia Scenes* (New York, 1897), 81. For a penetrating view of the politics of southwestern humorists, see Kenneth S. Lynn, *Mark Twain and Southwestern Humor* (Boston, 1959).

[29]*The Scotch-Irish in America*, Proceedings and Addresses of the Fourth Congress (Nashville, 1892), 130.

[30]George G. Smith, *Berry's Triumph: The Story of a Georgia Cracker* (Macon, 1888), 176.

[31]The earliest published reference to this etymology, to my knowledge, appears in a romance with a plantation setting by Caroline Gilman, published in 1838, cited by Richard H. Thornton, ed., *An American Glossary,* 3 vols., (New York, 1962), I, 218-19.

[32]Harper and Presley, p. 30.

Georgia in Literature:
A Sense of Place
HOLLIS L. CATE

The sense of place, so strongly suggested in the literature by Georgia authors, is unmistakable, whether one is reading the work of the nineteenth century humorists, the poetry of Sidney Lanier or the work of modern writers. For the beginning of Georgia literature, however, one must look back to the seventeenth century in which several poems about Georgia and Oglethorpe were written and published in England before and during the period of the first settlement of the province. The authors of the verses are unknown. Several poems appeared in *Gentleman's Magazine* in 1733. One was entitled "An Address to James Oglethorpe on His Settling the Colony of Georgia." Then in 1735, another verse referred to Oglethorpe's second voyage: "Another Britain in the desert will rise!" "Georgia, a Poem" and "Tomochichi, an Ode" also appeared in *Gentleman's Magazine* in 1736.[1] The latter poem, praising Oglethorpe, records the meeting of the old and new worlds:

> *What Stranger's this? And from what region far*
> *This wondrous form majestic to behold?*
> *Un'cloath'd, but arm'd offensive for the war*
> *In hoary age and wise experience old?*[2]

In the same publication, there appeared another poem entitled "To the Rev. Mr. Whitefield, on His Design for Georgia."[3] Finally, in 1978 appeared *Tomo-Chiqui* or *The American Savage: A Dramatic Entertainment*, which was probably written by playwright John Cleland.[4]

The first piece of satiric invective about the colony was published in Charleston in 1741.[5] Collaborating on the piece, Dr. Patrick Tailfer, Hugh Anderson and David Douglas complained that inhabitants of the colony could not import Negroes or rum and could not even own land in fee simple. The work was satirically dedicated to "His Excellency General Oglethorpe."[6] As Professor Davis points out, the attitude of the malcontents anticipates that held later by disgruntled Southerners toward the representative(s) of a controlling body.[7] The three authors took stabs at John Wesley as well, according to Jay Hubbell.[8]

After the colonial days, the humorists of the Old Southwest came into prominence. The best known Georgian of this group is, of course, Augustus Baldwin Longstreet of Augusta, but just a word about their brand of humor. Most of the stories are set around the turn of the nineteenth century. The narratives, for the most part, are in the form of the tall tale, and the writers, finding much to laugh at on the frontier, shared their embellished tales in the form of social realism. Of course, the realism was limited in that the speech of the frontiersmen, for instance, had to be censored. In any case, the humor of the Old Southwest was home grown and "no literature has been more a product of its time and place than the writings of the Southern humorists from around 1830 to until the Civil War."[9] Some of Mark Twain's work is in the tradition of the humor of the Old Southwest, and one even sees elements of it in the works of later writers such as William Faulkner and Flannery O'Connor.

As mentioned earlier, A.B. Longstreet is the Georgian who best represents this school in his well-known *Georgia Scenes*. Longstreet was the first Southern humorist to exploit backwoodsmen, crackers and poor whites.[10] He and other Southern humorists captured the flavor and accent of Southern speech, the dialect of it. Longstreet thought of himself as a social historian with his sketches of local scenes and was, in fact, the first humorist to write a full book of sketches. It is appropriate that Longstreet's *Georgia Scenes* opens with a piece entitled "Georgia Theatrics," for this sketch serves as a prologue of sorts for much of what follows it. Complete with concocted dialogue and sound effects, it describes a young bumpkin thrashing an imaginary foe and obviously enjoying himself very much. This sketch, as well as most of the other scenes, is essentially dramatic, including character and dialogue which reflect the drama of life lived during the first few decades of the nineteenth century in rural upcountry Georgia.

What Longstreet's scenes show is that the frontier was a

111

world unto itself, radically different from Savannah and Charleston. The world of the frontier was one of violence, cruelty, irrational behavior, oddities, abnormalities and folk speech. Since there were no theatres as such for the people of the frontier, the frontiersmen entertained themselves, and adlibbing came naturally. Longstreet's "The Fight," "The Horse Swap" and "The Gander Pulling" are therefore aptly named in that they are theatrics pure and simple. The author sets the tone with "Georgia Theatrics," the first sketch in the book. Encore after encore follows. Longstreet, like all humorists of the Old Southwest, focuses primarily on gatherings; there are those who do and those who watch, the entertainers and the entertained. Indeed all the world is a stage, including the frontier world of Augustus Baldwin Longstreet.

Although Longstreet is the best known Georgian who spun tall tales, he is not the only one. Richard Malcolm Johnston (1822-1898) was born in Oak Grove near Powellton in Hancock County. With his *Dukesborough Tales,* he opened up Southern literature to a national audience. A pivotal figure whose work had qualities of the Old Southwest humorists as well as those of Southern local colorists,[11] Johnston confined his sketches to strict geographical limits, revealing much of what Hancock County was and idealizing its past. In reading Johnston's tales, one learns of the peculiarities of a region and of its inhabitants. Joel Chandler Harris said that "the wit and humor of Georgia stand by themselves. They have no counterpart in any section of the country."[12] Harris surely included Johnston's wit and humor in his estimate. As Georgians, Johnston and Longstreet provide unique humorous insights into small town events, showing their concern for the common folk who were not always admirable but who were almost always funny. As stated in *The Literature of the South:* "For the first time there was a truly American character, shown in the guffaws of men of action ...."[13] Johnston, Longstreet, Harris and Bill Arp were all from upcountry, and for many years, there were no writers from the coast.[14] The action was in Middle Georgia, and Johnston and the others captured it. Significantly, Joel Chandler Harris wrote:

> *If you will take a map of Georgia, pick out Putnam County, and then put your finger on the counties surrounding it — Morgan, Greene, Hancock, Baldwin, Jones, and Jasper — you will have your thumb on the*

seat of Southern humor.[15]

This is quite a weighty remark when one considers the writers who were either influenced by Southern humorists or who used humor as part of their stock and trade, Faulkner and Twain included.

Bill Arp (1826-1903) was born Charles Henry Smith in Lawrenceville, Georgia. For Arp, the Southern woman was a symbol of cohesiveness; she held the family together and kept the family unit close. He stresses in his writing the wholesomeness of rural living, implying that what the rural Southern family stood for was the best the South had to offer. His writing reflected a Southern ideal of an orderly society, where everyone knew his place and was contented with it, blacks included.[16] There were no Nat Turners in the world of Bill Arp (or Johnson either, for that matter). Although Arp used dialect and grossly exaggerated misspellings in his writing, he is best known, probably, for his letters to "Abe Linkhorn," published in *Bill Arp, So Called* and written during and after the Civil War. Despite the country bumpkin pose, Arp, Smith's persona, is burning with defiance and sarcasm in his remarks to "Linkhorn." Arp, of course, intended to be funny in his remarks, but at bottom, he was a bitterly hurt Southerner by the war's end.

Like Bill Arp, Joel Chandler Harris (1848-1908) used dialect, but Harris concentrated on Negro speech rather than that of the semiliterate white. Born near Eatonton, Georgia, Harris was very much interested in the Negro folk tales which he later adapted for his famous Uncle Remus tales. In 1879, Harris mentioned Uncle Remus in one of his newspaper columns in the *Atlanta Constitution*, and since the readers were enthusiastic, several stories appeared in the paper. Harris' rabbit obviously symbolized the Negro who had to depend on his cleverness and his wit to get along in the world in which he found himself. In his stories, Harris used authentic folklore, and his Negro dialect is meticulously accurate. Regional writing, of course, caused readers in other regions to be conscious of a particular locale, and Harris, along with George Washington Cable, is one of the best known Southern local colorists. Jay Hubbell quotes the following dialogue from one of Harris' stories:

"Who is that lying there?" asked Joe.

> *"It's my old man, suh."*
> *"What is the matter with him?"*
> *"He dead, suh! But bless God,*
> *   he died free!"*[17]

This is unusual dialogue written by a Deep South writer of the nineteenth century. As Hubbell states, most Southern writers of the time would not have been this explicit about slaves' thoughts on freedom.[18]

One story, probably apocryphal, has it that a black woman from Boston went into a bookstore there and asked for a copy of the Uncle Remus stories. When the clerk brought the book, the woman thumbed through it, shook her head and said, "Oh, no, I wanted it in English." So much for language changes.

We now look at two nineteenth century Georgia poets, one briefly and one in more depth. Paul Hamilton Hayne was not Georgia-born, but he lived near Augusta at "Copse Hill" for twenty-five years. One of his poems, "The Aspects of the Pines," reads:

> *A stillness, strange, divine, ineffable,*
> *Broods round and o'er them in the mind's surcease*
> *And on each tinted copse and shining dell*
> *Rests the mute rapture of deep hearted peace.*[19]

Identifying the pine with our state, Hayne in the lines above senses the mystique invoked by the pines in the clay hill country he knew so well.

The live oak, not the pine, is our state tree, and another poet, Sidney Lanier, celebrates its beauty in his well-known "Marshes of Glynn." In fact, Lanier integrates the images of oak, marsh and sea in the poem. When the poet looked out over the expanse of those marshes, he knew a poem was forthcoming. Though not a great poet, Lanier was a sensitive one, and a poet so attuned to nature as he could hardly fail to see God in the expanse before him. It was like looking off into the infinitude of space and feeling God's presence in such limitlessness. While one can find God anywhere, Lanier easily found Him in the nature of coastal Georgia. Lanier had no modern ecological concern about the marshes enhancing the production of shrimp or about some other environmental concern; what he saw was the beauty of God's creation. He would have said: "Let's save the marshes for God's sake."

As for the oaks, Lanier claims one of them as well as the

marsh. Nothing suited Lanier better than sitting beneath that oak, as he suggests in "The Marshes of Glynn." He was very nearly pantheistic in his outlook, and he refers to the live oak as "Lord of the land." "The beautiful glooms" of the oaks provided him with the solace and seclusion he sought. Since Lanier was a sick man when he visited Brunswick, the inviting coast was an anodyne for him. He could certainly rest in peace beneath one of the coastal oaks, for he seemed to have a mystical attachment to them.

Thus, in his poetry, Lanier links three predominant images of Coastal Georgia: bodies of salt water, the marsh and the live oak. The poet made his way to the marsh's edge through the live oaks to gaze on the endless expanse of the marsh stretching toward the sea, the mysterious, powerful, life-giving mother. And so the poet, propped against the live oak, viewed the creek, the marsh and in his mind's eye, the sea, knowing he was with God.

As popular as "The Marshes of Glynn" is Lanier's "Song of the Chattahoochee" is a close rival. The opening lines have been recited many times: "Out of the hills of Habersham/Down the valleys of Hall ...." Indeed, the poem is the song of the river hurrying, winding, being held back, and Lanier achieves his characteristic use of meter, rhyme and onomatopoeia. In this poem, the poet has shifted his vision from the coastal plain to the Appalachian foothills, but the scene is still Georgia. There are ferns, the hickory, the poplar and "the chestnut, the oak, the walnut, the pine." Lanier wrote other poems which focus on the land in his native state. In "Thar's More in the Man Than Thar Is in the Land," Lanier reveals that a man named Jones left his farm in the clay hills of Georgia and moved to Texas where he expected to do better; but another man named Brown bought the place and made it pay, much to the chagrin of Jones who returned to Georgia after having failed in Texas as well. Lanier pleads in "Corn" for the planting of corn instead of cotton in the South. Corn becomes a symbol of reviving the land, a symbol of reclamation. The "golden treasuries of corn" were seen as the South's path to prosperity (Corn is now grown in Georgia much more extensively than cotton, a fact Lanier would applaud.).

Will Harben, a North Georgia writer not too well-known and probably not much read, made a contribution, nonetheless, as a local colorist. What Joel Chandler did with the Negro dialect in Middle Georgia, Harben of Dalton did with the speech of the mountaineers of North Georgia. We learn a great deal about the customs and lifestyles of the people of the region from reading Harben's books. Harben did not write about the downtrodden, poverty stricken Georgia farmers that we find in the fiction of Erskine Caldwell; his characters are honorable and persevering. They are people with drive, ambitions and the initiative to better themselves. Descended from English ancestors who settled Virginia and who later came south to the North Georgia hills, they were fundamentalists in religion and strong in their faith. Harben, however, could show the country preacher to be brutal and cruel in his fanaticism, and he unhesitatingly did so.[20] According to James Murphy, Harben knew the work of Longstreet, Johnston and Harris; therefore, his characters are closer to their types than to those of Mary Noilles Murfree, the Tennessee writer, or those of George Washington Cable. Harben's people are poor but not poor white trash; they are sociable yeoman farmers who gather in small groups and who act out of a sense of duty. Harben presents his black characters realistically, but on occasion, he does seem condescending. Like most of the white characters, they are, by and large, noble and proud individuals.[21] The main reason he used the Georgia background, Harben said, was that he had a sincere sympathy and affection for the people of his area, people who were the most unpretentious he had ever met.[22]

Margaret Mitchell's *Gone with the Wind*, published in 1936, hardly needs any commentary. It is one of the most widely read books ever, and it inspired the most popular movie of all time. For millions, the book *is* the ante-bellum South, despite the book's romantic flavor, and it is truly remarkable that a one-book author would have been such an outstanding success with the reading public. Stephen Vincent Benet wrote Miss Mitchell shortly after *Gone with the Wind* appeared: ". . . the story moves and has fire in it, and the reader sits up wanting to know what happens next."[23] The book created an image of Atlanta which will endure as long as the book is read and the movie is shown. When the book appeared, however, there were many Georgians still alive who had been born during or shortly after the Civil War and some who were born even before the war. To those born in the nineteenth century, the war was still a fairly fresh memory in 1936. What they had not seen, they had constantly heard about, and the book provided what must have been poignant nostalgia. For many Southern readers, the burning of Atlanta was the most moving incident of the war, far more than buildings burned. Hopes and dreams went up in smoke, too, and every Southerner knew it. Though some critics have questioned Miss Mitchell's powers of observation as a writer, the book is, nonetheless, the most widely read novel by a Southern author.

The three best known modern Georgia-born writers are Erskine Caldwell, Carson McCullers and Flannery O'Connor. They all established national reputations, and at their best, were praised by critics and the general reading public alike. Erskine Caldwell is the only one of the three who is still living. He was born in White Oak, Georgia in Coweta County in 1903, but he left the state when he was twenty-three years old.

Caldwell wrote of the poor whites, but the Old Southwest humor of Longstreet is not evident in the Caldwell's work. The dead pan humor of Bill Arp is replaced by a grotesque humor which many readers found and some still find revolting. For instance, some of the characters in *Tobacco Road* (1932) think that a rat eating the face of a corpse is funny. Whether Caldwell thought it funny or not, some readers no doubt stopped reading the book at that point, concluding that such people were not worth reading about. This is not to say, however, that Caldwell could not have written generally accepted hilarious scenes, many of which can be found in the paperback edition entitled *The Humorous Side of Erskine Caldwell,* published by Signet in 1951.

One reason, of course, for the difference in Caldwell's brand of humor and that of the humorists of the Old Southwest was that Caldwell was writing in the post-Depression years. While Jeeter and the other Lesters could get into much more trouble and a different kind of trouble in a car during the Depression, the characters of the earlier humorists could not with a horse and wagon. There was not as much talk among the nineteenth century characters of being hungry as in Caldwell's fiction when he is focusing on social reform. The earlier creations could be ornery, conniving, devilish characters, but they laughed at the right things.

As indicated earlier, to look at the literature of Georgia is to look at people and the land. With Caldwell the same is true. What of the people and what of the land? In much of his fiction, Caldwell condemns the land owners for being incompetent stewards; indeed, he condemns the land tenure system itself. He implies that many agrarian problems would have been solved by the institution of collective farming. As it happened, the land was exhausted along with the people. In *God's Little Acre* (1933), for example, Will Thompson abandons all hope of making out on the farm. Losing all hope in the land and thinking that the odds are stacked against him, he must make his world the world of the mill.

The breakdown of the rural community in Caldwell's work is obvious. The objection of some critics, however, to the breakdown is that it is always attributed to outside forces, to the system, not to the characters themselves, who are people that some South Georgia readers would say were just "plain sorry." William Faulkner writes of poor whites, too, but for the most part, they persevere in the hope that time will play a redeeming role. In this sense, works such as *Still Rebels, Still Yankees* and *I'll Take My Stand* can be contrasted with what is implied in Caldwell's works, but they cannot be compared.

No one can dispute the popularity of Caldwell's books, for they have sold in the millions and have been translated into many languages. The stage version of *Tobacco Road* ran longer than any other play in the history of the American theatre. While critics have never referred to him as a "great writer," Caldwell received high praise from his fellow Southerner, William Faulkner. Caldwell has also written some fine stories, including those in *Georgia Boy* (a title particularly appropriate in the context of this paper). This book has no social message, its only apparent purpose being to entertain by way of one humorous sketch after another.

In 1932 when *Tobacco Road* appeared, however, a great hue and cry arose from the citizenry of Georgia. They charged that a native son had betrayed his birthright. Just three years earlier, there had been a similar reaction (for different reasons) by the people of Asheville, North Carolina to Thomas Wolfe's *Look Homeward, Angel.* Wolfe later wrote *You Can't Go Home Again,* but in time's scheme of things, both he and Caldwell found they could go home again. The folks in Asheville found that Wolfe's being famous was not so bad, and the Georgians outgrew their insecurities as they watched their state overcome the effects of the Depression. "Even if Caldwell was right, it doesn't matter now" was the attitude of some; however, some bitterness among Georgians still persists. They will never forgive Caldwell for presenting what they would call a flawed synecdoche; that is, he had depicted a part as in fact the whole.

Carson McCullers is not associated with Georgia as readily as Flannery O'Connor because the former writer left the state and O'Connor did not. McCullers' early life in Columbus, Georgia, however, is important in the interpretation of *The Heart Is a Lonely Hunter* and *A Member of the Wedding;* for both have autobiographical overtones. Indeed, she once said that all her major works had a Southern focus because she could not separate herself from her region.[24] Thus, four of her major works have small town settings: *The Heart Is a Lonely Hunter, A Member of the Wedding, The Ballad of the Sad Cafe* and *Clock Without Hands.*

Carson grew up in Columbus when Negroes were servants in white middle-class and upper middle-class families. She must have remembered the dusty streets, the Negro shacks and the perpetual heat of summer. All in all, the image of her hometown had to be a depressing one.[25] The people of Asheville reacted to Wolfe's depiction as some Columbus natives did to Carson's work. They indicated that she must have gotten her ideas from what went on across the river in "Sin City," referring to Phenix City, Alabama.[26]

McCullers grew up, of course, in the midst of the black-white relationships in Columbus, but as a child she could not understand the "White Only" signs. Black people prepared white people's food and tended to their children, but they were not supposed to drink from the same water fountains or eat in their restaurants. McCullers never did resolve the paradox.[27] In her work, black men and women are not stereotypes, not just background figures.[28] She seemed determined that none of her black characters would even remotely resemble the stereotyped Stepin Fetchit character portrayed in 1930's films. McCullers did not live to old age, but her niche in American literature is secure. Tennessee Williams, a past friend, highly praised her work, as did Gore Vidal. She was an extremely sensitive writer who has no peer in capturing the essence of alienation and loneliness.

A contemporary of McCullers who did not leave the state was Flannery O'Connor. O'Connor's view is predominately a religious one which she reinforces by using distortions and grotesque descriptions. The Bible on the one hand and humor on the other were certainly a winning combination for her. Her characters are sometimes fanatical, sometimes warped in their religious outlook, but rarely is there no theological focus at all. Her characters' preoccupation with religious matters, if not overt, seethes beneath the surface. Man, as a sinner, either ducks God's grace or thinks he has found it when he has not. One such person is Mrs. May in the story "Greenleaf." Mrs. May goes to church, but she is not what anyone could possibly call a good Christian. She is self-righteous and highly critical of others, but she cannot remove the mote in her own eye. Finally, the bull which she wants Mr. Greenleaf to dispose of indeed disposes of her, suggesting her own iniquities.

O'Connor, of course, was a Roman Catholic, Southern writer, and her primary focus in her fiction clearly reveals that she is. She lived, however, in what some people would term the Bible Belt of the South, a predominately Protestant region. As a native Southerner and a practicing Roman Catholic *writer* living in Middle Georgia, O'Connor thought of herself almost as an anomaly in terms of her faith, though she always remained true.

One of her well-known stories with a strong religious emphasis is "A Good Man Is Hard to Find." When the grandmother in the story mentions Jesus, the Misfit tells her that Jesus had thrown everything off balance. The Misfit does not believe in the divinity of Christ, but he cannot get what is said about Christ out of his mind. For the Misfit, the Christian mystique becomes the fixed idea, and as the story reveals, speculation replaces belief as O'Connor knew it had in the modern world. At the end of the story, the Misfit is far from being saved, but even his victim, the grandmother, fails to achieve grace. Being a proper Southern woman did not assure grace, though she might have thought it did.

As alluded to earlier, O'Connor's fiction has a strong religious focus; but as Stanley Hamby points out, without her comic sense, her Catholicism could have given her work a distractingly didactic and sentimental flavor. On the other hand, if she had no theological framework, her humor would have been far too caustic.[29] As it is we see in her work an effective balance of the two. Hamby shows in his thesis that O'Connor's humor is, in some ways, not too far removed from that of the humorists of the Old Southwest. While the earlier writers do not include a Christian framework, both they and she make use of violence, cruelty, vulgarity and illiteracy. There is also a common focus on abnormalities and physical oddities.[30]

Similarly, both O'Connor and the earlier humorists have an "irreverence for prettification inspired by sentimentality," and both she and they incisively deflate pretentions and ridicule false values. O'Connor's story "The Patridge Festival" exposes one aspect of pretentiousness peculiar to the South, the "gala affair."[31] The earlier humorists also enjoyed poking fun at gatherings which were called for various reasons. The swindler or con man appears in O'Connor's work as he had in the earlier fiction.[32] Such a character is generally expected to appear in the work of any Southern writer because the earlier humorists had been so successful in creating and developing him. O'Connor uses such a character in both "Good Country People" and "The Life You Save May Be Your Own."

It should be obvious that some omissions in this paper are as glaring as some inclusions. In this brief essay, I have not commented on William Tappan Thompson and Harry Stillwell Edwards, two early Georgia humorists. I have not mentioned Caroline Miller, author of the well-known *Lamb in His Bosom*, a book which focuses on the wire grass country of South Georgia and is set in ante-bellum days. I also did not refer to the shy North Georgia poet and novelist, Byron Herbert Reece, who quietly went his way attending to his craft, and neither have I mentioned Marion Montgomery who has published poetry, short stories, novels and criticism. When a literary history of Georgia is written, all these writers will receive their just recognition and rightly so.

NOTES

[1]Richard Beale Davis, *Intellectual Life in the Colonial South*, (Knoxville: University of Tennessee Press, 1978), III, 1503.

[2]Davis, III, p. 1504.

[3]Davis, III, p. 1504.

[4]Davis, III, p. 1505.

[5]Davis, I, p. 62.

[6]Davis, III, p. 1399.

[7]Davis, III, p. 1399.

[8]Jay B. Hubbell, *Southern Life in Fiction*, Eugenia Dorothy Blount Lamar Memorial Lectures (Athens: University of Georgia Press, 1960), p. 69.

[9]*The Literature of the South*, ed., Richard Croom Beatty et al. (Chicago: Scott Foresman, 1952), p. 111.

[10]Hubbell, p. 73.

[11]Bert Hitchcock, *Richard Malcolm Johnston* (Boston: Twayne, 1978), pp. 44-45.

[12]Hitchcock, p. 134.

[13]Beatty, p. 113.

[14]Hubbell, p. 70.

[15]Hitchcock, pp. 134-135.

[16]James C. Austin, *Bill Arp* (Boston: Twayne, 1969), pp. 34-35.

[17]Hubbell, p. 84.

[18]Hubbell, p. 85.

[19]Beatty, p. 333.

[20]James K. Murphy, *Will N. Harben* (Boston: Twayne, 1979) pp. 140-142.

[21]Murphy, pp. 52-53.

[22]Hubbell, p. 80.

[23]Richard Harwell, ed., *Margaret Mitchell's Gone with the Wind Letters, 1936-1949* (New York: Macmillan, 1976), p. xxviii.

[24]Margaret McDowell, *Carson McCullers* (Boston: Twayne, 1980), p. 16.

[25]Virginia Spencer Carr, *The Lonely Hunter: A Biography of Carson McCullers* (Garden City, N.Y.: Doubleday, 1975), p. 6.

[26]Carr, p. 18.

[27]Carr, p. 21.

[28]McDowell, p. 145.

[29]Stanley Hamby, "Flannery O'Connor's Humor: A Study of Background and Approach," Thesis, Georgia Southern College, 1973, p. 75.

[30]Hamby, pp. 7-20 *passim.*

[31]Hamby, pp. 22-27 *passim.*

[32]Hamby, p. 44.

Georgia Women
And The Suffrage Movement
A. ELIZABETH TAYLOR

The suffrage movement had its beginning before the Civil War, but Georgia women did not become involved until the latter part of the nineteenth century. In accord with the laws of the state, Georgia women were allowed neither to vote nor to hold office. Since similar restrictions existed elsewhere, they were inclined to accept this condition as normal. In the privacy of their own minds, some doubted the fairness of such restrictions, but only rarely did they make their objections known.

One of those who questioned the justice of woman's unequal status was H. Augusta Howard of Columbus. The daughter of a prominent family, Augusta was born in Muscogee County in 1865. She was educated in Columbus and in Staunton, Virginia where she spent two years in advanced study. During these formative years, she had no contact with the votes-for-women agitation. Her intellectual interests motivated her to read widely; and through her readings, she became acquainted with the ideas of John Stuart Mill whose *Subjection of Women* is one of the classics in the history of feminism. A thoughtful observer of life around her, she noted that her mother, a widow, was required to pay taxes. Since the mother could not vote, Augusta reasoned that she was being taxed without representation, and hence unjustly.[1]

In July, 1890, Augusta organized the Georgia Woman Suffrage Association at a meeting in her home, the ante-bellum mansion known as Sherwood Hall. Besides Augusta, the only persons who joined at this time were her mother and four sisters. She was not discouraged, for she had realized that the Association's initial membership would be small. She thought, however, that "more could be effected by a few organized individuals than the same number unorganized."[2]

The Georgia Woman Suffrage Association became an affiliate of the National American Woman Suffrage Association and invited to membership all persons favoring justice for women, men as well as women. Individuals could become members by paying dues of one dollar per year. Local suffrage clubs could become auxiliaries of the state association.[3] Membership increased very slowly, and for a while, it seemed as if the Association would remain a family affair. Then a few outsiders began joining, and by 1894, there were members in five counties. The Association's total membership, however, was less than twenty.[4]

The Howard ladies held regular meetings at Sherwood Hall. They found themselves alone, however. There is no record of any other Columbus citizens joining the Association during the 1890's. Local opinion was strongly against woman suffrage; and instead of the support for which they had hoped, they encountered bitter hostility. In 1893, Augusta stated that the "opposition at Columbus . . . (was) of the most malignant and underhand sort, scrupling not an insult, lying and slander."[5] Two years later, a contemporary reported that the animosity toward the Howard ladies amounted almost to persecution.[6]

The task of educating and changing public sentiment was an enormous one; therefore, it was essential that the suffragists promulgate their ideas in every possible way. As a publicity device, the Association printed slogans on its stationery. One such statement was "Taxation without representation is tyranny — WOMEN ARE TAXED." Another was "Governments derive their just powers from the consent of the governed — WOMEN ARE GOVERNED." Still another was "Political power inheres in the people — WOMEN ARE PEOPLE." Although the Association sought the support of the press, newspapers were reluctant to publicize the cause. Some editors felt that suffrage news was of little interest, while others feared that it would offend their readers and hurt circulation.

An exception was the *Union-Recorder* of Milledgeville. On January 19, 1892, it introduced a new feature entitled "Woman's Rights Column" by H. Augusta Howard of Columbus. The *Union-Recorder* published this column for nine months, with the last article appearing on September 20, 1892. No reason was given for its discontinuance.

The suffragists wrote letters to members of the state

legislature. They distributed thousands of leaflets and pamphlets. One very effective piece was entitled *Prominent Georgia Men in Favor of Woman Suffrage.* Of the men quoted was Gunby Jordan of Columbus who thought that women taxpayers should have a voice in the expenditure of public funds. Another was Walter B. Hill of Macon, later to become Chancellor of the University of Georgia, who stated that there was "no rational argument against woman suffrage." State legislator William H. Fleming of Augusta considered it a matter of "abstract justice," while Charles W. Hubner of Atlanta called it an "inalienable right." Other men quoted were Will N. Harben of Dalton, J. Colton Lynes of Atlanta, Walter H. Johnson of Columbus and William C. Sibley of Augusta.[7]

In January, 1892, H. Augusta Howard and her sister, Mariam Howard Dubose, went to Washington to attend the annual convention of the National American Woman Suffrage Association. They were the first delegates from Georgia ever to attend and were among the youngest women there. They soon won the favor of the assemblage by their earnestness, their enthusiasm and their personal attractiveness. It was reported that they "were the delight of the convention" and that every reference to Georgia was received with applause.[8] While in Washington, Augusta was one of several suffragists who spoke briefly at a hearing of the Judiciary Committee of the United States House of Representatives. The following year, Augusta and Miriam once again went to Washington to attend the N.A.W.S.A. convention, and in 1894, they returned accompanied by their sister, Claudia Howard Maxwell.

Traditionally, the National American Woman Suffrage Association had held its annual conventions in Washington, but some of its members thought that the organization should meet in other cities as well. When the choice of a convention site for 1895 was before the assemblage, Atlanta, Cincinnati, Detroit and Washington were suggested. Augusta Howard had extended the invitation to meet in Atlanta. In support of this invitation, she addressed the convention:

> *The Georgia papers and the far Southern papers still insist that women do not want the ballot. Until you hold a convention in the South and prove to them that this is not so, they will keep on saying it is. In Atlanta, if the convention should go there, there can be no doubt that the Grand Opera House, which is one of the*

largest auditoriums in the United States, could be secured, and it could be packed from ceiling to pit. While a great many of them would come to laugh, many of them would go away with N.A.W.S.A. membership tickets in their pockets .... I believe that an effort would be made by Atlanta and the prominent business men, as well as the Georgia Woman Suffrage Association, to make the next convention a successful one. While Atlanta is not in sympathy with the movement, she is always ready to help Atlanta.[8]

When the vote was taken, Detroit received seven, Washington thirty-nine, Cincinnati fifty-seven, and Atlanta sixty-seven. Subsequently, the delegates from Michigan and New York changed their votes to Atlanta, thereby giving Atlanta a total of ninety-four and making it the official choice for the next convention.[9] At the time that Augusta Howard extended the invitation, there was no suffrage organization in Atlanta. On March 21, 1894, however, a league was formed. It began with a membership of forty men and women, with Mary Latimer McLendon as president.[10]

As the date of the convention approached, interest in Atlanta augmented. A reporter for the *Constitution* questioned a number of men about their attitude toward votes-for-women. Some, including the mayor of Atlanta, preferred not to discuss the matter; some were definitely opposed. One Atlantan, J.W. English, expressed his views as follows: "When women assume the voting responsibility, they must take up all other duties of citizenship. They must be soldiers, be eligible for places in Congress, for governorships, and for the Presidency ....I, for one, do not want any petticoat government. I do not want women to be soldiers, and I certainly don't want them at such places as our average polling places." Of the men questioned, only one favored suffrage, and his support was definitely low-key. J.R. Lewis said, "If they want to vote, let them."[11]

The convention assembled on January 31st with the Aragon Hotel as headquarters. Ninety-three delegates from twenty-eight states and many visitors from all parts of the nation were in attendance, making the convention in Atlanta in 1895 the first large assemblage of suffrage advocates ever held in the South. The most famous person attending was seventy-four year old Susan B. Anthony, President of the National American Woman Suffrage Association. Another distinguished delegate was sixty-seven year old Anna Howard Shaw, a long-time crusader for temperance and women's rights. Among the younger women was thirty-six year old Carrie Chapman Catt who was later to serve as the Association's president during the suffrage movement's concluding years. The most outstanding among the Southern women was forty-five year old Laura Clay of Kentucky, the daughter of Cassius M. Clay and chairman of the Association's Committee on Southern Work. Other Southern women of prominence were Ella C. Chamberlain of Florida, Lide A. Meriwether of Tennessee, Caroline E. Merrick of Louisiana, Josephine K. Henry of Kentucky, Virginia Durant Young of South Carolina and Elizabeth Lyle Saxon of Louisiana.

During the convention, reports were made and business conducted in the morning and afternoon sessions. Addresses by prominent individuals were delivered during the evenings. In discussing the progress of the movement, Susan B. Anthony stated that there were two equal suffrage states — Wyoming and Colorado — and noted with pride that Colorado had three women in its legislature. Robert T. Hemphill of South Carolina maintained that the woman's cause was advancing in spite of centuries of prejudice against it. Josephine K. Henry of Kentucky said that women were fighting for their freedom with "no weapon save argument and no wealth save the justice of their cause."[12] Henry C. Hammond of Georgia denied that voting was outside of "woman's sphere." He doubted that woman had a "sphere," but if she did, voting should certainly be in it.[13]

Before an audience of two thousand in DeGive's Opera House, Anna Howard Shaw refuted the charge that women's rights were in conflict with nature. She stated: "We ask for nothing which God did not give us. God created nature, and if our demands are contrary to nature, trust nature to take care of herself without the aid of man."[14] The following day, Susan B. Anthony presided over a mass meeting sponsored by the Atlanta Equal Suffrage League. She told her listeners that the purpose of the suffrage movement was to bring dignity to woman and to give her "that responsibility and influence to which she is entitled." As a disfranchised person, she has "to beg for every crumb she gets."[15]

The Atlanta convention was considered a pleasant and cordial one. The city made the visitors feel welcome, and some local citizens entertained them in their homes. Two large receptions were given in their honor, one sponsored by the Georgia Woman Suffrage Association and the other by Mrs. W.A. Hemphill, who was assisted by the wife of Governor W.Y. Atkinson.

The press, however, reacted less favorably. The *Constitution* stated that Atlanta had been glad to entertain the suffragists, but expressed the opinion that Georgia women had all the rights that they needed.[16] The *Augusta Evening News* doubted that the majority of women wanted the ballot.[17] The *Columbus Enquirer-Sun* commented: "We may presume that Atlanta is now in her element and happy. She is entertaining the charmed circle of worshippers of the most interesting modern fad, the woman suffragists, with the venerable and esteemed Col. Susan B. Anthony at the head."[18] The *Greensboro Herald* stated that it would favor votes for women were it not for the South's large Negro population.[19] The only Georgia paper to endorse female suffrage was the *Sunny South*, a weekly published in Atlanta and edited by Colonel Henry Clay Fairman.[20]

After the convention, Susan B. Anthony, her sister Mary, her niece Lucy, Anna Howard Shaw, Harriet Taylor Upton and Bessie Gilmer traveled to Columbus for a three-day visit with the Howard family at Sherwood Hall. The visit seems to have been a private one, for the only public recognition of the suffragists' presence in the city was the publication of an interview with Susan B. Anthony by an *Enquirer-Sun* reporter.[21]

During the 1890's, the president of the Georgia Woman's Christian Temperance Union was Mrs. William C. Sibley of Augusta. Mrs. Sibley favored suffrage but apparently never joined the Association. Since the cause in Georgia was frequently viewed with suspicion and disapproval, many temperance advocates thought it wise to avoid identification. On one occasion at least, a convention of the Georgia W.C.T.U. was given permission to use some rooms in a church but with the understanding that the suffrage issue would not be discussed.[22]

In the spring of 1893, the temperance ladies outdid the suffragists by actually going to the polls in Augusta in the hope of influencing a referendum of prohibition. They spent the day there — praying and singing hymns. They were treated courteously by the men who came to vote, but were unable to carry the referendum for prohibition. It was said that the "men walked by them in sound of their prayers and songs and voted that whiskey should remain" in Augusta.[23]

The Atlanta N.A.W.S.A. convention of 1895 was a personal triumph for the Howard sisters. Yet, it was to mark the end of their prominence in the movement. A few months later, both Augusta and her sister Claudia resigned their offices as president and secretary of the Georgia Association.[24] No reason was given for their withdrawal. Perhaps they felt that they had made their contribution in launching the movement in the state, perhaps the lack of support in Columbus made them think that leadership from a larger and more sophisticated city would be more effective, or perhaps there were personal or family reasons. Whatever the cause or causes, their participation became occasional, and after a few years, ceased entirely. Augusta Howard was not forgotten, however. In recognition of her role as the pioneer in Georgia, the N.A.W.S.A. conferred a Certificate of Honor on her in celebration of the enfranchisement of women in 1920.

Augusta Howard's successor as president of the Georgia Woman Suffrage Association was Frances Carter Swift of Atlanta. After several months as president, however, she resigned; and Mrs. Mary Latimer McLendon, also of Atlanta, became president. The Association grew slowly, and at the close of the nineteenth century, consisted only of the group in Atlanta and a few members throughout the state.

In November, 1899, the Georgia Assocation sponsored a two-day convention in Atlanta. Meetings were held in the halls of the Georgia House of Representatives and were attended by large audiences. Both Georgia and out-of-state women delivered addresses. Mrs. Gertrude C. Thomas of Atlanta "reminded the audience that woman was not taken from the head of man — she is not his superior; she was not taken from his foot — she is not his inferior; but she was taken from his side, and there she should stand, his equal in the work of the world." Mrs. Virginia D. Young of South Carolina said that women should have an equal voice in making the laws under which they live. Miss Frances E. Griffin of Alabama maintained that women should not be expected to defend or justify their demand for the ballot. She said, "I am a human being, just as a man is a human being, and in common justice, it is not the place of one-half of the human beings in the world to sav what the other half should do."[25]

An important part of the convention's business was the adoption of resolutions. In introducing its report, the resolutions committee stated: "Women of Georgia are governed, their property taxed, but they have never been asked if they wanted to be governed or to pay taxes on their property. They have no voice in electing their law-makers or officers who are to execute the laws."[26] The convention then adopted a resolution stating that women should be exempt from taxation as long as they were disfranchised. It asked that they be allowed to serve on boards of education and that they be admitted to the University of Georgia. It also favored having women physicians on the staff of the state lunatic asylum.[27]

In addition, the convention adopted a resolution favoring a woman suffrage amendment to the United States Constitution. This action was significant in view of the fact that some Southern supporters of suffrage considered a federal amendment a violation of the rights of the states.[28] In the election of officers, Mrs. Gertrude C. Thomas was chosen to succeed Mrs. McLendon as the Association's president. Mrs. Thomas held this office until the election of Katherine Koch in June, 1900.

By 1902, the Georgia Woman Suffrage Association had fifty members, most of whom lived in Atlanta. Upon learning that the city was revising its charter, Mrs. McLendon, Miss Koch and several other women asked the revision committee for the right to vote in municipal elections. They made a strong appeal, but their request was not granted.[29] A few months later, Atlanta men voted on a proposed bond issue. The suffragists, in turn, protested their disfranchised status by placing at the polls large placards proclaiming: "Taxpaying women should be allowed to vote in this bond election."[30] In 1904, Mrs. Rose Y. Colvin succeeded Miss Koch as president of the Georgia Association. Two years later, in 1906, Mrs. McLendon once again accepted the presidency and held this office until 1921.

In 1909, Atlanta was again revising her charter. Once again the suffragists asked for municipal voting rights, appealing in the interest of women taxpayers. Unfortunately, their arguments failed to convince the charter committee, and women remained disfranchised.[31] In February, 1910, however, the city held a referendum on a three million dollar bond issue. The mayor and the president of the Chamber of Commerce asked the Federation of Women's Clubs to influence men to vote in favor of the bonds. Seeing the irony of the request, the suffragists used the occasion to display a poster showing "women of all sorts, sizes, and conditions, armed with brooms, umbrellas, rolling pins, etc. driving men to the polls."[32]

In spite of the efforts of its supporters, the Suffrage Association showed little increase in membership. Mrs. McLendon refused to be discouraged, however. She was convinced that Georgia women would eventually realize that they were "handicapped in the race for life, liberty, and the pursuit of happiness because they had not the ballot."[33]

During the second decade of the twentieth century, woman suffrage gained general acceptance throughout the nation. This favorable trend was reflected in Georgia. In 1913, the membership of the Georgia Woman Suffrage Association increased from two hundred and fifty to more than one thousand. Other suffrage organizations were formed in the state. In the spring of 1913, the Georgia Woman Suffrage League was organized with Frances Smith Whiteside as president. Mrs. Whiteside was principal of the Ivey Street School and was the sister of United States Senator Hoke Smith. By March, 1914, the League had five hundred members, most of whom lived in Atlanta. This organization worked chiefly with teachers and businesswomen.[34]

Also in 1913, a Georgia Men's League for Woman Suffrage was organized with Leonard J. Grossman, an Atlanta attorney, as president. This league seems to have had few members outside of Atlanta and was primarily a symbol of masculine support of the woman's cause.[35] The following year, 1914, a group of Atlanta women organized the Equal Suffrage Party of Georgia, with Emily C. McDouglad as president. The Party began with less than one hundred members but soon had auxiliaries in thirteen counties. Its more active branches were in Savannah, Augusta, Columbus, Macon, Athens and Albany.[36]

In 1917, a branch of the National Woman's Party was organized. The National Woman's Party, originally called the Congressional Union for Woman Suffrage, was led by Alice Paul, who had crusaded with the Pankhurst suffrage faction in England. It favored aggressive tactics, such as picketing the White House and burning President Wilson in effigy. Because of this militant agitation, some of its members were arrested and jailed. In the spring of 1917, the National Woman's Party sent two organizers to Georgia. They traveled throughout the state and spoke in several towns. At a meeting in Atlanta, they organized a Georgia branch. Mrs. Beatrice Castleton, an Atlanta attorney, was made chairman and she held the position for the duration of the votes-for-women movement.[37]

The Woman's Party engaged in no militant activities in Georgia. In fact, there seems to be no record of Georgia women engaging in militant activities anywhere. While members of the Woman's Party from many states went to Washington, picketed the White House, were arrested and sometimes jailed, it appears that no Georgia women were jailed for suffrage agitation in Washington or anywhere else. Also, there seems to be no evidence of police harassment of suffrage agitators in Georgia. The National Woman's Party's following in Georgia was small, but it maintained its organization for the duration of the movement. When the question of ratification of the Nineteenth Amendment was before the legislature, it sent lobbyists to Atlanta to urge approval.

The suffragists appealed to other organizations to endorse their cause. In many instances, they were successful, but they were not successful with the state's two most outstanding women's groups — the Woman's Christian Temperance Union and the Georgia Federation of Women's Clubs. The national W.C.T.U. had long been a supporter of votes-for-women, but it allowed each state to decide its own policy. In Georgia, many W.C.T.U. members favored suffrage, and a few local units endorsed it. The state organization, however, never went on record in its favor. For several years, the Georgia Federation of Women's Clubs avoided endorsement because opinion among its membership was divided. Finally, at a meeting in Columbus in 1919, the F.W.C. went on record in favor of suffrage, but the victory was a hollow one.[38] By this time, it was obvious that the cause was lost in Georgia and that enfranchisement would come only after a federal amendment had been adopted.

A large number of Georgia women was indifferent toward the suffrage issue. As disfranchised persons, they had survived and often prospered. Many felt that they could continue to do so, and therefore, were content to remain as they were. There were some women, however, who actively opposed their own enfranchisement. In Macon in May, 1914, one such group organized the Georgia Association Opposed to Woman Suffrage. Miss Caroline Patterson was elected president and Mrs.

133

Dolly Blount Lamar vice-president.[39] This Association formed no auxiliaries in other cities but did have members throughout the state.

When the Georgia legislature met in 1914, resolutions to enfranchise women were introduced in both houses. On July 7th, the House Committee on Constitutional Amendments sponsored a hearing at which Mrs. Mary Latimer McLendon, Mrs. Elliott Cheatham, Mrs. Rebecca Latimer Felton, Leonard J. Grossman and James L. Anderson spoke for suffrage, while Mrs. Dolly Blount Lamar and Miss Mildred Rutherford spoke in opposition. Mrs. Felton, a sister of Mrs. McLendon, asked: "Why should our women not have the right to vote? Why can't they help you make laws the same as they help you run your homes and your churches?" Mrs. Cheatham stated that government was public housekeeping and therefore was in woman's domain. Mr. Anderson thought that the vote rightfully belonged to women. Mrs. McLendon noted that Negro men could vote and asked why Southern women should not have the same right. In agreeing with Mrs. McLendon, Mr. Grossman explained that the enfranchisement of Negro women constituted no threat to white control of Georgia politics since Georgia was a one-party state and primary elections were closed to Negroes.[40]

Speaking in opposition, Miss Rutherford told the Committee that the State of Georgia had not "sunk so low" that the good men could not "legislate for the women." Mrs. Lamar denied that the majority of women wanted to vote and said that those who did were a "fungus growth of misguided women."[41] The opposition prevailed, and at the close of hearings, the Committee voted to report the measure unfavorable.[42] The Senate Judiciary Committee also conducted a hearing at which Mrs. Felton and Mrs. Cheatham spoke in favor of and Mrs. Lamar spoke against suffrage. Following the example of the House, the Senate Committee voted to submit an unfavorable report.[43]

During the 1915 legislative session, woman suffrage resolutions were introduced in both houses and were referred to the Committees on Constitutional Amendments. Both committees conducted hearings, and both voted to make unfavorable reports.[44] The suffrage cause fared no better in 1916. During that session, the House Committee on Constitutional Amendments reported unfavorable[45] and the Senate Committee failed to report. In 1917, the House Committee once again voted to submit an unfavorable report,[46] but the Senate Committee voted eight to four to recommend passage.[47] As fate would have it, however, this favorable report failed to help the suffrage cause since the Senate adjourned without taking action on it.

When the legislature convened in the summer of 1919, the Susan B. Anthony Amendment had been submitted to the states. Several had ratified and none had rejected it. The suffragists felt that there was little likelihood of Georgia's approving and hoped that the question would not be considered. Some members of the legislature, however, wanted Georgia to go on record against the proposed amendment. In the House on July 1st, therefore, J.B. Jackson introduced a resolution to ratify. This resolution was referred to the Committee on Constitutional Amendments which held a hearing on July 7th. On that occasion, Jackson amended his resolution to make it read *rejects* instead of *ratifies*. At the close of the hearing, the Committee voted fourteen to thirteen in favor of the resolution to reject.[48] When the resolution came before the House, some members asked that no action be taken. They were overruled, and on July 23rd, the resolution to reject the Anthony Amendment was adopted by a vote of 118 to 29.[49]

Meanwhile, the Senate had under consideration a resolution to ratify the Anthony Amendment. On July 16th, the Senate version was amended to read *rejects* instead of *ratifies*. On July 23rd, a motion to postpone action indefinitely was defeated by a vote of 12 to 33, and the next day, July 24th, the Senate voted 35 to 8 in favor of the amended resolution.[50] Thus, the federal woman suffrage amendment was rejected by both houses, acting separately.[51]

When the legislature convened in 1920, the Anthony Amendment had been ratified by thirty-five states. Only one more was needed. Some hoped that Georgia would yield to the trend, but the legislature stood firm in its opposition. On August 26, 1920, however, the Nineteenth Amendment was proclaimed part of the United States Constitution, and woman suffrage became the supreme law of the land. Georgia women were still unable to vote, however, because state election laws did not authorize it. They were not allowed to vote in the state-wide primary on September 8th nor were they permitted to vote in the general election in November. Finally, in 1921, the legislature passed an act enabling them to vote and hold office.[52] With this act, the suffrage movement in Georgia reached its conclusion. There was no longer any doubt about women's right to vote. Opposition was now a matter of history.

The question of the Anthony Amendment was still not entirely settled, however. In 1970, the League of Women Voters (an outgrowth of the Georgia Woman Suffrage Association) celebrated its fiftieth anniversary. In notation of this fact, Lamar R. Plunkett introduced in the Georgia Senate a resolution to ratify the Nineteenth Amendment. This resolution won quick approval in both houses and was signed by Governor Lester Maddox on March 27th. It stated that women had made an "outstanding record" in their use of the ballot and it was "only fitting and proper" that the Nineteenth Amendment be "ratified and approved."[53] Thus, Georgia was the forty-fifth state to ratify the amendment. The following year (1971), North Carolina became the forty-sixth, and in 1984, Mississippi became the forty-seventh. Louisiana remains the only one of the forty-eight states that has not ratified.[54]

NOTES

[1]Mrs. Miriam Howard Dubose to A. Elizabeth Taylor, January 5, 1943.

[2]H. Augusta Howard, "Progress of the Woman Suffrage Movement in Georgia," *Woman's Progress,* II, No. 2 (November, 1893), 82.

[3]*Constitution and By-Laws of the Georgia Woman Suffrage Association,* 1-4.

[4]Howard, "Woman Suffrage Movement," *Woman's Progress,* II, No. 2 (November, 1893), 82.

[5]*Ibid.*

[6]*Union Signal,* XXI, No. 7 (February 14, 1895), 4.

[7]*Prominent Georgia Men in Favor of Woman Suffrage* published by the Georgia Woman Suffrage Association, October, 1894.

[8]*Proceedings of the Twenty-Sixth Annual Convention of the National American Woman Suffrage Association,* 1894, p. 93.

[9]*Ibid.,* 110. On February 21, 1894, Augusta once again addressed the Judiciary Committee of the United States House of Representatives. On this occasion, she refuted the charge that enfranchisement would cause women to neglect their domestic duties.

[10]Mary L. McLendon, "Georgia," in Elizabeth Cady Stanton, et al. (eds.) *History of Woman Suffrage* (6 vols. Rochester and New York, 1881-1922), IV, 581.

[11]*Atlanta Constitution,* January 29, 1895.

[12]*History of Woman Suffrage,* IV, 245.

[13]*Ibid.,* 244.

[14]*Atlanta Constitution,* February 1, 1895.

[15]*Ibid.,* February 6, 1895.

[16]*Ibid.*

[17]*Augusta Evening News,* February 11, 1895.

[18]*Columbus Enquirer-Sun,* February 1, 1895.

[19]Quoted in *Atlanta Constitution,* January 31, 1895.

[20]*History of Woman Suffrage,* IV, 238.

[21]*Columbus Enquirer-Sun,* February 8, 1895.

[22]*Union Signal,* XXI, No. 20 (May 16, 1895), 11.

[23]*Ibid.,* XIX, No. 21 (May 25, 1893), 10.

[24]*Woman's Journal,* XXVI, No. 14 (April 6, 1895), 108; *Ibid.,* XXVI, No. 10 (March 7, 1896), 74.

[25]*Minutes of the Georgia Woman Suffrage Association,* 1899, pp. 14-15.

[26]*Ibid.,* 11.

[27]*Ibid.,* 12.

[28]*Ibid.; Atlanta Journal,* November 28, 1899.

[29]*N.A.W.S.A. Proceedings,* 1903, p. 70.

[30]*Ibid.,* 1904, p. 74.

[31]*Ibid.,* 1909, p. 75.

[32]*Ibid.,* 1910, p. 109.

[33]*Ibid.,* 1911, pp. 113-114.

[34]McLendon, "Georgia," *History of Woman Suffrage,* VI, 133-134.

[35]*Ibid.,* 126.

[36]Emily C. McDougald, "The Equal Suffrage Party in Georgia," *History of Woman Suffrage,* VI, 134-136.

[37]*Suffragist,* v. No. 66 (April 28, 1917), 7.

[38]*Columbus Ledger,* November 14, 1919.

[39]*Macon Daily Telegraph,* May 23, 1914.

[40]*Atlanta Constitution,* July 8, 1914. Rebecca Latimer Felton and Mary Latimer McLendon were sisters.

[41]*Ibid.*

[42]*Georgia House Journal,* 1914, p. 287.

[43]*Georgia Senate Journal,* 1914, p. 236.

[44]*Ibid.*, 1915, p. 520; Georgia *House Journal*, 1915, p. 1073.

[45]*Ibid.*, 1916, p. 354.

[46]*Ibid.*, 1917, p. 587.

[47]*Georgia Senate Journal*, 1917, p. 612.

[48]*Atlanta Constitution*, July 8, 1919.

[49]*Ibid.*, July 25, 1919; Georgia *House Journal*, 1919, p. 910.

[50]*Georgia Senate Journal*, 1919, p. 657, p. 677.

[51]Neither house adopted the other's resolution.

[52]*Acts and Resolutions of the General Assembly of the State of Georgia*, 1921, p. 107. Mississippi and Georgia were the only states that refused to allow women to vote in the November election in 1920.

[53]*Georgia Laws*, 1970 Session, p. 952.

[54]States that ratified after the Nineteenth Amendment had been incorporated in the United States Constitution were Connecticut (1920), Vermont (1921), Delaware (1923), Maryland (1941), Virginia (1952), Alabama (1953), Florida (1969), South Carolina (1969), Georgia (1970), North Carolina (1971), and Mississippi (1984).

Sports and Leisure in Georgia[1]
CHARLTON MOSELEY

When James Edward Oglethorpe and the original settlers arrived in Georgia in 1733, they were greeted by native peoples whom we may accurately call the first "true Georgians." These aboriginal people were members of the Creek confederacy; more specifically, they were Tomo-chi-chi and the Yamacraws, who were a small band of the Creek Indian Nation. The aid provided to the first Englishmen by this Indian band and the strong alliance formed between the remainder of the Creek Nation and the first generations of European settlers are a familiar story to most students of Georgia history.

The Indians who inhabited the Georgia region during the first half of the eighteenth century consisted primarily of two large tribes, with the largest tribe actually being a loose confederation of many small tribes called the Creek Nation. Among the tribal groups called "Creeks" by the English were the Yuchi, Hichitis, Tallapoosas, Alabamas and remnants of the Westo and Yamassee. The principal language was the Muskogean dialect, although other languages were spoken; and the Creeks dominated the valleys of the Chattahoochee, Flint, Ocmulgee and other creeks and rivers in Georgia. When the first Europeans arrived in the Georgia colony, the Creeks probably numbered as many as 30,000 people in 50 towns in Georgia and Alabama.[2] The second largest Indian tribe was the Cherokee Nation which inhabited the highlands of North Georgia, Tennessee and the Carolinas. The Cherokee were of Iroquoian stock and had migrated into the South centuries earlier. James Adair, a trader among the Indians, estimated the population of the Cherokee to be as high as 17,000 in 1755, with the tribe inhabiting as many as 64 villages.[3] Both the Creek and Cherokee had highly developed political and social systems, and they were excellent farmers who grew corn, squash, pumpkins and other edibles and supplemented their food supply by the hunt.

By the late eighteenth century, another Indian group had begun to play an important role in the lives of Georgians. This was the Seminole Nation which principally occupied Florida but ranged into southern Georgia. The Seminoles were actually an amalgamation of several fragmented Florida tribes, but were heavily influenced linguistically and culturally by the Muskogean Creeks from Georgia who joined the Seminole band in increasing numbers as whites pushed against the Indian frontier. Until their removal from Georgia in the early nineteenth century, these tribes were an integral part of the growth and development of Georgia as colony and state.

The Indian groups in Georgia consisted of people who, like all other people, worked to provide for their families, hunted to feed themselves and their dependants, made war to protect their villages and hunting grounds, and again like their brethren in other cultures, enjoyed art, music and various forms of recreation. The Georgia Indians, like many other native American groups, indulged themselves in music, dance and various games for a variety of reasons. While most of their activities were recreational in nature, the activities involved considerable ritual and often had religious significance. The Indian also firmly believed that music, dance and recreational activities were generally vital to the health and happiness of man, a concept still promoted by modern enthusiasts of sports and recreation. While the Indian enjoyed his games even before his contact with the European, it is apparent that the ball games and other competitive events became even more important after his military subjugation by the whites; for fiercely competitive sports events became a substitute for warfare.[4]

In music, Georgia Indians primarily used three instruments: the drum, rattle and flageolet. The drum was made in various ways, but the principal method was to construct it by partially filling an earthen pot with water and stretching a skin over the open end. The water effected the tone and could be used occasionally to moisten the skin covering. Another favorite method of making drums was to stretch skin over short sections of hollow tree trunks such as the black gum, resulting in drums that often measured thirty inches in length and fifteen inches in diameter. Drumsticks were usually made of maple, poplar or ash.[5]

Second in importance after the drums were the rattles, usually constructed of gourds. The Indian could achieve various tones or sounds by placing pebbles, corn or beans in the gourd and by varying the size of the gourd itself. The result from shaking twenty or thirty rattles was apparently an awesome sound, for one early observer noted that they "make such a terrible noise as would rather affright then (sic) delight any man."[6] The gourd rattles were usually highly decorated with paint and hung with feathers or other ornaments. Another effective rattle, often used by women, was made by filling turtle shells with pebbles and attaching them with straps to the lower legs. A loud, rhythmic sound was produced as the women danced. After contact with white traders, however, the Indian women often substituted brass bells for the turtle shells.[7]

The flageolet was a wind instrument, a kind of a primitive flute from a hollow cane or an animal bone and usually about twelve inches in length. It normally contained only two finger holes and produced a very plaintive sound. William Bartram said of the flageolet, "On this instrument they perform badly, and at best it is rather a hideous melancholy discord, than harmony. It is only the young fellows who amuse themselves on this howling instrument."[8] Despite Bartram's disaffection for the flageolet, however, he found Cherokee music made by the rattle and drum most pleasant. The Indian musical instruments, says Bartram, "accompanied with their sweet low voices, produce a pathetic harmony, keeping exact time together ... (and) it instantly touches the feelings of the attentive audience, as the influence of an active and powerful spirit; there is then an united universal sensation of delight and peaceful union of souls throughout the assembly."[9]

Music and dance generally pervaded the life of the Indians of the Southeast. Although warriors often went into battle to the beat of the drum and the wailing sounds of whistles, music also accompanied dancing in the villages. The dance provided recreation and leisure for the Indian, but it was as often an expression of the Indian's recognition of the powers of nature and his dependency upon nature for his survival. An example was the dancing at the Green Corn Ceremony, which marked the beginning of the new year among the Creek Indians. After considerable ceremony, fasting and replenishing of the fires in the village, the Creek males adorned themselves with white feathers in hand and hair and formed three circles about the great village fire. They sang and danced, accompanied by musicians with gourd rattles and two earthen drums. Before the dancing ended, the women were invited to participate and were usually quite eager and energetic in their dancing, wearing their finest clothes, beads and ear pendants in place, hair gleaming with bear oil and tortoise shell rattles strapped to their legs.[10]

Many of the Indian dances were named after animals, for the Indians firmly believed that their dancing and music had an effect upon the animals. Some of the Creeks, for instance, refused to do the Snake Dance during the summer months because they believed the dance made the snakes angry. This dance was normally reserved for the fall when the snakes had gone into their dens. Even then the Indians who participated would place their feet close to the fire so that the snakes could not see to bite them. The dancers would also warm their hands in the fire and then rub their eyes in the belief that this would give them an enhanced ability to see snakes and avoid them.[11] The Cherokee danced the Beaver and Raccoon Dances and pretended to kill these animals, skin the carcasses and prepare the hides. In the Buffalo Hunt Dance, men and women imitated the cows and bulls of the herd, pawing the earth and emitting loud bellows; and in the Bear Dance, the Cherokee sought to appease the bears they intended to kill in the belief that the bears had once been human themselves.[12] The Indians usually danced in a circle around a great fire and always in a counterclockwise direction. The exception occurred when the women joined the men in dancing, forming an inner circle and dancing in the opposite direction. William Bartram described three general types of dances: "martial, bacchanalian and amorous." The latter dance-type Bartram described as "extravagantly libidinous."[13] The dancing and feasting often lasted several consecutive nights.

Charles Hudson describes a Cherokee dance performed in the early part of the twentieth century and called the Booger Dance. It was quite bawdy in nature and was therefore something of an enigma since the Cherokee were generally considered to be one of the more morally refined and restrained Indian peoples. Those who were to participate in the dance usually gathered at a home in the neighborhood, and for a time, engaged in traditional social dances. Sometime later, a small group of Cherokee men would knock at the door — they were expected, of course — and when admitted, they entered disguised in sheets or blankets wrapped around their bodies and hideous masks, representing outsiders, including Northerners, Southerners, Frenchmen, Chinese, Negroes and others. The "strangers" would pretend to speak foreign languages, and they often adorned obscene names such as "Black Buttocks," "Sooty Anus" and "Big Phallus." Some masks were also obscene. One, in particular, was constructed from a gourd and modeled in the form of a male sex organ. The "strangers" would shout obscene comments to the women present, rush forward as if to catch and attack them and dance and make obscene gestures to them. Finally, the "strangers" left the dance to discard their costumes, and upon reentering the room, they deported themselves with all the decorum normally ascribed to members of the Cherokee Nation. The Booger Dance is an interesting commentary on a carefully orchestrated breach of the normally firm Cherokee code of sexual conduct.[14]

Georgia Indians also enjoyed themselves with various forms of ball play. The most popular form was similar to the game played by other Indian tribes throughout most of the eastern woodlands. Lacrosse, the national game of Canada, is an adaptation of the game which was played by Southern Indians with two wooden sticks about two feet long. One end of each stick was curved to make a cup to catch the ball and was framed with leather thongs. The ball was made of deerskin wound tightly around deer or squirrel hair. The game was played on flat playing fields which varied in size from about one hundred yards to as much as five hundred yards in length; and goal posts, established at each end of the field, resembled modern football goal posts except that the Indian version was about twenty feet high. Team sizes varied in number from as few as a dozen players to as many as several hundred, and the only rule seems to have been that the teams must be equal in number. The object of the game was to carry the ball to the goal post and throw it over the crossbar or against one of the upright posts. While the ball had to be carried in the ball stick's pocket, it could be thrown from one team member to another. Play began in the center of the field, with one of the elder men of the tribe throwing the ball into play. Once a team had possession of the ball, the opposing team could use almost any method to retrieve it, including tripping the ball player and tackling and beating an opponent with the stick.

This was a dangerous game which often resulted in serious injury and sometimes even death to some of the players. Sportsmanship was applauded and encouraged; serious rivalries developed between teams and individual members of teams; and some teams were accused of deliberately trying to disable the best players on the opposing side. James Adair recounts seeing players of one team deliberately break the bones of the opposing team members, although he was later told that this particular incident was caused by a feud between two Indian families "that might have raised their spleens, as much as the high bets they had then at stake, which was almost all they were worth."[15] Each time a team threw the ball over the goal post, a point was scored. Among the Cherokee, the first team to score twelve points won the contest, but the Creeks required a twenty-point total for the winning team. The games were occasionally played in as little time as an hour or less, but they frequently continued on for a full day.

Although ball playing was a sport of the summer months, the harvest season was the favorite time for play. The game was serious business to the Indian, and he went to considerable lengths to ensure victory. The players fasted from the evening meal before the day of the game until after the game was played, and they refused to eat certain animals for fear they would be physically affected. Eating rabbit, for instance, was avoided because it was believed that rabbit meat would frighten or confuse the athlete on the athletic field. They would not eat hot food or salt, and they were forbidden to touch a woman for seven days or more before a game. Also, the village medicine man went to great lengths to prevent a rival ball team from conjuring magical sabotage against the home team. Just as the players avoided certain animal foods, they used other animals in an attempt to improve their physical prowess and wore deer or cougar tails to improve their stamina and agility. The Creeks often painted animal symbols on their bodies to symbolize the conflict of the game and to improve their performance. The night before a ball game was usually given to dance and ritual as the players prepared themselves for the contest on the following day. The ball games were almost always contests between rival towns, and often ill will developed between winners and losers. When a team scored a point, it mocked the opposing team, imitating turkey gobbles to insult the opponents. One of the most common practices among the onlookers was betting on favorite teams, and often the betting left losers stripped of most of their material wealth, including clothing and even wives, when their team failed to achieve victory.[16]

While Indian women were allowed to play certain kinds of ball games, chunkey was restricted to males and was another favorite game among Indians of the Southeast. Unlike the ball game, it was usually played by Indians belonging to the same village. The game varied somewhat from tribe to tribe, but basically consisted of rolling a small wheel-shaped stone of about eight inches in diameter along a carefully constructed chunkey court. The court was about one hundred feet by twelve feet and was often made of packed sand. Normally, two men played against each other, and the object of the game was to roll the chunkey stone along the court. Before it stopped rolling, the two players would throw eight-foot poles toward the rolling stone. The player whose pole was nearest the stone when it stopped rolling scored a point, and if the stone actually touched the pole, the player scored two points. When a certain number of points was scored by a player, the game ended. As in most Indian games, betting by participants and by-standers was usually heavy, and the losers often left destitute.[17]

Indian music, dance and athletic contests were also closely related to the hunt, religious beliefs, nature and the preparation of a strong, competitive body and spirit for martial defense of the tribe. Similarly, in a considerable way, there was a relationship between many of the sports and leisure activities of the common man of Georgia in the colonial and frontier periods, a relationship which has to some extent continued into the twentieth century. According to the historian Everitt Dick, one of the outstanding features of frontier social occasions in the South was the fact that, with the exception of a wedding, almost all of the very earliest ventures were connected with work.[18] This statement, however, may not have been entirely true in all sections of Georgia, for historian Ulrich B. Phillips said that "in the mountain coves luxuries were never known, and leisure was mere loafing."[19] Nevertheless, there does appear to have been a strong correlation between the social and leisure activities of the common man and his need to provide food and shelter for himself and his family. Since primitive economic conditions in the South continued well into the twentieth century in the forms of the sharecropping and tenant farming culture of the region, many of these frontier-type leisure and recreational activities are still familiar to many rural Georgians, or at the very least, have not long been extinct.

In the South during the eighteenth and nineteenth centuries, one of the favorite recreations which support Everitt Dick's contention was the shucking bee, where friends and neighbors gathered at a local home to husk the corn which had been recently gathered and brought to the ricks or barns. Usually, the corn was divided into two even piles, the huskers assembled into teams and a frantic, intense rivalry developed as each group sought to husk their allotment of corn faster than the opposing teams. On occasion, the rivalry led to cheating as some members of a team would hide unhusked ears of corn in the shucked pile or furtively pitch them out of a window. Generally, however, the shucking events seem to have been very festive occasions, usually enlivened by the liberal imbibing of fiery, homemade spirits from gourds or bottles. Fiddles and banjos were often nearby, and once the husking was finished, a home-cooked feast was spread, followed by dancing which often lasted into the night. Any young man who discovered a red ear of corn during the husking was allowed to publicly kiss the girl of his choice during the festivities which followed.[20]

During the ante-bellum period, slaves were often allowed to join in the shucking contest if they were not too numerous.[21] In the lower South where blacks were more heavily concentrated, they were often allowed what might be properly called "work festivals" of their own, although the master's family might still participate in the event. Emily Burke, a school teacher in Georgia in the Eighteen Forties and a native of New Hampshire, recounted such an event:

> At about seven o'clock in the summer season, the colored people would generally begin to assemble in the yard belonging to the planter's residence. Here they would kindle little bonfires not only to ward off the mosquitos but because they are considered essential in the hot season to purify the air when it is filled with feverish vapors that arise from decayed vegetable matter. Then while two of their number are engaged at the mill (grinding corn), all the rest join in a dance around

147

the burning fagots. In this manner was spent the greater part of the summer evenings, and it was usual for the white members of the family to assemble on the piazza to witness their pastimes. And sometimes at the request of a favorite slave I have seen the white children engage in the waltz or take their places in the quadrille.[22]

Similar to the shucking bee was the quilting party which, of course, was primarily the domain of women who gathered over the quilting frame to turn out the beautiful patch-work quilts which are still a traditional American craft. On many of the plantations, the slaves were organized into quilting sessions which seem to have been as much for the pleasure and enjoyment of the blacks as for the necessity of making proper bed coverings. The slave quilting party was unique in many instances in that both males and females were involved in the sewing. Using darning needles and tracing their patterns with charcoal, the black men and women worked prodigiously. "Among the Southern field hands," said one observer, "the women can hoe as well as the men and the men can sew as well as the women ...."[23] The slave quilting party was first devoted to quilting and "the latter part to festivity and dancing."[24] On occasion, a particularly generous plantation owner would provide hams and pastries for the festivities.[25]

In fact, according to one authority, the average slave had a surprising number of liberties. He was allowed holidays at Christmas, Easter, the Fourth of July and on other occasions, and picnics and barbecues were often held, accompanied by athletic contests and dances. In Savannah during the antebellum period, when the local population turned out for parades to celebrate special holidays, the slaves were very much in attendance as well. In fact, a Northern visitor to Savannah in the Eighteen Forties relates that when military parades were conducted by the militia on holidays, all of the musicians were black and were dressed in the full uniform of the company to which they belonged. Also, a very common sight was black slaves carrying their master's children to the parades, to the mutual enjoyment of child and servant.[26]

In his book, *Roll, Jordan, Roll,* Eugene D. Genovese refers to slave recreations and leisure activities in a chapter entitled "De Big Times," and in an interesting but academic manner, he describes the varied activities of Southern slaves in their quest for fun and frolic during their leisure time. "All except the most unfeeling masters," writes Genovese, "threw Saturday night parties for their slaves once in a while."[27] Most masters also contributed material commodities for the fling in the form of a hog, chickens and even whiskey. If the masters of a plantation did not voluntarily provide material for their slaves, the latter often stole a few of the plantation chickens or a hog and created their own party, often inviting slaves from neighboring plantations to join in the festivities despite a normal nine o'clock p.m. curfew on most plantations.[28] Blacks particularly enjoyed music, singing and dancing, and while they owned few musical instruments, they were able to improvise. A gracious master might provide a banjo or fiddle for his slaves, but if not, they would make homemade drums, flutes and even banjos and fiddles. Spoons and dishpans made excellent percussion instruments and many of the slaves became adept at playing them.[29]

The longest and most festive holidays for slaves usually came at Christmas time when, says Genovese, "even harsh masters usually provided a three-day holiday ...."[30] Some masters even extended the period for a week and more, and there was usually a plantation Christmas tree and presents for the slaves. The masters often provided whiskey and eggnog and staggered the parties so that the slaves of one plantation might visit and be entertained at a neighboring plantation. The parties consisted of singing and dancing and great barbecues.

There were, of course, other holidays in addition to Christmas. Usually, there was a party at laying-by time, another at Thanksgiving and a great celebration on the Fourth of July. The slaves became very adept at wheedling additional holidays by insisting that they celebrate the master's or mistress' birthday, the wedding of one of the master's children, the master's return from a trip, or any other occasion which was an excuse for taking a day off from the fields and other chores. These celebrations did much to make slave conditions more bearable, but according to some critics of the peculiar institution, much of the generosity shown by the masters was a deliberate effort to quiet the slaves and lessen their natural animosity towards their bondage. Charley Hunt, a Georgia slave, summed it up succinctly when he said, "Anyway, dat one day on massa's place all am happy and forgits dey am slaves."[31]

Thus, some slaves in the South were allowed liberties. They were allowed to take holidays at Christmas, Easter and the Fourth of July among others, and the better masters allowed a half day on Saturday and all of Sunday free from work. The more thoughtful and kindly masters often organized picnics and barbecues for their slaves and provided food and refreshment for those occasions.[32] Emily Burke, the New Hampshire woman who became a school teacher in ante-bellum Georgia, recounts a slave holiday on a plantation about a day's journey from Savannah. Upon returning from church with the white family with whom she was staying, Miss Burke said:

> There a new scene presented itself to my view. The slaves had finished their tasks that had been assigned to them in the morning and were now enjoying holiday recreations. Some were trundling the hoop, some were playing ball, some dancing at the sound of the fiddle, some grinding their own corn at the mill, while others were just returning from fishing or hunting excursions. In this manner the Sabbath is usually spent on a Southern plantation.[33]

Frances B. Leigh, in her book *Ten Years on a Georgia Plantation Since the War*, described celebrations among blacks on the plantations of coastal Georgia in the postwar era. Leigh celebrated her birthday on the plantation, and when the field hands learned of the event, they came to the home to perform the Shout for the mistress. The Shout was apparently a combination of good fun, singing and religious celebration. All day, Leigh relates, the blacks brought little presents to her, including honey, eggs, flowers and other items. Then, in the evening,

> . . . about fifty of them, of all sizes and ages and of both sexes, headed by old Uncle John, the preacher, collected in front of the house to 'shout.' First they lit two huge fires of blazing pine logs, around which they began to move with a slow shuffling step, singing a hymn beginning 'I wants to climb up Jacob's ladder.' Getting warmed up by degrees, they went faster and faster, shouting louder and louder, until they looked like a parcel of mad fiends. The children, finding themselves kicked over in the general melee, formed a

150

circle on their own account, and went round and round like small catherine wheels.[134]

The Shout continued until it was stopped by the white mistress who relates that the blacks were in a frenzy of excitement and eager to continue their singing.[35]

The Shout, as it was called, was a common phenomenon among slaves who "got religion," especially those converted to Methodism. Since dancing was sinful, these blacks stopped dancing and the Shout evolved as a religious experience. One of the most common methods of doing the Shout was an assemblage of slaves (or free Negroes) singing while several of their number formed a circle or "ring" and began a special dance in perfect time to the music. It should be noted, too, that many poor whites developed religious practices very similar to the Negro Shout; however, it was generally agreed that the white "shouters" were a poor second to the black performers and that blacks usually held the poor white's efforts in considerable disdain. The slaves heartily disagreed with their critics who maintained that the Shout was, in fact, a form of dancing. In dancing, according to blacks, the feet crossed and in the Shout, the feet always moved parallel one to the other.[36]

In 1871, Leigh witnessed another postwar recreation among Negroes on Georgia's coastal plantations. Having given her Negroes a holiday, she went down to the river to witness boat racing by the blacks. "The river was crowded with boats of all sizes and shapes, in the midst of which lay the two elegant little race boats, manned by six of my men and six of the Altama negroes. Splendid fellows all of them, wild with excitement and showing every tooth in their heads, they were on such a broad grin."[37] The Leigh plantation blacks won two or three boat races in that day.[38]

In contrast, fighting was often considered a "sport" among white frontier Georgians. On the frontier, fights which broke out were attended by crowds of spectators and were often little more than "gouging matches" with the men fighting like animals, punching, kicking, biting and gouging while the excited on-lookers cheered them on.[39] Augustus Baldwin Longstreet, in his *Georgia Scenes,* depicts one of these events provoked by a disagreement between the wives of two men. "It is said," Longstreet wrote, "that a hundred game-cocks will live in perfect harmony together if you do not put a hen with them; and so it would have been with Billy and Bob had there been no women in the world."[40] But Billy and Bob were married, and when their wives engaged in a heated debate in a country store after the local militia had drilled, their husbands took up the matter and a fight was arranged on the courthouse square. As a large crown cheered the combatants on, Billy and Bob entered the contest, and in the "no holds barred" spirit of frontier fighting, soon had considerably maimed each other. Longstreet recounts the scene:

> *I looked and saw Bob had entirely lost his left ear and a large piece from his left cheek. His right eye was a little discolored, and the blood flowed profusely from his wounds.*[41]

Bill's condition was even worse:

> *Bill presented a hideous spectacle. About a third of his nose, at the lower extremity, was bit off, and his face so swelled and bruised that it was difficult to discover in it anything of the human visage, much less the fine features which he carried into the ring.*[42]

The fight did not end with these barbarities but continued until Bob had a finger bitten off by Bill and dirt rubbed in his eyes when he collapsed from exhaustion. Yet, after several weeks spent in recuperation, the two men met on the street, shook hands and remained friends.[43]

One of the cruelest sports among frontier Georgians and one which was popular throughout much of the South was gander pulling. Although gander pulling varied from region to region, it was an event which drew large crowds at almost any public gathering. Augustus Longstreet described the popular sport as it occurred in Augusta, Georgia in 1798. A circular path was laid out about forty yards in diameter around which a horseman would ride at considerable speed. At one point, a pole was erected on each side of the path and a rope was stretched between the two poles. Attached to the pole, swinging by the feet, was a gander whose feathers had been pulled from his neck and head and whose neck had been liberally greased. The object of the "pull" was the horseman's riding around the bridle path and pulling off the head of the gander. It was a difficult task because of the greased condition of the goose, the speed of the horse and the rider's standing in the stirrups to reach the fowl. Judges stood near the contact point, and if a horse reduced its speed too much, the supervisors would hit the horse on the flanks to increase the speed. The goose usually withstood many a wrench of its neck before some champion managed to end its suffering by breaking its neck or pulling its head from its body. The winner of the "pull" received a cash award consisting of the twenty-five cent fees charged to attend the contest and the mutilated goose. Gander pulling, says Everitt Dick, was enjoyed by "large crowds of both sexes and colors . . . ."[44]

Of all the sports in Georgia from the frontier experience to the present time, probably no other has equalled the enthusiasm for hunting wild game. In the early days of the colony and state, hunting was often necessary to provide meat for the table, but in more recent times, hunting has been less a necessity and more a demonstration of the primitive instinct for the chase. Mann Norton, a modern citizen of the North Georgia mountains, summarized the early twentieth century hunter by saying, "They really didn't have to hunt, but they liked the taste of wild meat." Another mountaineer, Lon Reid, agreed: "They didn't have to hunt. They had hogs and a garden. But they enjoyed it. They liked the chase, and they liked a change and fresh meat."[45] In the colonial period, hunting not only provided food for the table, but skins for clothing and trade as well.

Probably no game has been hunted more than deer, for deer were hunted in a variety of ways in the colonial era. Still prevalent today, the "still hunt" was quite popular and consisted of the hunter's locating a game trail or watering place and remaining in hiding until the deer approached. In contrast, however, some twentieth century Georgia hunters buy expensive platforms called "tree stands," devices which allow the hunters to climb trees more easily to await the deer. A second method of hunting, although quite illegal today, was hunting with fire. The hunter went into the woods at night with a large firebrand, and the deer, attracted to the light, could be easily killed. Today, a spotlight or the headlights of an automobile have the same effect, and this method is termed "night hunting." The third principal method of deer hunting involved chasing the deer with trained dogs. Hunters placed themselves in good locations called "stands" and waited until the hunting dogs drove the deer close enough to them to be shot; however, a hunter was never assured that the dogs would drive a deer in his direction. Thus, many a poor hunter spent a lonely, cold

153

day on his stand without the solace of even hearing the yelping of the dog pack in the distant swamps.

During the ante-bellum period, deer hunters sometimes used horses to follow the dogs during a hunt. Emily Burke, who sympathized with the deer, described one such scene in Georgia in the Eighteen Forties:

> Of all the amusements resorted to at the South by gentlemen to pass away time, I always looked upon deer hunting as one of the most cruel. When I saw a half dozen men on horse-back followed by as many hungry hounds, I always wondered how men could enjoy such sports. When I have seen them (the deer) panting for breath and almost dead with fear, shifting and turning, sometimes retracing their own steps to elude the hounds, my sympathies were always with the poor animals rather than the cruel hunters, and I always wanted to lend a helping hand to effect their escape. Deer hunting days are always hailed as the most joyous and merry, and, when the company was about setting out, the prancing of the horses and the barking of the hounds testified their eagerness to be in the chase. But I never could see these preparations without commiseration for the poor animals at whose expense all this merriment was to be purchased.[46]

Hunting squirrel was another popular sport. Thousands of Georgia hunters from the colonial era to the present have participated in the quest for these furry little creatures in Georgia's swamps and woodlands. In earlier days, the best site for hunting squirrels was near an oak grove where the animals came to feed on acorns. Similarly in modern Georgia, though squirrel hunters are not nearly so numerous, the hunter may hide in the edge of a wood near a pecan grove. Another traditional hunt in Georgia was the raccoon and opossum hunt. While the hunt for these animals still has its adherents in modern Georgia, the hunt for the wily 'coon and 'possum was especially popular among poorer whites and blacks, from the North Georgia mountains to the Okefenokee swamp. 'Coon and 'possum hunting was done at night. The hunters armed themselves with a rifle and a lantern or pine knot torch, and with the dog on a leash, they were off to the woods. After the dog was released in prime 'coon or 'possum territory, the hunters usually reclined under a tree to enjoy the usual storytelling, smoking and tobacco chewing. When the dogs found a trail and their mournful baying resounded through the woodlands, the hunters followed. The hunters could tell immediately when the chase had ended by the tone of the dog's barking and the stationary position of his frenzied baying. While some hunters shot the raccoon from the tree, others climbed the tree and chased the raccoon out of the tree so the dog could be rewarded by making the kill. Roast raccoon was considered good food by most families of rural Georgia, and a platter of baked 'possum, surrounded by roasted sweet potatoes, was a real delicacy![47]

While such hunting forays may seem cruel to the modern Georgian who secures his food from the local Piggly Wiggly or Big Star grocery store, hunting had a two-fold purpose for the frontier Georgian: the hunt provided an outlet from the day-to-day drudgery of earning a living, and it put food on the table. During the ante-bellum period, for example, slaves were allowed to hunt, and they eagerly seized this pleasure because it put venison, rabbit, duck, 'coon, 'possum and other wild game on the table.[48] Many poor sharecroppers and tenant farmers supplemented their meager diet of corn bread, syrup, greens and pork with flavorful and nutritious wild game; thus, hunting was often a sport of necessity among poor families.

Just as hunting was both a recreation and necessity, so was fishing, but it did not involve elaborate tackle and baits or expensive junkets to the coast. "Common man fishing" required a pole cut from the nearest woods and a minimum of tackle and paraphernalia. The fisherman walked, rode in a wagon or drove an antique car to the nearest creek or river, armed with his pole, a can of worms dug out of the barnyard, or perhaps, a jar filled with grasshoppers captured in the nearest corn field. If the trip to the local fishing spot was successful, the table would soon be heaped with a platter of fried fish and "corn dodgers" or "hush puppies"; and if the catch was large enough, the neighbors or friends might be invited in for a "fish fry," one of the most popular leisure activities in the rural South.

If the creeks dried up during a summer, the "common fisherman" might try one of several methods of obtaining fish. One of these methods was seining for fish. Those who could afford to buy a good net or seine attached a six-foot pole at each end of the seine and pulled the net through the water, scooping up the fish and dragging them up on the bank. The process usually required a strong man on each end of the seine. One or two of the younger boys followed the seine, and if the netting became entangled on a root at the bottom of the water hole, their job was to unloosen it without letting the fish escape. Often times, the women remained on the bank to remove the fish from the net and place them in a wet sack. For those who could not afford a seine, a number of feed sacks carefully sewn together served the same purpose. Seining a creek or running waterway is quite illegal. The old-fashioned art of "muddying" the small holes of water in a creek was another method. An entire family usually took part in the venture which consisted of entering the water hole with hoes and literally stirring the water until it became muddy, causing the fish to come to the top of the water seeking oxygen. Then the fish could be easily scooped up in small homemade nets or caught with the bare hands. While few sophisticated moderns would consider these methods fun, they were the poor man's recreation, and they filled his dinner table with fresh fish. There were several perils in seining or "muddying" a creek fishing hole, including being caught by the game warden or being bitten by a poisonous water snake. Nevertheless, the participants enjoyed themselves and their efforts usually yielded fish at supper time![49]

A recreation which grew out of the sport of hunting was the shooting match. A very common pastime during the frontier era, it continues to be popular in many rural areas of Georgia in the twentieth century. The shooting match normally involved a number of gunmen who bought chances in the match. If they won the event, they might take cash, beef, turkey or other rewards as a victor's treasure. The match usually involved placing an "X" on a block of wood and positioning it against a tree fifty or sixty yards away. Each contestant fired his shot and his bullet hole was carefully marked. After the shooting was finished, a judge declared the winner, but often a "shoot off" was necessary because of the extremely able marksmanship of the participants. In shotgun competition, the "X" was placed on a block of wood which was tossed into the air and fired on by the contestant. Since a shotgun scattered many shots, a separate block was provided for each contestant. The shooter who put the most shots near the crossing of the "X" received the prize in the contest. Another variation of the shooting match was the "turkey shoot" in which a live turkey was tethered by the foot behind a log thirty or forty yards away. Since the turkey tended to hide himself behind the log, it was necessary for the hunter to "gobble" and encourage the timid fowl to raise its head above the obstruction. When the turkey did raise its head, the shooter had a brief instant in which to fire. Of course, target shooting was often done in the spirit of competition with no other reward than the pride of accomplished marksmanship. James Silk Buckingham, a foreign traveler who visited Georgia in 1839, described a parade of the militia in Savannah and the shooting contest which followed:

> . . . the companies that turned out on that occasion were well dressed, well disciplined, and had as perfectly martial an air as the National Guards of Paris, to which, both in uniform, stature, and general appearance, they bore a marked resemblance. During their exercises of the day, they fired at a target with rifles, and put in their balls with extraordinary skill. They are habituated to this practice, it is true, from their youth upward, for almost every boy of fourteen or fifteen has a horse and a rifle. Shooting matches are therefore frequent, and in deer-shooting they have almost daily opportunities of trying their aim; as the wild deer are here so abundant that they are shot in the woods within a mile or two of the town; and venison is therefore to be seen on almost every table.[50]

While there may be those who would debate whether tobacco chewing was a recreation or sport, there was almost universal use of the weed by all ages and sexes in Georgia during the frontier period. The universality of the tobacco chewing cult in the nineteenth century has been aptly described by the foreign visitor James Silk Buckingham:

> One most disgusting feature of all the oratory that I have yet heard in the Southern States, is the constant interruption to the flow of their discourses, by the almost equally copious flow of their saliva, from their excessive use of tobacco. In the churches, at public lectures, in private parties, or in public assemblies, you hear every minute the sound of the labial ejection, and its fall upon the floor; while the chewers roll about the offensive and blackened mass in their mouths, as

though it was all that was worth living for. Each young man carries in his waistcoat pocket, not in a box, but open, a flattened square mass of black compressed tobacco, like a piece of Indian rubber. From this he cuts off, from time to time, whether in the company of ladies or not, a large piece, and, taking the expended quid from his mouth, he flings it out of the window, or in any near corner, and replaces it by the new one, which he forthwith begins to roll about like any ruminating animal.[51]

Buckingham continued with this query: "How is it that the ladies of America, married and unmarried, do not with one voice and one accord, refuse the approach of lips so filthily defiled, and turn with disgust from the offensive spitting in their presence and at their very feet, does, I confess, surprise me as much as anything I have ever seen in this country."[52] He concluded by saying that the practice of tobacco chewing " ... should be left to the savage tribes, with the tomahawk and the scalping-knife, the warwhoop and the rum-bottle, but be banished forever from a people claiming to be polished and refined."[53]

Considerably more polished and refined than the tobacco cult witnessed by Buckingham in 1839 were the school orations and barbecues in ante-bellum Georgia. Annual examinations at the academies and small community schools were an excuse for a community gathering throughout the state in the Eighteen Forties. The examinations were often set to coincide with the Fourth of July celebrations, and hundreds of people came to hear students and public leaders give speeches and orations, sprinkled with public singing. There was usually a barbecue with tables to provide eating space for scores of visitors. Emily Burke, the New Hampshire-born school teacher, wrote that the word "barbecue" is "a term that means at the South, one or more swine roasted whole. These feasts are prepared and given in the woods in a most rural manner." Barbecuing has apparently changed little in the South since the Eighteen Forties, for Burke described what is still a very common procedure:

Animals cooked in this way are generally undergoing the roasting process at least one night previous to their being served up. Pits are dug in the ground and then filled with live coals, which are frequently renewed from another great fire at a little distance kept constantly burning for that purpose.[54]

Burke also documented the conviviality, noting that "the last course at these entertainments is usually made up of healths to friends, songs, toasts, and speeches upon political or scientific subjects, according to the pleasure of the speaker."[55]

Almost any meeting provided an excuse for hundreds of lonely people in rural America to come together for fun and frolic. The camp meeting was no exception. It provided fire-and-brimstone preachers the chance to dwell on the dangers of hell fire and to save souls, and in reality, hundreds of people attended merely because of the spectacle which the gathering of large numbers of people provided.[56] One source points out that in Sparta, Georgia in 1807, approximately three thousand people, white and black, attended a camp meeting and slept on the ground at night.[57] Emily Burke noted that in North Georgia all events were reckoned from the date of the last camp-meeting, even death or illness or marriage. A typical Georgia camp meeting had a tabernacle at the center of the grounds — a huge open-sided building very similar to a public market. Facing the tabernacle and forming a square were the homes and family dwellings. Near one of the camp grounds in the Eighteen Forties someone had built a saloon for those who came for the excitement of the meeting and had little concern about their personal salvation. "While the fervent and incessant prayers of the righteous ascended on high like holy incense from within the camp," wrote Emily Burke, "curses and blasphemies were poured forth from the throats of those who had encamped round about this place."[58] Those attending the camp meeting transported food, furniture, beds and other materials needed for the days and nights they spent; and the young people, dressed in their finest clothes, used the occasion to talk and court. Each family residence had an earthen hearth about six feet square and one foot high, and each night a fire was kept burning until around midnight. Burke says:

The older members of the families would seat themselves beneath the piazzas to witness the pastimes of the children, all collected together to vie with each other in the dexterity of trundling the hoop, throwing the ball, jumping the rope or running races, in all of which sports the dogs sustained a part with caninish glee running to pick up the fallen hoop, bringing back the ball that had bounded too far and in the race often outstripping all the children.[59]

Each morning the worshipers were summoned for prayers by a hunter's trumpet. There were usually four sermons each day, the first at eight o'clock in the morning and the last usually at four in the afternoon. The slaves were an integral part of the camp meeting. While most of the house servants attended meetings with their masters in the tabernacle, the other slaves, who were exempt from labor during the camp meetings, were usually provided for at a meeting somewhat removed from the tabernacle. The white preachers shared turns preaching to the slaves. According to Emily Burke, this was desired by the slaves themselves so that they could more completely enjoy "freedom in speaking, singing, shouting and praying they could not enjoy in the presence of their masters ...."[60] Writing to a friend, Northern-born Burke continued:

I can never recall the scenes connected with a Southern campmeeting but with emotions of the deepest interest and pleasure, and, when with a retrospective glance of the mind's eye, I review scenes such as I have described in these letters, my soul invariably thirsts for a return to Southern life.[61]

The sports, leisure and recreational activities of early Georgians were obviously varied and often unique, and they were reflective of the lives of the common man in Georgia, whether red, white or black. There has been no effort in this essay to describe the recreations of the highly organized, urbanized and affluent social classes of this era; rather, the focus was on the simpler life-style of the era. Even then, this discussion was restricted necessarily to only a few of the more popular activities; therefore, it has omitted such activities as cock-fighting, bear-baiting, candy pulls, cane grindings, dancing, hog kills, and doubtless, scores of other events which enlivened the personal experiences of generations of Georgians and which, in many instances, are still enjoyed in one form or another today.

NOTES

[1]This paper is an examination of a few of the many sports and leisure activities of the "common Georgian" during the colonial and frontier experience. It purports to relate the sports and leisure activities of the Georgia Indian, slave, free black, poor white and small farmer. It does not include to any great extent the leisure activities of the upper classes or the planter aristocracy; nor does it attempt to examine the modern leisures of any class of Georgians. Lastly, the paper is only a cursory overview of the subject and certainly makes no pretense at being a thorough examination of the diverse and many faceted entertainments of this earlier era.

[2]Alvin M. Josephy, Jr., editor, *The American Heritage Book of Indians* (New York: American Heritage Publishing Co., Inc., 1961), p. 146.

[3]Quoted in Glen Fleischchman, *The Cherokee Removal, 1838* (New York: Franklin Watts, Inc., 1971), p. 7.

[4]For an excellent summation of music, dance and games among Southern Indians, see Charles Hudson, *The Southeastern Indians* (Knoxville: University of Tennessee Press, 1976), pp. 400-426.

[5]John R. Swanton, *The Indians of the Southeastern United States.* Bureau of American Ethnology Bulletin, no. 137 (Washington, D.C., 1946), pp. 624-626.

[6]*Ibid.,* pp. 626-627.

[7]*Ibid.,* 626-628.

[8]William Bartram, *Travels of William Bartram,* ed., Mark Van Doren (New York: Dover Publications, 1928), p. 396.

[9]*Ibid.* Also see Swanton, *Indians of the Southeastern United States,* pp. 624-629.

[10]Hudson, *Southeastern Indians,* p. 374.

[11]*Ibid.,* p. 403.

[12]Grace Steele Woodward, *The Cherokees* (Norman: University of Oklahoma Press, 1972), p. 50.

[13]Bartram, *Travels,* p. 396.

[14]Hudson, *Southeastern Indians,* pp. 407-408.

[15]Samuel Cole Williams, ed., *Adair's History of the American Indians* (Ann Arbor: University Microfilms, Inc., 1966), p. 429. Also see Hudson, *Southeastern Indians,* pp. 376-426; Woodward, *The Cherokees,* pp. 50-53; James A. Maxwell, ed., *America's Fascinating Indian Heritage* (Pleasantville, N.Y.: The Reader's Digest Association, Inc., 1978), pp. 97-99.

[16]See Hudson, *Southeastern Indians,* pp. 376-426; Williams, *Adair's History,* pp. 428-429; Woodward, *The Cherokees,* pp. 50-53; Swanton, *Indians of the Southeastern United States,* pp. 674-680; Bartram, *Travels,* p. 398.

[17]For an excellent account of chunkey, see Williams, *Adair's History,* pp. 430-431; Swanton, *Indians of the Southeastern United States,* pp. 682-684; Woodward, *The Cherokees,* pp. 52-53; Hudson, *Southeastern Indians,* pp. 421-425.

[18]Everitt Dick, *The Dixie Frontier: A Social History of the Southern Frontier from the First Transmontane Beginnings to the Civil War* (New York: Octagon Books, 1974), p. 125.

[19]Ulrich Bonnell Phillips, *Life and Labor in the Old South* (Boston: Little, Brown and Co., 1948), p. 342.

[20]Dick, *Dixie Frontier,* pp. 129-130; Eliot Wigginton, editor, *Foxfire 1* (New York: Anchor Press, 1973), pp. 362-366.

[21]Dick, *The Dixie Frontier,* p. 130.

[22]Emily Burke, *Pleasure and Pain: Reminiscences of Georgia in the 1840's* (Savannah: The Beehive Press, 1978), p. 40.

[23]*Ibid.,* pp. 89-90.

[24]*Ibid.*

[25]*Ibid.* Also see Rebecca Latimer Felton, *Country Life in Georgia in the Days of My Youth* (Atlanta: Index Printing Co., 1919), p. 53; *Foxfire 2,* pp. 369-370.

[26]Burke, *Pleasure and Pain,* pp. 26-27.

[27]Eugene D. Genovese, *Roll, Jordan, Roll: The World the Slaves Made* (New York: Vintage Books, 1976), p. 569.

[28]*Ibid.,* p. 571.

[29]*Ibid.*, p. 572.

[30]*Ibid.*, p. 573.

[31]Quoted in Genovese, *Roll, Jordan, Roll*, p. 580. For an excellent summation of slave recreations, see in *Ibid.*, pp. 566-584.

[32]Dick, *The Dixie Frontier*, p. 95. Also see "Basil Hall" in *The Rambler in Georgia*, edited by Mills Lane (Savannah: The Beehive Press, 1973), p. 66.

[33]Burke, *Pleasure and Pain*, pp. 49-50.

[34]Frances B. Leigh, *Ten Years on a Georgia Plantation Since the War* (New York: Negro Universities Press, 1969), pp. 59-61.

[35]*Ibid.*

[36]Genovese, *Roll, Jordan, Roll*, pp. 233-234, 238, 240.

[37]Leigh, *Ten Years on a Georgia Plantation*, pp. 196-197.

[38]*Ibid.*

[39]Dick, *The Dixie Frontier*, p. 140.

[40]Augustus Baldwin Longstreet, *Georgia Scenes: Characters, Incidents, etc., in the First Half-Century of the Republic* (New York: Harper & Brothers, 1897), p. 69.

[41]*Ibid.*, p. 78.

[42]*Ibid.*,

[43]*Ibid.*, 78-81.

[44]*Ibid.*, pp. 147-159; Dick, *The Dixie Frontier*, pp. 141-142.

[45]Eliot Wigginton, editor, *The Foxfire Book* (New York: Anchor Press, 1972), p. 249.

[46]Burke, *Pleasure and Pain*, p. 65.

[47]*The Foxfire Book*, pp. 254-256.

[48]Dick, *The Dixie Frontier*, pp. 95-96.

[49]The author confesses to considerable personal experience during his youth in the art of seining and "muddying" for fish.

[50]"James Silk Buckingham" in *The Rambler in Georgia*, p. 140. For a good description of shooting matches, see

Longstreet, *Georgia Scenes*, pp. 274-297. Also see Dick, *The Dixie Frontier*, pp. 142-144.

[51]"James Silk Buckingham" in *The Georgia Rambler*, pp. 169-170.

[52]*Ibid.*, p. 170.

[53]*Ibid.*

[54]Burke, *Pleasure and Pain*, pp. 72-73.

[55]*Ibid.*

[56]Foster Rhea Dulles, *A History of Recreation: America Learns to Play* (New York: Appleton-Century-Crofts, 1965), pp. 80-81.

[57]Dick, *The Dixie Frontier*, p. 96.

[58]Burke, *Pleasure and Pain*, p. 94.

[59]*Ibid.*, p. 95.

[60]*Ibid.*

[61]*Ibid.*, p. 96.

A FAILURE OF WILL
OR INTIMIDATION?:
UNIONIZATION IN GEORGIA AND THE SOUTH

LESLIE S. HOUGH

In 1980 about 323,000 Georgians, or 15.1 percent of the nonagricultural labor force, were members of a trade union. This compares with a national percentage of union members among such workers of 25.2, 10 percent more than Georgia.[1] While one in four nonfarm workers in the nation as a whole belonged to a union, only about one in seven Georgia workers held a union card. What factors are responsible for the fact that union growth has been retarded in the South when compared to the rest of the United States? Is it something that unions have done, or failed to do, or is it something about the region itself and its people that explains the divergent experience of the South with respect to union organization?

Unions have certainly erred during their organizing attempts in the South. The most common failing has been to allocate too few resources to Southern campaigns. Throughout the twentieth century, Southern trade union leaders have urged the international unions for which they worked to give them more staff and money to help in their organizing efforts.[2] During periods of time when those resources were provided, the results of such campaigns were sometimes encouraging. But often the effort expended during organizing efforts in the South did not seem to justify the expenditure of dues from union members in the North. Organizing drives in the South were also handicapped by the fact that the union infrastructure that nourished new unions in many parts of the North simply did not exist in most of the South. Plants were often organized by union members from other locations in their community. When difficult campaigns led to strikes or lockouts, Northern workers were more likely to be able to depend on their fellow trade unionists nearby for both monetary and

165

moral support. In towns and cities across the South where a number of workers were organized, success in later campaigns was more likely. Workers at nonunion plants were more likely to have had union experience at other work sites. Unions were simply more a part of the social fabric outside the South.[3]

This argument does not answer the underlying question as to why Southern communities were not as receptive to the union organizer as were towns and cities in other parts of the country. This question will only be answered by looking at the South itself. Something about either Southern workers, or the managers, and other leaders of Southern communities must hold the explanation for the variant experience of unions in the South. Have workers in the South simply not been receptive to the message brought by the union organizer, or have other influences been brought to bear on the will of the workers? This essay seeks to answer that question.

One overwhelming reality of the economy in Georgia and the South until the beginning of the twentieth century was the dominance of agriculture. Georgia had more owner-operated farms than wage earners through 1900.[4] Most Georgians worked the land either for themselves as tenant or share farmers, or as agricultural laborers. Farmers have made extensive use of cooperative mechanisms for marketing and other purposes, but they have not formed unions, with rare exceptions.[5] This fact meant that most workers in Georgia were by the nature of their work quite unlikely to join or form unions.

Beginning in the 1880's, however, Georgia's nonagricultural labor force began to expand rapidly, more than doubling during the decade from fewer than 25,000 to more than 51,000.[6] Another major development involving workers both in Georgia and the rest of the nation occurred in the 1880's. The first great national labor union, the Knights of Labor, which had begun in the late 1860's in Philadelphia, spread rapidly through Georgia, the South and elsewhere during the mid-1880's. The Knights boasted of nearly 6,000 members in Georgia in 1886 and 1887.[7] With a nonagricultural work force of about 40,000, nearly fifteen percent of Georgia's workers held membership in the Knights in the late 1880's. By comparison, less than seven percent of the nation's total nonagricultural labor force were members of the Knights. While all statistics from the era, particularly claims made by the Knights to a large membership, have to be taken with caution, there is no reason to believe that they reflect any regional bias. The obvious conclusion is that a Georgia worker was about twice as likely as his counterpart elsewhere in the country to have been a member of the Knights.

One other point should be made about the experience of Southern workers with the Knights of Labor. While the Knights were cautious on racial matters, they stood for equality of opportunity both in the work place and within the union itself. Problems between the races did surface within the organization, but in the context of the South in the 1880's, the Knights were quite progressive on racial matters. They suffered criticism from the Southern power structure based on their policies of racial moderation, but the principal reason for their overall decline was not racial but practical. The Knights had little success in winning significant economic gains for their members, both North and South, and their membership left the Knights in droves as the 1880's drew to a close.

There is further strong evidence that Southern workers of the late nineteenth and early twentieth centuries were favorably disposed toward joining together to better themselves. American workers had always used the frontier as a means of protesting unfair work conditions. Individual workers quit their jobs and sought opportunities elsewhere. As the frontier began to close and workers found themselves increasingly drawn from farm to factory or mill, a collective response to perceived injustice on the job became more common, North and South. The most common manifestation of this response was the strike.

Nearly 50,000 work stoppages involving over 8.5 million workers took place nationwide between 1887 and 1905.[8] During this period, the Southern worker was actually more likely to have been a striker than the average worker in the United States. From 1880 to 1910, Southern industry grew even more rapidly than in the country as a whole. Southern workers represented only about 2.5 percent of the nation's nonagricultural labor force in 1880; the region employed over 4 percent of such workers in 1910.[9] During those same years, the South was the home of from 6.75 percent to 8 percent of all American strikers, and from 5 percent to 9 percent of all strikes in the nation took place in the region.[10]

A Southerner was therefore about twice as likely to have participated in a strike during the two decades closing the last

167

century and the first decade of the twentieth century. This is strong further evidence for reassessing the stereotype of the tractable Southern worker during the building of the "New South."

What conclusions can be drawn from the success of the Knights of Labor in the South and the relatively high rate of participation in strikes among Southerners during the late nineteenth and early twentieth centuries? Southern workers appear to have been anything but docile, and in fact, they were rather more militant than their Northern counterparts. If this is true, then what has happened since then to alter the attitudes of Southerners toward unionization and militant job actions?

One hint at the shaping of the attitudes and actions of Southern workers is hidden in the previously cited statistics on strikes and strikers at the turn of the century. Typically, Southern workers were less successful in achieving their objectives in a strike when compared with workers in other parts of the country.

Most strikes that took place during the period were essentially defensive in nature. When business conditions deteriorated, as they frequently did, the first recourse of management, both in the South and elsewhere, was to cut wages. Workers often felt compelled to strike in such situations, since the wages of the average worker were already low. Cuts sometimes threatened to drive the standard of living of working class families below the subsistence level. In such a situation, the loss of a strike represented a double disaster for the workers involved, since the wage cut stayed in force and the families' financial reserves, if any, had likely been exhausted during the strike. Wages were generally lower in the South than in other parts of the country, in any case.

Strikes for union recognition were also relatively common during the late nineteenth and early twentieth centuries, and these strikes were also often lost, with management often benefiting from the help of sympathetic government officials.

Finally, the blacklist was a fact of life for most participants in unsuccessful strikes. Relocation or extended unemployment were often the ultimate consequences of a strike, particularly for the Southern worker.

It is clear that the situation of the striker forced back to work in the South at the turn of the century was desperate indeed. This fact could not have failed to impress both those workers and others in their communities regarding the risks involved in strikes, whether within or outside the trade union structure. In fact, after the turn of the century, though the number of strikes in the South continued at a high level, the number of strikers involved in each strike diminished steadily, from an average of 262 workers per strike in the period 1887-1894 to an average of only 124 workers in the period 1901-1905.[11] All the while, the number of workers in the average enterprise was increasing, both in the South and elsewhere. This reduction in the size of strikes might reflect a spread of the strike response to small shops, but it certainly also suggests a reluctance on the part of the Southern workers, especially in large plants, to take on management in a strike.

Let us now look at several incidents from the 1880's to the 1930's that helped to shape the thinking of workers in Georgia and the South toward unions and strikes. The first case is that of the Savannah black laborers' strike of 1891.

The actual origins of the 1891 strike date from at least ten years earlier when an unsuccessful strike by black workers seeking wages of $2.00 a day resulted in the death of four dock workers at the hands of company police. In 1891, Savannah's laborers formed the Labor Union and Protective Association (LUPA). Many Savannah workers, over a thousand in fact, had the experience of membership in the Knights of Labor during the 1880's. It is possible that LUPA represented a revival of the Knights, though the main precipitating factor was certainly a cut in wages to $1.10 per day. Even that amount was often not realized by the workers, since their actual rate of pay was from $.125 to $.15 per hour, frequently for only three or four hours a day. Wage cuts coincided, surprisingly, with the period of time when cotton bales and naval stores were pouring into Savannah from upcountry for shipment by sea through the city's port. LUPA saw an opportunity to turn a wage cut into a raise, so its members demanded an increase of $.05 per hour, insisting on a quick answer to their demand from management, the Central Railroad of Georgia. The railroad both transported most of the goods to the port and undertook the loading of cotton and naval stores onto waiting ships. Savannah's corporate and political leadership responded to the wage demand by calling up the local militia and ordering more ammunition from the state arsenal.

The response of the union was to call a strike but to counsel also quiet and caution, urging its members not to picket the dock area of Savannah. Instead, the strikers depended on publicity and "walking delegates" to discourage strikebreakers from coming to Savannah and to avoid panic in the city itself. The solidarity of Savannah's black workers was such that the railroad was forced into a compromise of $.025 per hour wage increase, a settlement which was rejected by the union.

This decision may have been a fatal error on the part of the workers, for it seemed to solidify the resistance of Savannah's business community to the strikers. The Central Railroad redoubled its efforts to recruit strikebreakers and sought to isolate the strikebreakers from LUPA agents. The union had been split by the rejection of the compromise wage offer. It wavered in its resolve to continue the strike and then took a rather militant stance, demanding that the compromise settlement be embodied in a contract between the union and the railroad, thus formally recognizing LUPA. This was a most difficult objective in light of late nineteenth century realities. The only union contracts in force in Georgia at the time were in the building and printing trades. These unions had been in existence for many years, and their members were white. The demand for a contract was summarily rejected by management, a blacklist was threatened and the strike was lost when many union members returned to work.[12]

The 1891 strike is illustrative of the difficulty faced by workers in late nineteenth century Georgia. No matter how militant and united, workers and their union faced management determined to resist labor's demands, along with a hostile political leadership. The workers who returned to the docks were forced to accept lower wages. All the strikers had lost several weeks of earnings, and since many lost their jobs to strikebreakers, all were worse off than before the strike.

Another example of an attempt by Georgia workers to form a strong union occurred during the 1920's. This was also a difficult period for unions, for American business was promoting the American plan, seeking to establish open shop conditions and depriving unions of any effective power. This example is, however, a great contrast to the short-lived union of black Savannah dock workers. The organization was the Atlanta Public School Teachers' Association. The association had affiliated in 1919 with the American Federation of Teachers (AFT), becoming Local No. 89 of the AFT. It grew to become the largest teachers' union local in the United States by the late 1920's. Local No. 89 was led for many years by a remarkable woman, Mary Barker, who also served as president of the AFT on the national level in the late 1920's.

Unfortunately, racism was a major stumbling block in the path of Local No. 89 and its efforts to build a strong teachers' union in Atlanta. From its beginnings in the early twentieth century, the association had excluded black teachers from membership. Black teachers were being paid less than whites, and the Atlanta City School Board exacerbated racial tensions by granting a raise to black teachers and reducing white teachers' pay a similar amount. The Scottsboro Case of 1934 was also a very divisive issue for the members of Local No. 89. Mary Barker, a racial moderate, urged the local to support a fair trial for the Scottsboro defendants and was effectively eliminated as a leader of the local by these racial animosities. The issue of race ultimately destroyed Local No. 89, for after the 1954 Brown v. Board of Education decision, the AFT expelled the local when it refused to integrate.[13] Again, a combination of internal division within a union and hostility from outside was successful in weakening and then destroying the union.

It is impossible to discuss the fate of unions in Georgia and the South without reference to the textile industry. Georgia textile workers were certainly active in textile unions in the late nineteenth century, including both the Knights of Labor and its successor in textiles, the International Union of Textile Workers (IUTW). The Knights had more textile workers organized in Augusta, Georgia in the 1870's and 1880's than in any other American city. One of the largest strikes staged in the history of the textile industry to that date took place in Augusta in 1886.[14] The president of the IUTW in the late 1890's, Prince W. Greene, was himself a Georgian, and the union was dominated by its Southern locals. Another union, the United Textile Workers of America (UTWA), replaced the IUTW as the major national textile union in 1901.

The next year, a major strike of 7,000 textile operatives occurred in Augusta, Georgia. Although the UTWA counseled the workers against a strike, the Augusta operatives walked out anyway. Management locked out those textile workers not

171

already on strike and imported strikebreakers from nearby South Carolina. The UTWA was able to provide $10,000 in support to the strikers, but that was not enough. The strike was lost after two months, and the strikebreakers kept their new jobs, forcing many strikers to leave Augusta to find work.[15]

Textile employers learned a lesson from the Augusta strike. They learned that a firm stand against a union's demands and the importation of strikebreakers could defeat nearly any effort by a labor organization. Textile workers sensed a certain futility in strikes, and perhaps in unions, and the leaders of the UTWA were also disheartened by the failure of one of their largest locals, a key to success in organizing Southern mills.

Atlanta was the scene of the next struggle — the Fulton Bag and Cotton Mills in 1914-1915. Nearly 2,000 workers were involved in a year-long struggle under the sponsorship of the UTWA, with workers evicted from their company homes and the establishment of a tent city for the strikers. Again, the strike failed when management imported strikebreakers and refused to deal with the strikers.

The next major push to organize textile workers in Georgia took place in Columbus, Georgia in 1919, when 7000 operatives struck over the issue of work hours. An eight-hour day, forty-hour week was sought, and the Columbus strikers did gain some concessions, though one striker was killed and several others wounded. Textile workers numbering over 2000 walked out in Macon later in 1919. Black strikebreakers were employed and the strike was broken.[16]

The most concerted effort on the part of Southern textile workers to organize themselves was in 1934, a year of hope and despair for the operatives. The National Industrial Recovery Act had just passed, and it called for a code of fair competition for all major American industries, including textiles. The code included a minimum wage, maximum workweek of 40 hours, abolition of child labor and sanctioned collective bargaining between labor and management. The Depression had driven textile management to desperate measures, and it appeared that textile workers might be allowed to form unions and negotiate for their long-sought goals, including better wages and shorter hours.

The hard-pressed textile industry did not find it profitable to comply with the code, however, and workweeks for textile workers fell to thirty or fewer with proportional reductions in wages. Meanwhile, the UTWA took advantage of the codes to organize as many textile operatives as possible. By May, 1934, the union claimed two-thirds of the nation's textile workers as members. There is little evidence of that proportion of Southern operatives in formal union local organizations at that time, but many Southern workers were aware of the UTWA's efforts to organize the nation's textile operatives. Employers in the South resisted union organizing, as they had for decades. By the summer of 1934, relations between labor and management in Georgia's textile mills were very tense. Trouble began in Columbus at the Georgia Webbing and Tape Company when a thirty-year old textile worker and UTWA member, W.R. Sanders, was killed while walking the picket line. Further clashes followed in Macon.

On Labor Day, September 3, 1934, 400,000 textile workers struck the nation's mills. Nearly 45,000 Georgia operatives, about 75 percent of the total, joined the strike. The Southern Textile Manufacturers' Association, headed by Bibb Manufacturing Company's president, W.S. Anderson, responded by hiring 800 company police. Characterized by the textile workers as thugs, they included the notorious New York strikebreaker, Pearl Bergoff, nicknamed the "Red Demon." Two strikers were killed during the first week of the work stoppage in Georgia, and on Thursday of the second week of the strike, Eugene Talmadge was reelected governor in the all-white Democratic primary, having promised repeatedly never to call out troops to quell a strike. The following day, the entire Georgia National Guard was mobilized and the state was declared to be under martial law.

Military justice prevailed in all parts of Georgia, including suspension of the *writ of habeas corpus*. A camp was set up at Fort McPherson in Atlanta, where German POW's had been interned during World War I. The barbed wire and circumstances of the strikers imprisoned there led the press to term it a "concentration camp." Another striker was killed at Aragon, Georgia on September 16, and nearly all the UTWA leaders were rounded up and held without charges. A fourth striker was beaten to death by National Guardsmen when he moved too slowly after being ordered away from Callaway Mill property in LaGrange. By late September, the strike was broken, and most strikers and all union members were out of a job.[17]

The mill owners had won and textile workers learned more vividly than ever that unions in the mills meant grief. From the record of efforts to organize unions in Georgia and the South, a clear picture emerges. Many Georgia workers have shown an interest in forming a union, particularly when they were defending their own basic interests. When they have, the result has usually been strident, even violent opposition from employers, with politicians either openly or duplicitously supporting the employers in their resistance. Racism has often been an effective tool in splitting groups of workers or dividing workers from the public. The impact of the media on the coverage of labor disputes has nearly always had a negative effect on labor's interests in a crisis. One question still remains: If given a free choice, would most Georgia workers join unions? The fact is that we shall never know.

NOTES

[1]Courtney D. Gifford, ed., *Directory of U.S. Labor Organizations, 1982-1983* (Washington, D.C., 1982), 68.

[2]Robert C. Dinwiddie, "The International Woodworkers of America and Southern Laborers, 1937-1945" (Georgia State University, 1980), 94, 95; International Woodworkers of America, District 4 Records, Southern Labor Archives, Georgia State University.

[3]Most of the literature on the history of the labor movement in Georgia and the South consists of local studies, often focusing on a single conflict between labor and management. The only serious attempts to write a history of labor in the South are F. Ray Marshall, *Labor in the South* (Cambridge, Massachusetts, 1967); Marc S. Miller, ed., *Working Lives: The "Southern Exposure" History of Labor in the South* (New York, 1980); Gary M. Fink and Merl E. Reed, eds., *Essays in Southern Labor History: Selected Papers, Southern Labor History Conference, 1976* (Westport, Connecticut, 1977); and Merl E. Reed, Leslie S. Hough, and Gary M. Fink, eds., *Southern Workers and Their Unions, 1880-1975: Selected Papers, The Second Southern Labor History Conference, 1978* (Westport, Connecticut, 1981). Marshall treats the period

before the 1930's only briefly, and Miller makes no effort to cover the period prior to 1900.

[4]Donald B. Dodd and Wynelle S. Dodd, *Historical Statistics of the South, 1790-1970* (University, Alabama, 1973), 20, 21.

[5]The Southern Tenant Farmers Union (STFU) was a notable exception, and other unions in agriculture, like the United Farm Workers Union, trace their heritage back to the STFU.

[6]Dodd and Dodd, 20, 21.

[7]Melton A McLaurin, *The Knights of Labor in the South* (Westport, Connecticut, 1978), 171.

[8]*Historical Statistics of the United States: Colonial Times to 1970, Part I* (Washington, D.C., 1975), 179.

[9]Dodd and Dodd, 4-61.

[10]Marshall, 30-33.

[11]Marshall, 30-33.

[12]Mark V. Wetherington, "The Savannah Negro Laborers Strike of 1891" in *Southern Workers and Their Unions*, 4-21.

[13]Two works treat the history of the Atlanta Public School Teachers Association. The first of these is a doctoral dissertationn by Joseph W. Newman, "A History of the Atlanta Public School Teachers' Association, Local 89 of the American Federation of Teachers, 1919-1956" (Georgia State University, 1978). The association existed for several years prior to its affiliation with organized labor. That period of its history is detailed in Wayne J. Urban, *Why Teachers Organized* (Detroit, 1982), 44-65.

[14]LeeAnn Whites, "Southern Ladies and Millhands: The Domestic Economy and Class Politics; Augusta, Georgia, 1870-1890" (University of California, Irvine, 1982), 232.

[15]Dennis R. Nolan and Donald E. Jonas, "Textile Unionism in the Piedmont, 1901-1932" in *Essays in Southern Labor History*, 48-53.

[16]Nolan and Jonas, 54, 55.

[17]John E. Allen, "Eugene Talmadge and the Great Textile Strike in Georgia, September, 1934" in *Essays in Southern Labor History*, 224-243.

GEORGIA AGRICULTURE SINCE THE CIVIL WAR*

GILBERT C. FITE

For three quarters of a century after the Civil War, agriculture in Georgia remained remarkably the same. It was characterized by small farms, low production and poor people whose main crop was cotton. While some change occurred on individual farms throughout the two generations after 1865, it was not until the late 1930's that fundamental change began to occur on a broader scale in the state's principal agricultural regions. In the thirty years after World War II, a virtual revolution took place on Georgia farms. The shift was from small one-and two-mule cotton farms to large, highly mechanized operations that depended on other crops and livestock for their income. Why the old patterns of agriculture persisted so long and the reasons for the rapid changes after about 1935 are the theme of this essay.

At the close of the Civil War in 1865, much of Georgia agriculture was in serious disarray. Millions of dollars worth of crops, livestock, buildings, fences and other farm property had been destroyed by Sherman's army in the latter part of 1864, leaving thousands of farmers and planters in dire straits. To make matters worse from the planters' viewpoint, the slaves had been freed, and the planters no longer had a controlled labor supply as had been the case under slavery. Who, and under what circumstances, would plant and harvest the crops?

The major question facing planters was how to develop a new labor system based on free workers. Planters had land, but no one to work it. At the same time, most freedmen had no land; they possessed only their labor. How could land and

---

*Small parts of this article have been published in the author's *Cotton Fields No More*, a larger study of Southern agriculture since 1865.

labor be brought together in farming operations that would be satisfactory to both landowner and worker? This was not a problem for small, largely self-sufficient farmers in North Georgia or farmers and ranchers in the wire grass region. These areas had never had many slaves or much hired labor, and the farms were mainly self-sufficient family operations. But in the Southern Piedmont and across Central and Southwest Georgia, the old plantation belt, the matter of labor supply was of crucial importance.

At first planters tried to hire newly freed blacks for cash wages; however, many planters did not have cash for this purpose. Besides, the planters complained of not having sufficient control over their workers, and they believed the cost of supervision and management of wage labor was too high. Negroes, as well, did not like the wage system because it reduced their independence and seemed to preclude them from becoming landowners. Thus, after a few years of experience with different kinds of labor arrangements, the sharecropping system developed. Under this type of farm organization, a landowner made an agreement with a worker to farm some 20 to 40 acres of cultivated land which was about the acreage that could be worked by a man and his family. On many 40 acre tracts, it was common to have 20 acres of cotton and 20 acres of corn. Besides the land, the owner also furnished a house, tools, seed and a mule for plowing. At the end of the year, the cotton was divided equally, while the sharecropper received two-thirds of the corn. There were actually many different arrangements for dividing various crops.[1]

Lacking money for living expenses until harvest, both black and white sharecroppers had to obtain advances of money or supplies until the crop was sold. Landowners, who were also merchants in many instances, commonly advanced $6 to $10 a month in cash or supplies to the sharecropper family from about March to November. Interest rates on this credit were extremely high. The Georgia Commissioner of Agriculture reported in 1875 that farmers in the state were paying an average of 44 percent interest on advanced supplies.[2] At the the end of the crop year, the cotton was sold in hopes of repaying the advances and having something left to improve the farm family's standard of living. In many cases, however, the sharecropper's half of the cotton would not bring enough to settle his debts, and he sank into perpetual bondage to his creditors. Sharecroppers were actually wage workers who were paid with a share of the cotton. In most cases, they represented farmers at the lowest end of the economic scale and were barely a notch or two above the strictly farm wage laborers.

Other kinds of tenancy were also developing in Georgia and throughout the South. Farmers who had some capital in the form of machinery and livestock but not enough to buy a farm rented land on a share or cash basis. The farmer who furnished his own machinery, seed, fertilizer and other operating needs usually got two-thirds of the crops, while cash tenants paid the landlord a fixed amount of money or so many bales of cotton. But even these more independent farmers needed credit for living and operating expenses, and to meet these needs, many of them were forced into the crop lien system. Under this plan, merchants loaned farmers money and took a mortgage on the crops, livestock and other property as security for the loans.

All types of tenancy rose rapidly in Georgia after 1870. While a few freedmen were able to acquire farms of their own, most of them remained sharecroppers and tenants. Moreover, an increasing number of white farmers experienced a similar fate. By 1880, some 45 percent of Georgia's farmers were classified as tenants. This figure rose to 60 percent by 1900 and reached a high of 68 percent in 1930. The highest rate of tenancy was among blacks in the plantation areas of the Lower Piedmont and Southwest Georgia. For example, in Burke county in 1900, over 90 percent of the 3,223 black farmers were either share or cash tenants. For the 9,466 white farmers in the county, the figure was nearly 50 percent.[3]

Besides a rapid growth in tenancy, Georgia had an increasing number of small unproductive farms. In 1860, the state's 62,000 farms averaged 430 acres each. This was plenty of land on which to raise both crops and livestock, but during the succeeding decades, the size of operating farm units got smaller and smaller. By 1880, the average size farm in Georgia was 200 acres, or less than half as large as twenty years earlier; and by 1900, farms averaged only 117 acres. In 1925, the average size farm in the state had declined to 86 acres. The trend was for large landowners to divide up their acreage into small cotton farms that would be worked by a sharecropper or tenant family.[4]

The average size of farms, however, tells only part of the

story. Georgia farmers, like most Southern farmers, cultivated very small acreages. The average acres of cropland harvested in 1880, the first year such information is provided in the census, was only 46. The cropland harvested gradually decreased until by the late 1920's it was only 32 acres per farm. On such small acreages, a farmer could not grow enough of the main crops of cotton and corn to provide a decent living for himself and his family. In the late nineteenth century, most Georgia cotton growers did not produce more than 140 to 150 pounds per acre, and corn made only 8 to 12 bushels per acre.[5]

During the late nineteenth and early twentieth centuries, Georgia farmers devoted most of their attention to growing cotton. Production of cotton had grown faster than that of other crops in the 1850's, and the high prices right after the Civil War caused farmers and planters to concentrate further on cotton. In 1860, for example, Georgia ranked fourth in cotton production; but from 1870 to the 1890's, it was second among the states in the number of bales produced. In 1900, it dropped to third place below both Texas and Mississippi, but cotton was king in the state throughout the late nineteenth and early twentieth centuries. Of the 224,000 farms in Georgia in 1900, cotton was the principal source of income for 160,000 of them, or about 70 percent. Cotton provided 59 percent of the value of all crops sold by Georgia farmers in 1899.[7]

Why did so many Georgia farmers concentrate on growing cotton to the exclusion of other crops and livestock? One important reason was that much of the state was ideally suited for that crop. Moreover, cotton returned the highest cash income per acre of any major field crop except tobacco, which was not grown widely in Georgia before 1900. Corn, the state's other leading crop, did not have a good commercial market. Its value was in food and feed for livestock rather than as a cash crop. Speaking before the Georgia Agricultural Society in 1878, J.R. Respass of Schley County declared that "cotton was the most money-making crop . . . in the world," and another Georgian said that "cotton affords the greatest profits to farmers."[8] It was the main crop that farmers depended on for cash income, and landlords viewed it as the premier crop. Raising cotton also required relatively little supervision by landowners, and it could always be used as security for credit. Thus, cotton seemed to have advantages for both tenants and landlords. The crop fastened itself on Georgia farms in the

1870's and 1880's, and its hold was not broken until the late 1930's.

Georgia farmers, of course, also raised other crops and livestock. Corn occupied more acreage than any other single crop. In 1899, Georgia had 3,477,000 acres of corn compared to 3,343,000 acres of cotton. Corn, as mentioned above, was used mainly for human food and feed for livestock. Georgia farmers also raised small amounts of wheat and oats. Rice, which had been an important crop in the lower coastal region before the Civil War, lost its position to the western producers in Louisiana, Texas and later in Arkansas. In 1899, there were only 624 farms in Georgia where rice was the principal source of income.[9]

Some farmers raised peanuts, pecans, fruit, vegetables and other specialized crops. Much of this production, however, was used in family consumption rather than as cash crops. For example, peanuts were commonly raised and then eaten by hogs which rooted them out of the ground. On the other hand, a few specialties produced cash income. Georgia became known as the peach state as farmers around Fort Valley began to ship peaches to Northern markets in the 1870's. Samuel Rumph of Marshallville began developing the Elberta peach in 1872, and by the 1880's, it had become a popular variety. Another Rumph, Lewis H., also of Marshallville, developed the Georgia Belle peach. In the 1890's, the number of peach trees in Georgia increased from 2.7 to 7.6 million. Although unstable markets and peach diseases, particularly the peach scab, hurt peach growers, in 1898 Georgia producers shipped 3,000 carloads of peaches to Northern markets.[10]

Georgia farmers also raised livestock; however, except in a few regions of the state, the numbers were small. In 1860, Georgians had over one million cattle and calves, but after the Civil War, farmers concentrated on cotton at the expense of cattle raising. In 1900, there were about 100,000 fewer cattle in the state than forty years earlier, and only 70 percent of the farmers had any cattle at all.[11] Many of the poorer farmers, particularly the sharecroppers, had no milk cows, which meant that their diets lacked milk and butter. Middle and upper-class farmers usually had several head of cattle, including milk cows, a situation which contributed to their better financial position. In the wire grass area of South Georgia, most farmers were actually herdsmen and small ranchers up to the mid-1880's. As the timber companies cut and sold the trees and railroads entered the region, commercial crop farming began to replace the society of herdsmen; and by the turn of the century, cotton was rapidly becoming a major crop in that area as well as in most other sections of the state.

Most farmers had one or two mules or horses to provide power on their farms. Many sharecroppers did not own any work stock but used a mule furnished by the landowner for plowing. Larger farmers and planters usually had several head of mules and horses. Since pork was a staple in the Southern farm diet, most farmers kept hogs; however, hog numbers declined after 1860 when they exceeded 2 million and did not reach that figure again until 1920.[12] Farmers also kept barnyard chickens for eggs and meat for Sunday and holiday dinners. In short, while a majority of Georgia farmers kept livestock, most of the holdings were small and cattle and hogs did not provide much cash income. Cotton, for example, brought farmers about $10 million in 1899, more than the value of all domestic animals on farms.[13] Out of 224,000 farms in 1900, only 10,706 received most of their income from livestock.

Raising a single commercial crop on small farms left tens of thousands of Georgia farmers in severe poverty. Many farm families, both black and white, were unable to make more than $150 to $200 a year. The census for 1900 gave the average labor income for Georgia farmers as $158 in 1899. Farmers in Georgia, like those throughout most of the South, were distinguished by their poverty. This first became clear when a special census was made of cotton farmers in 1880. It was found that many sharecroppers and tenants had cash incomes of less than $100 a year. Describing the situation in parts of the state, a reporter for the Census Bureau used such phrases as "sometimes without bread for their families," "in a destitute condition," and referring to blacks in Troup County, "many are in a worse condition than they were during slavery."[14] Of course, not all farmers were destitute. Those who cultivated more acres, owned some livestock and managed well had incomes of $500 to $1000 a year, and a few made even more.

It is clear, however, why so many Georgia farmers were poor. They simply did not produce enough to pay their operating costs and to provide a decent living. Under the circumstances of the time, their small farms had too little output.

The farm population grew rapidly during the late nineteenth and early twentieth centuries, placing too much demand on the developed agricultural resources. For example, between 1860 and 1920, the number of farms rose from about 62,000 to 310,000. There was some expansion of total land farmed, but it did not keep up with the development of new farms. The amount of cropland harvested in Georgia rose from 6.4 to 9.6 million acres between 1870 and 1910, an increase of about 50 percent. The number of farms, however, more than doubled, rising from 138,626 to 291,027. Consequently, the average cropland harvested dropped from 46 to 33 acres per farm during those 40 years.

Additionally, many of the small cotton farms lacked a proper resource base. They either had too few acres for crop and livestock production, or they did not provide full-time productive work for the farmer and his family. Georgia farmers were among those throughout the South who were underemployed. An observer in Northwest Georgia wrote in 1880 that "the average laborer in cotton production of the country makes a support by working half his time."[15] There were many reports of this kind. In contrast to the Midwest, where farmers were occupied tending their livestock during the winter months, Georgia cotton farmers had little if any productive work between cotton harvest and spring planting. The net wealth produced was so small that, except for a few unusually good years, Georgia's one-and-two-mule farmers had only a mere subsistence.

The manuscript census of 1880 reveals the situation as it existed among so many Georgia farmers. A random sample of 10 farmers in Harris County in Southwest Georgia illustrates the low productivity and meager incomes. Of the 10 farmers from the same community, five were owners and five were sharecroppers. One sharecropper had only 13 acres of cultivated land, while two farmed 35 acres each and the others 25 and 40 acres. Three owners farmed 20 acres each, while the two other owners had 40 and 45 acres under cultivation. Both sharecroppers and owners in this sample had small operations. All of them had a milk cow or other cattle.

The value of production, sold or used at home, varied in 1879 from a low of $160 to a high of $650. The average was $325 per operator. About half of this was in the form of cash and the rest was imputed value of commodities used on the farm. One sharecropper who farmed 35 acres raised 50 bushels of corn and six bales of cotton. He received half of the cotton, or three bales, which at 10 cents a pound would bring him about $150. He also grew 50 bushels of corn, about 35 of which he would receive, but this would not bring him any cash. He also raised 6 bushels of wheat which would fetch some $4. Thus, the total cash income for this black family of three, an unusually small family for the time, was around $150. One of the white owners who lived nearby raised the same amount of cotton and corn, but he was better off because he did not have to share any of his production with a landlord, although he had operating expenses to pay. However, both of these plantation belt farmers, one black and one white, had very meager incomes. In Jackson County in the northeast part of the state, the situation was better. There the farms were larger, farmers had more income from livestock, and their incomes averaged about twice as high as the sample in Harris County.[16]

A detailed study of conditions in Brooks County in South Georgia in 1914 showed a clear relationship between the size of farm and family income. Farms with only 33 acres of cropland — and there were tens of thousands in that category throughout the state — had an income of only $226 a year and a labor income of only $59 annually.* On the other hand, farms with an average of 111 acres of crop area produced an income of $768 with a labor income of $193. Moreover, researchers have found that farmers with larger operations had a more varied and better quality diet. In short, the study concluded that "the larger farms support a much higher standard of living as well as furnish larger net returns in other forms."[17]

How could Georgia farmers improve their condition? One possibility was to increase the size of their farms so they could produce more crops and livestock. Another approach was to produce more per acre. If farms were to be enlarged, farmers would need more work animals and more machinery, but Georgia farmers had relatively little machinery and equipment with which to work. The census of 1900 found that the average investment in implements and machinery on Georgia farms

---

*Labor income is defined as the amount left after "the earnings of farm capital, or interest upon the value of the farm and equipment, is subtracted from farm income." Most farmers, of course, did not use such sophisticated bookkeeping practices.

averaged only $44 compared to $253 in Iowa. Sharecroppers and tenants commonly had only from $15 to $30 worth of machinery and equipment, usually consisting of hoes, shovels and perhaps a cheap plow. In order to get greater production on small acreages, farmers needed to plow and cultivate better, rotate their crops and apply the right kind and amount of fertilizer. As the agricultural reformers argued, farmers must apply science and technology to their agricultural practices if they intended to raise their incomes and standard of living.

One Georgian who believed that farmers should rely on scientific agriculture to increase their productivity was Farish Furman. Furman, a Middle Georgia planter who lived near Milledgeville, was a graduate of the University of South Carolina and a lawyer, and he began farming part of his land in 1878. Furman, emphasizing intensive farming, believed that farmers could profit only if they produced more per acre. He stressed that eroded and exhausted soil must be improved if productivity were to rise, which meant restoring both humus and nutrients to the land. Working with H.C. White, Professor of Chemistry at the University of Georgia, Furman determined the elements needed to maintain and build up soil fertility. Besides applying phosphoric acid, potash, lime and some other minerals, he wanted to restore humus to the soil. Thus, he developed a "formula" consisting of livestock manure, cottonseed, acid phosphate and potash, which he mixed into a compost heap. He then applied this mixture to his cotton fields, and by spreading this "compound" to 60 acres of cotton, he increased production from 8 to 47 bales between 1878 and 1881. One visitor to Furman's plantation in the fall of 1882 said: "I literally saw a wilderness of cotton," while the Secretary of the Georgia State Agricultural Society reported that he had never seen "sixty acres of such cotton in my life, and I'm an old farmer."[18]

The so-called "Furman's formula" received wide publicity through farm journals, newspapers and agricultural society meetings. Henry W. Grady of *The Atlanta Constitution* praised Furman's approach to increased efficiency. Through publications and lectures, especially in Georgia, South Carolina and Alabama, Furman popularized aspects of scientific farming and was instrumental in stimulating the growing movement for agricultural reform not only in Georgia but throughout the South.

Farish Furman was only one of many farmers and agricultural organizations who insisted that farmers must apply science and technology to farm production. The Georgia Agricultural Society and the State Department of Agriculture also urged farmers to change to modern methods. Part of the idea behind scientific agriculture was the call to place less emphasis on cotton and diversify production by raising other crops and livestock. Agricultural journals were also in the vanguard in emphasizing diversification and lessening dependence on cotton. In October, 1890, the *Southern Cultivator*, published in Atlanta, argued that farmers should produce more of their own food and stressed the importance of raising livestock. In his January 1, 1902 editorial, the editor of the *Southern Cultivator* observed that changes were beginning to appear in the Georgia countryside: "Those who have adhered, blindly, to the old idea of shallow scratching and all cotton, have not made money. Those who made their soil deep and fine have reaped a rich reward for their labors. Those who have raised home supplies and food crops for sale are prosperous." Daily, he continued, more and more farmers were trying "new and better methods of farming."[19]

At the same time, the College of Agriculture at the University of Georgia was urging farmers to improve their operations. Faculty members at the college were doing research in plant science, chemistry and other subjects important to scientific advances on the farm, but it was some years before the institution's impact was really felt. Farmers tended to scorn book farming, and besides, most of them were not in a financial position to make changes. In 1887, congress provided $15,000 to each state to set up an agricultural experiment station, and in 1889, the Georgia Experiment Station in Griffin was established. The Georgia Experiment Station began experiments and studies on a wide range of topics — breeds of cotton, dairying and fertilizers among others — but relatively few farmers ever ordered the bulletins even though they were free.

While there was a growing body of scientific knowledge available to farmers from around 1890 onward, most of it was not getting to the mass of Georgia farmers. Thus, in order to get more up-to-date information in the hands of producers, farmers' institutes were organized. These were usually two or three-day affairs where farmers met to hear lectures on crop rotation, soil conservation, mechanization and other practical topics. This was a type of adult education, but lecturing to farmers did not cause many of them to change their farming practices. In the early twentieth century, Seaman H. Knapp developed a program of demonstration plots or farms. Working for the USDA, Knapp got individual farmers who would follow the advice and suggestions of his farm agents, and these cooperating farmers served as models to others in the community. In other words, farmers were shown by demonstration how improved fertilization, rotation of crops, production of livestock, better machinery and raising more feed could improve a family's income. By 1912, there were hundreds of demonstrator farmers throughout the South. Georgia had its share.[20]

Most farmers in Georgia, however, as well as those throughout the rest of the South, continued in their old ways. This was highly frustrating to the agricultural reformers in the College of Agriculture, at the experiment stations and in the offices of editors of farm papers. Why did farmers persist in their old ways? Why did they not diversify their crops, raise more livestock, adopt soil conservation practices and do other things that would improve their condition? Why, in other words, did Georgia farmers refuse to adopt technology and scientific methods as advised by Farish Furman and many other Georgians? In 1909, cotton still occupied 57 percent of the cropland in Georgia, a slightly higher percentage than in 1899.

In the first place, there was widespread resistance to so-called book farming. The President of the Georgia State Agricultural Society told the assembled members in 1876 that the Society had begun "under popular derision."[21] Those trying to reform agriculture, he continued, had been faced with sarcastic statements and were ridiculed for talking about book farming and scientific agriculture. Moreover, habit and tradition were strong throughout Georgia and the entire South.

More important, however, was the fact that many landowners, including merchants and absentee owners, opposed their sharecroppers and tenants growing any commercial crop other than cotton. As mentioned earlier, most planters found cotton the most valuable cash crop and the most profitable crop for small farm owners. Furthermore, diversification and scientific agriculture required different kinds of tasks and decision-making by farm laborers, whether they were sharecroppers or small independent operators; and there was a vast difference in the skills required to operate a dairy farm or to grow cotton. Many Georgia planters and farmers believed that sharecroppers and tenants could not successfully manage more diversified and complicated agricultural operations, and to switch away from cotton would have greatly increased the cost of supervision and management. Moreoever, the entire credit structure was built on the production of cotton. Money was advanced to growers on the crop, and it was the only collateral accepted by most merchants. Obtaining a loan from a merchant to buy cows or hogs was almost unthinkable. The lender reasoned that his security might die or be eaten, and he would be left holding a worthless note.

Finally, of course, scientific agriculture required additional capital. Everything that the agricultural reformers recommended — soil conservation, switching to livestock and mechanization — cost money. There were two main sources of capital. It could be borrowed or accumulated from savings from current production, but most Georgia farmers were unable to save anything. A farm family who took in $200 to $300 a year or less had nothing left over. Indeed, thousands of Georgia farmers were constantly in debt just for their day to day and month to month living expenses. From a lender's point of view, most Georgia farmers were poor credit risks for capital loans. Furthermore, before the New Deal, the sources of capital were very limited. Actually, because of poor credit facilities and lack of a productive enterprise, Georgia farmers were in no position to get credit for agricultural improvement.

Many Georgia farmers attributed their poor economic position to outside influences. They complained about high railroad rates, extortionate interest charges, marketing expenses and high prices for the things they had to buy. They saw other economic groups organizing in order to set prices for their goods and services, while hard-working producers out on the land had no control over either what they received for their products or what they paid for purchased supplies. As they viewed their economic situation, the farmers saw organization as one means to alleviate at least some of their problems. It is not surprising, then, that when the Farmers Alliance with its emphasis upon forming producer and consumer cooperatives swept westward from Texas in 1887 and 1888, thousands of Georgians joined the crusade. By 1889, some 100,000 Georgia farmers had joined the Farmers Alliance.[21]

Farmers throughout the state organized scores of cooperatives to handle farm supplies and to market their cotton. This, they believed, would reduce their costs of operation and give them higher prices. Besides organizing cooperative business enterprises, leading alliance members sought public office. In 1890, Thomas A. Watson of Thomson was elected to the House of Representatives on a platform critical of big business and monopolists. Georgians also elected less well-known alliancemen to congress, placed a friend in the governor's office and sent a majority to the legislature. However, farmers failed both in politics and in business. Most of the Alliance cooperatives soon failed because of lack of business experience, inadequate capital, opposition from local businessmen and a weak commitment to cooperative principles. Politically, there were not enough representatives and senators in Washington to push through basic agrarian reforms. The election of William McKinley in 1896 represented defeat for agricultural reformers in Georgia and elsewhere.[22]

Despite their failures at economic organization and political action in the late 1880's and early 1890's, Georgia farmers did not give up trying to improve their condition through organization. The Farmers Union, organized in Texas in 1902, spread to Georgia the following year, and soon many farmers joined ranks with the new organization. The purpose of the Farmers Union was to discourage "the credit and mortgage system" and "to assist members in buying and selling." This meant the establishment of business cooperatives. Farmers Union members were mainly interested in controlling cotton marketing. By 1907, some 80,000 farmers in the state claimed membership in the Farmers Union, and they formed scores of cotton cooperatives. In 1906, Charles S. Barrett of Union City, a founder of the Farmers Union in Georgia, became national president of the organization. However, the Farmers Union was no more successful than the Alliance. Its cooperatives failed and by 1914 the organization was all but dead in Georgia and the South. Georgia farmers could look back 15 or 20 years and see very little positive results from their organizing and political efforts.[23]

Despite some improvement on American farms in the early twentieth century, the so-called Golden Era did not touch many Georgia farmers. Only occasionally did higher cotton prices bring better times. In 1903, 1905 and 1907, cotton brought more than 10 cents a pound, compared to 5 to 7 cents during much of the 1890's, but these prices were temporary aberrations. The years from 1909 to 1914 were really difficult ones for most cotton growers, and it was not until the demands of World War I pushed farm prices up that farmers in Georgia and the rest of the South enjoyed some real prosperity. By the fall of 1916, there were reports of unprecedented good times for many Georgia farmers, both white and black. A large cotton crop of 1,821,000 bales brought an average of nearly 20 cents a pound. Such a price had been unheard of since just after the Civil War. The crop placed about $180 million in farmers' hands.[24]

Farmers throughout the state flocked to town to buy clothes, furniture and even automobiles. In the fall of 1916, black farmers around Valdosta were "having as good a time as if it was Christmas." Some farmers in the area were buying Fords, while others were "discarding Fords and buying higher priced cars." One black farm wife in the area bought a new dresser and placed it on the front porch for all to see![25] The good prices continued through 1919 when Georgians and other Southern cotton growers realized 35 cents a pound for their cotton. Although authorities estimated that farmers in Georgia lost 20 percent of their crop in 1919 to the boll weevil, producers realized nearly $200 million from cotton sales. Income from cotton had been even higher in 1918 because of unusually heavy production and small boll weevil losses.[26]

The new found prosperity, however, was short lived. Postwar cotton prices dropped to only 15 cents a pound by the fall of 1920, and Georgians suffered extremely heavy losses from the boll weevil. The situation became so serious in some plantation areas that farmers were forced to quit growing cotton. For example, in Morgan County east of Atlanta, farmers had raised 35,504 bales in 1919, but boll weevils reduced the crop to only 7,064 bales in 1921. Some farmers in Morgan and Greene Counties simply left the area, but others began to see the necessity to abandon cotton and turn to livestock and other crops, including many Georgia farmers in the plantation areas. Some observers believed that the boll weevil did more to encourage diversification than all of the advice handed out by the College of Agriculture and the farm press.[27]

It was, therefore, the boll weevil and low prices which caused

Georgia farmers to reduce their cotton acreage. In the early 1920's, there was some substitution of livestock and other crops for cotton, and in other cases land remained idle. By the mid-1920's, however, ways had been developed to reduce boll weevil damage, and as cotton prices recovered, farmers returned to their traditional crop. In 1924, there were only about 3 million acres of cotton harvested in the state compared to more than 5 million in 1919. In 1926, however, farmers planted nearly 4 million acres, and while there was a slight decrease in intervening years, in 1930 the figure stood at about 4 million. Cotton was still king among Georgia farmers on the eve of the Great Depression.

One important development which had begun to take shape in the 1920's was the decline in the number of black farmers. Georgia had 130,187 Negro farmers in 1920, more than any other state except Mississippi. Most of them were sharecroppers and tenants; only between 10 and 12 percent had become landowners. However, for several thousand blacks or their children in Georgia, movement from slavery to land ownership represented a remarkable economic advance.

During World War I, many blacks left Georgia and migrated north in search of industrial jobs. This trend continued strong in the 1920's. There were 43,398 fewer black farmers in the state in 1930 than a decade earlier, representing a drop of about 33 percent compared to a decline of only 7 percent for white farmers. This "whitening" of Georgia agriculture accelerated during the 1930's and 1940's and later as blacks sought off-farm opportunities. Black farmers forsook farming because they could not get credit to buy land, the New Deal cotton reduction program and growing mechanization began to destroy sharecropping and industrial employment offered a better situation.[28]

As one views Georgia agriculture at the end of the 1920's, it is clear that little agricultural change had occurred during the previous two generations. The work of men like Farish Furman, professors in the College of Agriculture and scientists at the experiment stations had brought only minimal change. The boll weevil probably had more effect in causing farmers to change their agricultural practices than all of the advocates of scientific farming. But if one compares Georgia farming in the late 1920's with conditions in the 1880's, there are many more similarities than differences. Indeed, for most sharecroppers and tenants, as well as many owners, conditions were getting worse.

As mentioned earlier, the average cropland per farm in 1930 in Georgia was only about 32 acres, less than in 1910. Cotton was still the main cash crop. While fewer acres of cotton were grown in 1930 than in in 1909 or 1919, planting was above that of the mid-1920's. Some 206,000 of Georgia's 255,000 farms grew cotton in 1929. At the advent of the Great Depression, most Georgia agriculture centered around small cotton farms, and the call for self-sufficiency and diversification had gone largely unheeded. Other crops and livestock were produced, but they played a minor role compared to cotton. Tobacco was one major cash crop that developed rapidly after 1909, but as of 1929, there were only around 18,000 tobacco farms in the state. In 1930, about 70 percent of farm income came from crops and only 30 percent from livestock.

If incomes had been low and conditions bad on many Georgia farms before 1930, they became much worse with the advent of the Great Depression. With cotton bringing as little as 5 cents a pound and other farm products selling at extremely low prices, living standards fell even lower for thousands of Georgia farm families. In 1931, many Georgia farmers became excited over Governor Huey Long's plan not to plant any cotton in 1932, for it was believed that this drop-a-crop campaign would force prices upward. Governor Richard B. Russell, Jr. and most other Southern governors, however, refused to go along with that program, and surpluses and low prices continued.[29] Farmers were desperate by the time Franklin D. Roosevelt was inaugurated in March, 1933.

The New Deal brought major changes to Georgia agriculture and to farming throughout the entire South. The federal agricultural programs implemented after 1933, along with developing technology, began to bring needed adjustments. The cotton acreage reduction program finally achieved what agricultural reformers had been advocating for years — the planting of less cotton, the production of other cash crops and the raising of more livestock. Moreoever, price supports, payments for not growing cotton and tobacco, and after 1934, peanuts assured a dependable income to farmers with sufficient acreage. Money received for reducing production gave farmers funds for capital expansion in the form of land purchases and acquisition of machinery. In 1934 alone, government payments to Georgia farmers in the cotton program exceeded $10 million.[30] With a reduction in cotton acreage, farmers had more land available on which to raise cattle, and conservation payments also helped farmers shift to livestock.

Meanwhile, D.W. Brooks was approaching farm problems from another angle. Critical of how farmers operated, he urged farmers to improve their agricultural practices to increase efficiency and to get together and organize cooperatives. After teaching agriculture at the University of Georgia, Brooks organized the Cotton Producers Association in 1933, an organization that finally grew into Goldkist, the third largest farmer cooperative in the nation. Brooks believed that farmers could improve their condition by getting together and selling their cotton and purchasing their fertilizer and other supplies on a cooperative basis.

By the late 1930's, Georgia farmers were purchasing more machinery, enlarging their operations and increasing the productivity of agricultural workers. For years officials at the College of Agriculture and the experiment station had been urging farmers to become more efficient. Efficiency of labor could be greatly increased, they said, by utilizing more machinery. Still in 1940, only 3.8 percent of the farmers in the state had a tractor, but the trend toward tractor farming, however, was definitely underway.

Government programs and mechanization were gradually changing the structure of Georgia agriculture. Between 1930 and 1940, the average acreage of cropland harvested on Georgia farms rose from 32 to 40 acres. During that same period, the number of farms decreased by nearly 40,000, from 255,000 to 216,000. Not only were farms getting larger, the number of sharecroppers and tenants was declining. Some of them were forced off the land under the acreage reduction program and the use of machines did away with the need for so much labor. Tenancy dropped from 68 to 60 percent in that same decade, and as mentioned above, the decline in the number of black farmers was especially rapid. In 1930, there were some 86,000 black farmers in Georgia, but by 1940, the number had dropped to 59,000, a loss of about 27,000.[31]

If the New Deal and developing farm technology were laying the foundation for a new agriculture in Georgia, World War II brought further changes. The high wartime prices and the non-farm jobs that became available to the surplus farm population greatly contributed to changes that were already well underway. Nonfarm jobs pulled tens of thousands of people off Southern farms and helped to bring the relationship between population and land into a better balance. Shortages of farm labor also encouraged farmers to mechanize. By 1950, nearly 25 percent of Georgia's farmers had a tractor, compared to less than 4 percent a decade earlier. Another major breakthrough occurred in 1941 when International Harvester marketed its first spindle type cotton picker.[32]

For many years cotton farmers had dreamed about a machine that could successfully pick cotton. Until that happened, labor requirements would be heavy and mechanical efficiency would not be achieved in cotton production. So long as cotton had to be picked by hand, farmers had to maintain a reliable labor supply. Many farmers were discouraged from turning to tractors for ground preparation as long as they had to keep labor on the farm for hoeing and picking. Nevertheless, there were strong efforts in the 1930's to develop a successful mechanical cotton picker. During this decade, the Rust Brothers conducted experiments with a mechanical cotton harvester, but it was not until after International Harvester developed its single row picker in 1941 that mechanized harvesting really began.

Near the close of World War II, Walter S. Brown, Director of Agricultural Extension, interviewed several agricultural leaders in the state and wrote an article on the future of farming in Georgia. D.L. Floyd, chief statistician of the crop reporting service, explained that Georgians had cut their cotton acreage, they were growing more peanuts, small grains, legumes and hay and the livestock and poultry industries were expanding. Yet, as another authority pointed out, there was still a problem of finding "cash enterprises to replace cotton." H.P. Stuckey, Director of the Coastal Plains Experiment Station at Tifton, said that farmers could increase their efficiency by using more machinery, increasing acre yields and improving the quality of their output. He explained that in the past "our production per man or per family has been too small to provide an adequate living."[33]

More than anything else, it was the increasing use of tractors which permitted farmers to solve the problem of low productivity. In 1948 and 1949, the Georgia Agricultural Experiment Station published two studies on the use of tractors in the Piedmont and Coastal Plains. Using survey methods, researchers got information from 68 farmers in five Piedmont counties and 64 producers in two Coastal Plains counties, and they compared the operations of the farmers before and after they obtained one or more tractors. These studies showed that similar trends prevailed in both areas. Tractor farms were larger, and farmers grew relatively fewer row crops such as cotton and corn and more small grains, pasture and forage. The tractor farmers also had more hogs, milk cows and beef cattle. While some farmers with tractors continued to maintain work stock, the numbers gradually decreased; however, the largest farms were those using both tractor and mule power. The general pattern was for a farmer to buy a tractor and use it in conjunction with his work stock for several years, but as farmers found that tractors and other machinery could do more and more of the farm work, they gradually sold off their mules. From 1945 to 1955, the number of mules in Georgia decreased from about 156,675 to 68,016.

As farms with tractors got bigger — the acreage rose 29 percent in a period of only five or six years in the Piedmont counties surveyed — the number of sharecroppers declined. But when the sharecroppers left, it did not mean that the land was abandoned. The old sharecrop land was incorporated into larger mechanized operations, and the farmer planted more of his land to grains and forage crops. It was the shift away from cotton that destroyed most opportunities for sharecroppers, and blacks left in large numbers "mainly because of the unfavorable cotton situation to seek more favorable employment elsewhere." While sharecropping continued through the 1950's and even into the 1960's, it declined rapidly during those years.

Tractor farmers not only tended to have larger farms; they also cultivated more acres of cropland. In the group studied, the average cropland rose about 65 percent after farmers obtained a tractor. The great expansion on the farms was in grain, with the average small grain acreage per farm rising from 21 to 55 acres under tractor power. There was also a substantial increase in the acreage of lespedeza, grass, hay and forage, reflecting more emphasis on livestock. Of the five Georgia Piedmont counties studied, farmers increased their beef cattle numbers by 174 percent, and the number of dairy cows rose 52 percent.

When farmers were asked about the advantages of tractors, they emphasized that they could farm more acres and accomplish work better and faster. They were impressed with the timeliness of getting jobs completed. Farmers found that one of the greatest advantages provided by tractors was that of increased power, which was essential, for instance, for genuine land improvement. Mule power was not sufficient to change cropping patterns from, let us say, cotton to grass and back to cotton or corn. Farmers also reported that the tractor was very important as a tool for soil conservation and building pastures. "I couldn't have fall and winter pasture without power equipment," one farmer declared in 1945. Mule power was inadequte for deep plowing, good terracing, removing stumps, rocks and hedge rows and filling ditches. If farmers were going to enlarge their grain and hay production, they needed enough power to get the required machinery over more acres. By 1946, of the farmers surveyed in the Piedmont of Georgia, about two-thirds of them had mowing machines and grain combines. To improve the quality of plowing and cultivating, they required power beyond that which could be furnished by one, two or even four mules. The tractor, then, proved to be a major facilitator of change in Georgia agriculture as well as throughout the rest of the South.[34]

Increased use of machinery on Georgia farms was only one cause of the agricultural revolution that was changing the face of the state's farming. The use of chemicals and the improvement of plant and livestock breeds were also of fundamental importance. By the late 1940's and 1950's, chemicals were changing several aspects of farming. Not only were more and better fertilizers being used to increase production, but insecticides and herbicides were applied to cut losses from damaging bugs and weeds. Improved crop breeds, properly fertilized and protected from insects and weeds by herbicides and insecticides, greatly increased the productivity of some crops. Peanuts is an excellent example.

Scientists at the Georgia Experiment Station at Tifton conducted experiments following World War II that greatly increased the production of peanuts per acre. Their work involved developing a better variety of peanut, improved fertilization, chemical weed control and better cultural practices. The results were dramatic. In the 1930's, Georgia farmers produced between 600 and 700 pounds of peanuts per acre. By 1978, the average was 3,300 pounds.[35]

While there had been a slow growth of livestock on Georgia farms before World War II, in 1944 livestock production was only about equal to what it had been in 1919. In a few sections of the state, such as Morgan and Greene Counties, dairying had developed on a substantial scale, but this was the exception rather than the usual things. By the 1940's, however, a series of events was finally coming together to make commercial dairying and beef cattle production feasible on a broad scale throughout the state. These factors included the availability of capital generated by high wartime and postwar prices, better credit facilities, the development of more productive and nutritious grasses by plant geneticists, tractor power which was so essential to shift from row crops to grass, adequate medical treatment for animal diseases and improved marketing facilities. Apart from scarcity of capital, the major deterrents to increasing dairy and beef production in Georgia and throughout the South had been the lack of good permanent pasture, the need for breed improvement and the matter of reducing losses from disease and pests. Science played a major role in solving all of these problems.

In some parts of the state such as South Georgia, it was essential to abandon the open range and go to fenced pastures. As late as the 1940's, for example, large numbers of cattle in the Coastal Plains region ran at large in the woods where they existed on rough native grasses, weeds and brush much as animals had done in the 1870's and 1880's. Consequently, the cattle were small and their meat was tough. Also calf losses were heavy, partly because of weak and undernourished cows, and these native brood cows would often go a year or more before rebreeding, reducing the normal number of calves.

For years progressive farmers and agricultural scientists had been preaching the need for better pastures and hay crops. They realized that a thriving livestock industry rested on adequate and nutritious feed, but except in a few areas, little progress had been made. One Georgian who grew up on a farm in the early twentieth century said that he had never seen an improved pasture until after he graduated from the Agricultural College in Athens in 1923. A key problem was developing suitable grasses for the Southern soils and climate.

In the 1930's, scientists at the Coastal Plains Experiment

Station in Tifton began a concentrated effort to breed grasses that would thrive in the South and lay the foundation for a profitable livestock industry. Nebraskan Glenn W. Burton, agronomist and plant geneticist, joined the research staff at Tifton in 1936 and began working to improve grasses. The idea of planting grass was not initially popular with many farmers; indeed, native Bermuda was the scourge of cotton farmers who had for years fought it with hoe and plow. They looked askance at anyone who was trying to improve the worst weed they had to contend with in the cotton patch. Recognizing these attitudes, Burton did not publicize his early grass experiments.

In 1943, Burton released his famous Coastal Bermuda for general farm use. By the late 1940's, thousands of acres of the grass were being planted in the state. More Alta Fescue and other grasses were also being sown. As one observer wrote in 1947, "Those old, eroded cotton fields are beginning to look pretty nice with a blanket of lush-growing grass." Unlike the situation in the Midwest and Great Plains, researchers found that it was absolutely necessary to fertilize Southern pasture lands to get the needed nutrition and production. Much of the research at the experiment station dealt with the kind and amounts of fertilizer that would produce the best growth. While more acreage was devoted to pasture, it was the quality of the grass and forage that made such a great difference in Georgia's livestock and dairy industries.[36]

The federal government, through the Soil Conservation Service, provided valuable help to farmers who wanted to shift land from cash crops to grass and forage for livestock. The SCS provided funds on a cost-sharing basis to seed and reseed thousands of acres of pasture and to construct hundreds of farm ponds. The Soil Bank Act of 1956 offered even greater enticement to farmers and landowners to reduce their cultivated cropland. Under this law, entire farms could be taken out of production in return for cash payments, and much of the idled land was subsequently planted to grass and trees. Probably no single thing did so much to change the landscape of Georgia and some other Southern states as the Soil Bank.

Besides better feed, Southern livestock men needed improved breeds. There had been efforts here and there throughout the South to upgrade the quality of cattle, and there were herds of purebred Herefords, Black Angus and other breeds scattered across the state prior to World War II. The Experiment Station at Tifton had a purebred cattle herd in the 1930's, but most Southern cattle were small and scrubby. In the late 1940's and early 1950's, Georgia farmers imported an increasing number of high quality bulls to improve their herds, but often cattle from Texas and the Midwest were subject to diseases common in the warmer and more humid Southern climate. Consequently, many Southerners imported Brahma blood lines from Texas which produced hardy and larger animals more resistant to disease than some other breeds.

As indicated earlier, diseases and damaging insects had always plagued Southern farmers who engaged in the beef cattle or dairy business. While Texas fever had been largely brought under control by the 1930's, the screwworm became a scourge throughout much of the Southeast after 1934. Effective chemical treatment of the worms that burrowed into animal flesh became available in the 1940's and made it easier for farmers to deal with that problem. Vaccinations for various diseases and insecticides to kill flies, grubs and other insects also helped to improve the health of cattle and increase profits for the developing livestock industry.

Commercial dairying developed rapidly in Georgia after World War II. Growing urban markets for fluid milk made dairying increasingly attractive to farmers in a position to take advantage of that demand. For many years, farmers adjacent to the larger cities had specialized in milk production, but except in a few areas, progress had been slow before 1940. Besides the poor pastures and low productivity of Southern cows, dairymen had serious marketing problems, including lack of adequate transportation and refrigeration. Additionally, most Georgia farmers did not have electricity before World War II.

By the 1940's, however, a whole series of interrelated developments was taking place to make dairying in Georgia a much more feasible enterprise. Pasture and feed improvement, availability of capital, better roads, refrigerated milk tanks on farms, refrigerated tank trucks that regularly picked up a farmer's milk, along with the growing town and urban markets, combined to encourage commercial dairying throughout the state. In the 1940's and 1950's, dairy farmers also began to import high producing Holstein cows from Wisconsin and elsewhere. In 1938, production of milk per cow in Georgia was only 3,380 pounds a year; in 1961, it was 4,940 pounds; and by 1978, the figure was 10,116.[37] This reflected dramatic changes in breeding, feeding and care of dairy cows.

One of the most important developments in Georgia agriculture after about 1940 was the development of the commercial poultry industry. Up to the 1930's, commercial poultry production had centered largely in New England, the Middle Atlantic States and the Midwest, but there was a number of people who believed that the South offered good possibilities for poultry production. The Georgian who promoted the expansion of broiler production in the state was Jesse Dixon Jewell, a feed dealer in Gainesville. In 1936, he began providing chicks and feed to farmers on credit and then bought back the mature chickens for marketing. Former cotton farmers were familiar with this kind of short term credit because storekeepers had customarily advanced supplies or cash at the beginning of the growing season in return for a mortgage on the crop. Gradually, Jewell made arrangements with bigger feed processors to supply him with even larger quantities of feed which he, in turn, sold to farmers on credit. He developed a "businessman-farmer team" which grew into the agribusiness concept. Poultry raising, especially in North Georgia, slowly began to change from a sideline or barnyard activity to genuine farm business.

Jewell's next step was to establish a hatchery, and in 1940, he built a processing plant in Gainesville where the birds were prepared for market. By World War II, he had an integrated operation where he hatched the eggs, contracted with farmers to raise the chicks on feed that he supplied from his mill to growers on credit and finally processed and marketed the birds. Farmers provided the housing, labor and management in return for an assured market. On this foundation, poultry expanded in Georgia until it became the most important source of farm income.[38]

By the 1960's and 1970's, the agricultural revolution in Georgia had produced a radical change in the state's farming. Farms had gotten fewer and much larger. In 1940, the average size farm in Georgia was only 109 acres; by 1978, it was 234 acres. The average size of commercial farms selling more than $2,500 worth of products was 312 acres. Moreover, Georgia agriculture became increasingly white, for by 1974, there were only about 2,963 black farmers left in the state, compared to 130,000 in 1920.

The rural landscape had changed drastically as millions of acres were planted to grass and trees. The mule and cotton, important for so long on Georgia farms, were no longer even symbols. The mule was gone and cotton played only a minor role in the state's agricultural economy. In 1978, cotton and cotton seed provided only about 2 percent of the state's cash farm income compared to nearly half in 1930. Cotton had been replaced by soybeans and peanuts to some extent, but mainly by grass and trees.

Crops which had produced about 70 percent of the farm income in the late 1920's accounted for only 44 percent of the income in 1978. Livestock — cattle, calves, dairying and hogs and especially poultry — had become the highest producers of income on Georgia farms. Livestock and its products were responsible for 56 percent of the farm income in the state in 1978, and poultry and eggs alone accounted for 34 percent of that figure. The five leading producers of farm income in the late 1970's were poultry and poultry products, peanuts, hogs, soybeans and dairy products. This is a vastly different picture than that presented from the 1870's to the 1940's.

Scientists and farm leaders such as Farish Furman, D.W. Brooks, Glenn Burton, and Jesse Jewel played an important role in Georgia's agricultural change. Their work and that of others supplemented the broader influences of science and technology and the actions of the federal government to produce change, even revolution on Georgia farms. The federal government with its cotton reduction program, the price support program, payments for conservation and agricultural credit began to break the barriers which had held back agricultural change in Georgia and throughout the South. These programs helped to provide the capital for a more highly mechanized agriculture, while scientists, supported by the USDA and the agricultural experiment stations, showed how productivity could be increased by growing better crops and livestock.

The changes that occurred after the 1940's left Georgia with only about 38,000 commercial farms in 1978. They were larger, more efficient, and except in times such as 1977 and 1983, more profitable. However, problems remained, and no doubt more shifts and changes are in store for Georgia agriculture. While modernized farmers have problems, most of them are not sorry that the old mule and cotton generation is gone.

FOOTNOTES

[1]A great deal has been written on sharecropping. See Ralph Schlomowitz, "The Origins of Southern Sharecropping," *Agricultural History*, 53 (July, 1979), pp. 557-75; Joseph D. Reid, "Sharecropping as an Understandable Market Response: The Post-Bellum South," *Journal of Economic History*, 33 (March 1973), pp. 106-128; and Robert Higgs, "Patterns of Farm Rental in the Georgia Cotton Belt, 1880-1900," *Journal of Economic History*, 34 (June, 1974), pp. 468-80.

[2]*Annual Report of the Commissioner of Agriculture*, State of Georgia, 1875 (J.H. Estill, Public Printer, 1875), p. 55.

[3]*Twelfth Census of the United States*, 1900, Agriculture Pt. I (Washington, 1902), pp. 68-69.

[4]*1950 Census of Agriculture*, II, General Report (Washington, 1952), p. 54.

[5]*Ibid.*

[6]*Ibid.*, Pt. II, p. 423.

[7]*Ibid.*, p. 422.

[8]*Transactions of the Georgia State Department of Agriculture* (Atlanta, 1878), p. 468; and *Publications of the Georgia State Department of Agriculture*, 12 (Atlanta, 1886), p. 202.

[9]*Twelfth Census of the United States*, 1900, Agriculture, Pt. I, p. 396.

[10]*Ibid.*, Pt. II, p. 704; see also Willard Range, *A Century of Georgia Agriculture, 1850-1950* (Athens: University of Georgia Press, 1954), pp. 110-111.

[11]*1950 Census of Agriculture*, II, General Report, pp. 400-401.

[12]*Ibid.*, p. 426.

[13]*Twelfth Census of the United States*, 1900, Agriculture, Pt. 1, pp. 423 and 426.

[14]United States Census Office, *Reports on Cotton Production in The United States*, Pt. II (Washington, 1884), p. 173.

[15]United States Census Office, *Report on Cotton Production in the United States* (Washington, 1884), Pt. II, p. 173.

[16]Manuscript Census of Agriculture, Harris County, Georgia, 1880. District 55, p. 8; and Jackson County, District 48, p. 21.

[17]E.S. Haskell, *A Farm-Management Survey in Brooks County, Georgia*, USDA Bulletin No. 648 (May 1, 1918), p. 33.

[18]Lester D. Stephens, "Farish Furman's Formula: Scientific Farming and the 'New South,'" *Agricultural History*, 50 (April, 1976), pp. 377-90.

[19]*The Southern Cultivator*, 60 (February 1, 1902), p. 8.

[20]See Roy V. Scott, *The Reluctant Farmer: The Rise of Agricultural Extension to 1914* (Urbana: University of Illinois Press, 1970).

[21]Range, *A History of Georgia Agriculture*, p. 139.

[22]Robert C. McMath, Jr., *Popular Vanguard, A History of the Southern Farmers' Alliance* (Chapel Hill: University of North Carolina Press, 1975); Theodore Salautos, *Farmer Movements in The South, 1865-1933* (Berkeley: University of California Press, 1960); and C. Vann Woodward, *Tom Watson, Agrarian Rebel* (New York: The Macmillan Company, 1938).

[23]Salautos, *Farmer Movements in the South*, chap. 12.

[24]*Yearbook of Agriculture*, 1921 (Washington, 1921), p. 611-12.

[25]"Cotton's Magical Rise Enriching The Nation," *The Literary Digest*, 52 (December 9, 1916), p. 1519.

[26]*Yearbook of Agriculture*, 1921, pp. 611-612.

[27]James S. Fisher, "The Modification of Rural Land Occupance System: The Central Georgia Piedmont" (Ph.D. diss., University of Georgia, 1967), pp. 70-75.

[28]*United States Census of Agriculture*, 1954, II, General Report (Washington, 1956), p. 1046.

[29]*Atlanta Georgian*, September 16, 1931.

[30]*Yearbook of Agriculture*, 1935 (Washington, 1935), p. 696.

[31]*United States Census of Agriculture*, 1954, II, General Report, p. 1046.

[32]See Walter W. Wilcox, *The Farmer in the Second World War* (Ames: Iowa State University Press, 1947); Gilbert C. Fite, "Recent Progress in the Mechanization of Cotton Production in the United States," *Agricultural History*, 24 (January, 1949), pp. 19-28.

[33]Walter S. Brown, "Georgia Farm Leaders Face the Future," *Progressive Farmer*, 60 (April, 1945), p. 14.

[34]J.C. Elrod and W.T. Fullilove, *Cost and Utilization of Tractor Power and Equipment on Farms in the Lower Piedmont*, Georgia Experiment Station Bulletin 256 (Experiment, Georgia, January (1948); and J.C. Elrod, *Cost and Utilization of Tractor Power and Equipment on Farms in the Coastal Plain*, Georgia Experiment Station Bulletin 260 (Experiment, Georgia, June, 1949).

[35]Glenn W. Burton, *Our Role in Feeding the World* (University of Georgia College of Agriculture, 1976).

[36]Interview with Glenn W. Burton, June 14, 1982; J.J. Inskeep, "Grass Boom in Dixie," *Farm Journal*, 71 (September, 1947), p. 58.

[37]See the appropriate tables in *Agricultural Statistics* for the years cited.

[38]Gordon Sawyer, *The Agribusiness Poultry Industry, A History of Its Development* (New York: Exposition Press, 1971).

PART II
IDEAS AND RESOURCES
FOR TEACHING GEORGIA HISTORY

INTRODUCTION

CHARLES STEPHEN GURR

Most frequently, Georgia history is taught in the fourth and eighth grades of public and private schools, at the undergraduate level of colleges as a state requirement for graduation and at the upper and graduate levels of many of Georgia's colleges and universities where the focus is on research in topical areas. As with most history courses, the techniques employed in the teaching of Georgia history are fairly traditional — lectures, texts, readings, and frequently, as units or parts of courses in United States or Southern history. Increasingly in recent years, however, there is a trend toward the expansion of the study of Georgia history to include the growing interest in local and community history.

The study and teaching of Georgia history goes back almost as far as the history itself. There were individual students of Georgia's past in the first generation of Georgians, and frequently these were ministers who made a study of their colony and state as a high level hobby, the results of which often became the basis for more professional efforts in the mid and late 19th century. Thus, as an indication of the value placed on the orderly gathering and study of Georgia history in the first half of the nineteenth century, the Georgia Historical Society was chartered in 1839, barely one hundred years after the first settlements at Savannah.

Just when Georgia history was formally introduced into the curriculum is a matter of conjecture. No doubt, the earliest of school rooms included an effort to inculcate the "proper respect" for the state's founders and made some gesture toward depicting the basic historical context of Georgia's, the region's and nation's establishment and evolution. Depending on the contemporary events, history in America — national, regional, state or local — has not infrequently been the tool of the times. Times of crisis, especially times of conflict, have given rise to renewed emphasis on history in American classrooms, and no doubt, Georgia history was to flourish as the times demanded: in justification of anti-English sentiment coincident to the War of 1812, in defense of the expansion of slavery to the American Southwest at the time of the war with Mexico, and most certainly, in conjunction with the great "War Between the States" in the 1860's. The pace of this move to "history for a purpose" was accelerated in the post-Civil War years, during Reconstruction and later with another intent in the era of imperial expansion and war with Spain. The twentieth century linked American history to the causes of the two World Wars, and the respective regions, states and local settings found their place in support of the historical justifications called into play at these junctures. Georgia history, in content and in emphasis, experienced the shifting focus and design attendant to the wider national and regional developments.

Focusing specifically on the goals of Georgia history, a fundamental step in this effort to contribute to the teaching of Georgia history, one finds it interesting to examine the historic evolution of such goals and purposes. It is necessary here, however, to limit this review of goals to some examples drawn from those writings that were specifically intended for use in the classrooms of Georgia. An examination of the more broadly cast studies of Georgia history or the more refined detailed works on some rather narrow element of the state's history might reveal a much wider (or narrower) goal focus and is, therefore, not especially germane to the present study.

The text writing of state history had its origins in the late 19th century, with a number of state history series being produced by a booming publishing trade fad resulting, in considerable part, from the public school movement's national growth. Georgia, as did many other states, began a state-wide school program in the 1870's and was therefore among the target markets for national publications of school books. Together with the school movement was a "professionalization" of history, the first Ph.D.'s being granted in American universities during this period. History was getting several "shots in the arm."

An 1893 volume by Frances Letcher Mitchell, entitled *Georgia Land and People,* provides a distinct purpose and goal for the teaching of Georgia history at the end of the 19th century:

> *The liberty we now enjoy was won by the help of Georgians with the sword, with the pen, and with fiery words of eloquence in political assemblies. If there lives a Georgian with heart so dead that it swells not with pride when he hears the great names of Georgia's warriors, statesmen, and poets, may he go down to his grave 'unwept, unhonored, and unsung.'*
>
> *Patriotism is a virtue that elevates character, leading men to right feeling and lofty sentiments. To claim kindred with the noble and great is in some degree to wish to be like them. To love our State should not be merely a matter of pride, or simply a sentiment, but a principle.*

The man credited with writing Georgia's first "school book" history of the state is Lawton B. Evans, whose *A History of Georgia For Use in Schools* was published in 1898 and went through many editions, providing the basic source of teaching Georgia history into the 1930's. In his preface, Mr. Evans reveals in part his purpose:

> *The author has tried to represent in this book the leading facts of the history of Georgia .... This book is written for pupils of from twelve to fifteen years of age. Though not descending to childish narrative, the author has endeavored to make the story easily understood .... Pictures of many Georgia men are given for the first time in history .... The faces of these commanders (Civil War Generals) in the great struggle are thus presented to the youth of the State, who will look upon them with gratification and pride. (Preface, 1898 Edition)*

A later edition of Lawton's book (1932) delineates the purposes even more specifically:

> *The author of this book has endeavored to present*

the leading facts in the history of Georgia, in order to instruct the youth of the State in the annals of their forefathers, and to inspire them with a love for their own institutions. The main events in the history of the United States are included in the narrative in order to show the closeness of relation between State history and the affairs of the nation at large .... The author hopes that by the study of the history of Georgia in its connection with the other States which compose the United States, the child will gain the proper understanding of the meaning of State rights and State pride, without interfering with or diminishing that larger patriotism that comprehends the entire country .... The author feels confident that the children of the schools will feel an abiding interest in the narrative contained in these pages, and, inspired with a deep love for their State, will enter upon their citizenship with a high and noble patriotism. (Preface, 1932 Edition)

Empire Builders of Georgia, copyrighted first in 1951 and carried through a number of editions into the mid-1960's, offers a veiw of Georgia history's purpose that is half a century beyond Evans' first statement:

Our youth must be aware of the changing times, alert to seize opportunities, and ready to help meet the problems .... Young Georgians will build a happier world if they have a knowledge of the living past. They will be able to build more wisely if they are trained to think through their situations, to profit from an understanding of the trials and errors of those who have lived before them in this region .... This book is written for young Georgians. It offers to help them set their goals as they begin the great adventure of building their lives in their own state. **Empire Builders of Georgia** *points the way toward making Georgia a better state in which to live .... Young Georgians may be helped to decide what characteristics of present-day Georgia should be kept and what should be changed. (Preface, 1983 Edition)*

E. Merton Coulter's *A Short History of Georgia* went through a number of editions and was used widely as a text at the high school and college levels around the state between

1933 and 1976. Nowhere in this volume, however, is there a stated goal other than to provide "a short history of Georgia brought down to the present ...." Coulter went on to say that he hoped "it will be of value both to the general reader and to the student." (Preface, 1933 Edition) The 1977 *A History of Georgia* (Kenneth Coleman, *et al.)* was a product of the interest of then Governor of Georgia, Jimmy Carter, who asked Kenneth Coleman, Dean of Georgia Historians, to take the lead in the writing of a new history of Georgia. In his foreword, then President Carter vaguely alluded to the purposes behind his original interests in having a new history written:

> *Like most Georgians, I am deeply attached to the land .... Through our love of the land, we share a common bond and become a community .... This family and community spirit was essential to Georgia's early settlers. This same spirit has withstood the test of time and circumstance. We were able to make it through the Revolutionary and Civil wars and still retain many of our original values and traditions .... This fine history explains the roots of these traditions. (Foreword, 1977 Edition)*

In the 1980's, Georgia State Department of Education guidelines for curricula briefly note the basic skills related to Georgia history in the public schools. At the fourth grade level, one specific social studies guide calls for the development of an awareness unit on Georgia — past, present and governments (sic). The guidelines for the eighth grade are more detailed:

CONCEPTS

Identifies geographic and environmental patterns of Georgia.

Describes historical development in regard to political, economic, social, cultural development.

Identifies ethnic groups and linguistic patterns.

Describes cultural expression of values (art, music, literature) as related to Georgia.

Discusses modern Georgia in regard to communication, transportation, urbanism.

Discusses social issues in modern Georgia.

Explains state and local government.

Describes the interdependence of Georgia and the United States in regard to local, state and national relationships (political, economic, social, cultural).

(**Source:** *Georgia State Department of Education Basic Curriculum Content for Georgia Public Schools,* Draft, 1984)

As mentioned earlier, local history has become an important development in the study of state history. The history of Georgia, along with the history of most other states, is benefiting from the recent movement toward emphasis on local and community history in America. Major grants and funding have been available over the past ten years for the purposes of research, teaching and dissemination of history at its most immediate level — locally. A major National Endowment for the Humanities grant to the Family and Community History Project at the Newberry Library in Chicago has given hundreds of state history scholars a chance to relate state history to local and community history, and the result has been a boom to state history all over the nation. Major "state histories" are being researched and written as a part of this movement, and several valuable state-based student projects and competitions are providing much needed incentives to those interested in history at a level nearer to home than U.S. history in its broad context. National "History Day" projects are in fact creating good state history.

The move into local and community history has made more obvious than ever the fact that students learn by doing and more and more options are becoming viable for the Georgia history classroom teacher. The linking of Georgia's history to Hall County history or to Ty Ty history or to Buford, Georgia history creates the immediacy of place which makes students feel part of the history that has so far seemed to have passed them by when it is considered only in terms of major battles and leading men and women. Outside the path of Sherman has until recently been stark ground for Civil War history in Georgia. With the new local focus, however, the history of that dark period can be found in the fields and lanes of local communities, battle scars or no. The fact that the local student can be and really cannot avoid being part of local history is a wide open invitation to rejuvenate Georgia history. The specific opportunities are limitless provided the mind is open and the imagination is allowed to run freely.

Given the evolving goals and purposes of Georgia history as expressed by authors, historians and educational institutions, there is a need to translate the teaching of the history of Georgia into "ground level" terms: what *has* gone on, what *is* going on and what *should* go on in the Georgia history classrooms. During the summer of 1983, the Georgia Endowment for the Humanities, through generous grants, encouraged an effort to look into and to attempt to improve the teaching of state history in Georgia. Three state institutions of higher education, Georgia Southern College, Columbus College and Georgia Southwestern College, received matching grants designed to bring together teachers of Georgia history from across the state for the purpose of contributing to the improvement of Georgia history instruction in the schoolrooms of the state. Teachers from public and private schools in Georgia shared several weeks of ideas, experiments, failures, successes and questions related to the teaching of Georgia history in the middle grades and ways in which instruction might be improved.

The teachers brought to the seminars a variety of backgrounds and experiences, for there were some with as much as thirty years in the classroom or as little as six months, some with years of teaching Georgia history or very little experience with the subject. The ability levels of their students ran the full range, and the amount of emphasis and time permitted for Georgia history in their respective curricula varied greatly. For several weeks, the participants in the seminars investigated teaching methods and resources in Georgia history, participated in field trips to historical sites in the state and heard from experts in a number of areas related to the teaching of Georgia history. The three seminars and the combined experiences and ideas of the participants produced many resources for teaching Georgia history effectively and creatively. What follows are brief suggestions to aid both experienced and inexperienced teachers of Georgia history in bringing their subject alive for their students.

Ideas And Resources For The Classroom

Tips on Getting Started
in the Georgia History Class

Many of the good ideas emerging during the Georgia Southwestern summer seminar had to do with the process of beginning a class. Our discussions, of course, were about the beginning of a Georgia history class, but many of the tips that were shared are applicable for any class. Perhaps some of these will be helpful.

1 . On the first day of class, *devote the entire period to an orientation session.* Provide your students with handouts that outline specific requirements and objectves, and call for information about your students that you may need in planning for the future work of the group. (A letter to parents including this would be helpful.)

2 . Organization is a major key to effective teaching. *Take pride in your own ability to organize and emphasize that to your students.* Get them off on the right foot by setting a good example and helping them follow. Provide a file folder for each student for his/her own use for your class. (They may not have it the next day, but it gives the initial impression of your sense of order and its importance.)

3 . *Discuss* with your students the handout materials that you give them. Do not simply read your requirements; give the students solid ideas about why you have these requirements and how you arrived at them. Give them your *most basic* goals for the class (*not* factual information memorization but the "why" behind your specific detailed objectives).

4 . One of the favorite beginning tips is *taking photos of yourself* and family or friends, brothers, children, car, hobby, etc., and *passing them around* in an effort to establish your own "identity" outside the classroom. Students are interested in you.

5 . *Have students write about themselves.* Be sure to read this before the next day, and where appropriate, acknowledge some of the things you learned about them.

6 . Each teacher likes too establish his/her own "tone" or degree of formality for the classroom. Choose your own and SET IT THE FIRST DAY. If you want a traditional setting and fairly rigid and demanding responses, let your students know it. If you let them know what you expect IN ADVANCE, then they can and will adjust to your style. THINK IT OUT first, however. Remember, it's much easier to lighten up than to toughen up. Your personal appearance and the appearance of your room are most significant in this whole process.

7 . *Appoint a class secretary* for the first week or so; then perhaps have the students elect secretaries every "x" number of weeks. The class secretary can be of help to you and serve as a helpful partner for both you and the students in reconciling what students think went on and what you think went on. Let the class secretary report "minutes of the class meetings" as you see fit, helping with checking deadlines, etc.

CHRONOLOGICAL GUIDES FOR THE STUDY OF GEORGIA HISTORY

The teachers in the Georgia Southwestern summer seminar considered the history of Georgia in terms of four major time periods: 18th Century, Early 19th Century, Late 19th Century and 20th Century. Based on their experiences with the common organizational plans of textbooks and their opinions that 8th grade students follow chronological treatments better than they do topical divisions, the teachers determined that a basic guide pattern should be developed for each period. What follows are the key elements of these guides together with complete sample periods as developed in the seminar.

TIME LINES

For each period, a basic time line was drawn and marked with three types of benchmarks: political developments, economic trends and social and cultural events. Additional items of national or worldwide significance were indicated for purposes of relating state history to a larger frame of history.

TOPICAL OUTLINE

For each period, a three to five item outline was drawn up, and for the most part, these correspond to the three foci indicated on the time lines: political, social, economic.

OBJECTIVES

For each of the time periods under consideration, the seminar participants spelled out objectives, drawing on the emerging State Department of Education criteria. These were drawn in such a way as to call for student skill development in conjunction with the utilization of specific data or information grounded in the history of Georgia. Recognition, description and analysis were common to many of these objectives.

ACTIVITIES

Given the variety of interest and ability levels among students in the 8th grades of Georgia, it seems incumbent upon Georgia history teachers to provide as wide a variety of experiences as possible in their classroom activities. Familiar activities such as field trips, map work and films were combined with more recent classroom innovations such as role playing, oral history projects and genealogy. These are indicated in the various time periods.

EVALUATIONS

An important part of the teaching of any course is the evaluation process. For each unit guide, the seminar participants suggested what they considered appropriate forms and examples of questions/or activities to be used for purposes of evaluation of the students' progress and the value of the instructional methods used.

SITES AND SOURCES

During the seminar, there was a special emphasis on the value of history outside the classroom, both in field trips and through local resources in the form of individuals, records and related base data. The fact that more and more historic sites are being developed in Georgia and more and more local history is being brought to light naturally draws attention to the need for the field experience, an occasional problem given the recent demands for the reduction of time outside of the classroom in Georgia schools.

OTHER SOURCES

Fortunately, not all of Georgia's important historic resources are fixed-place objectives or buildings that require a trip beyond the physical limits of the classroom in order to benefit from them. Increasingly, state and local history is drawing on the human resource in the form of the local people who lived and made the history of their place. Seminar participants addressed this important source in their unit guides along with the growing variety of nonhuman but portable raw materials of state and local history such as the photograph, newspaper, diary and artifact. Important in this category, too, were the lists developed for the contacts around Georgia who have some specific knowledge about the infinite variety of subtopics within our history such as railroads, Indians, etc.

BIBLIOGRAPHY

For each chronological unit the participants developed a basic, twelve item bibliography. The criterion was that the work not only make a basic contribution to the knowledge of the period but that it be readily available in most school, local or regional libraries.

EIGHTEENTH CENTURY GEORGIA

Social/Cultural/Economic/Political

	1700	'32	'33	'40	'52	'54	'63	'75	'83	'88	1800
Ga. Trust Developed		—									
Royal Charter		—									
Savannah Founded			—								
War With Spanish				—							
Bethesda Established					—						
Trust Ends						—					
1st Gov.						—					
Wrights's Eco. Leadership							—				
Ga. Gazetta Established								—			
Rise of Revolution								—			
Break With Gov. Wright									—		
Turning From British Pattern - Peace of Paris									—		
Independence From Britain										—	
U.S. Const. Ratified											—

TOPICAL OUTLINE

I. **Indian Cultures Prior to and after Oglethorpe**
    A. Evidence of Native Americans Prior to Europeans
    B. Spanish Interactions with Indian Cultures
    C. The English Relationship with the Indians

II. **The Founding of the Colony**
    A. The Empire's Needs
    B. Oglethorpe and the Trustees
    C. Planning and Executing the Trust

III. **Social, Cultural and Economic Conditions**
    A. The People Who Came
    B. Living in the Colony of Georgia
    C. A Mixture of Cultures
    D. A Controlled and Dependent Economic Pattern

IV. **Political Structure in the Colony**
    A. The Charter and the Trust
    B. Evaluation of the Trust
    C. Royal Government in Georgia
    D. Challenges to Royal Authority

V. **Revolutionary War in Georgia**
    A. The Break with England
    B. American Offensive
    C. British Offensive
    D. War in the Back Country

OBJECTIVES

Students should be able to:

1. Recognize how the Indian culture was changed by the introduction of English and European customs and values.

2. Cite and explain reasons for the establishment of the Georgia colony.

3. Provide a description of Georgia's changing social, cultural and economic conditions in the 18th century.

4. Analyze the conflicts and processes that led to changes in Georgia's government.

5. Provide a description of Georgia's role in the Revolution and the influence of the other colonies on her.

ACTIVITIES

1. Field Trips: note the examples of recommended sites which follow — plan ahead and follow up!

2. Maps of Georgia: the Colonial Period is a good time to develop basic "map knowledge" of Georgia and the Southeast.

3. Visual Interpretation: have student groups develop exhibits which illustrate life or events in early Georgia.

4. Role-Playing: individual "dramatic readings," group "plays" or "guides" for exhibits in Number 3 above.

EVALUATIONS

Written and Oral Presentations

Written Examinations

Construction and Interpretation of Charts, Maps and Graphs

Exhibit Development by Teams

SITES AND SOURCES

1. **Savannah Historic District — Georgia's First Settlement (1733)**
   a. Yamacraw Bluff
   b. Town Squares
   c. Colonial Cemetery
   d. Pirate's House
   e. Savannah Riverfront

2. **St. Simons Island — Example of Georgia as a Buffer Colony**
   a. Fort Frederica*
   b. Colonial Cemetery

    c. Site of Battle of Bloody Marsh

    d. Christ Church

(*The film "This Is Frederica" is available from the National Park Service.)

3. **Darien, Georgia — Example of Early European Settlement in Georgia (1721)**

    a. Fort King George Historic Site and Museum

    b. Historic District

4. **Kolomoki Mounds and Museum, Ocmulgee Mounds and Museum, Columbus Museum's Permanent Indian Exhibit as Examples of Indian Cultures in Georgia.**

NOTE: If field trips are not possible, teachers may visit these sites and make slide presentations and tapes for use in the classroom.

OTHER SOURCES

In conjunction with the American Bicentennial Celebration during the 1970's, the Georgia Commission for the Bicentennial and the Georgia Department of Education published a series of thirteen booklets on various aspects of this period of Georgia's history. These booklets deal with social, cultural, political, economic and military subjects, are illustrated and have suggested activities, bibliographies and teacher's guides. They were written especially for middle grades level students in Georgia history. Contact the Georgia Department of Education for availability.

BIBLIOGRAPHY

Abbot, W.W. *The Royal Governors of Georgia.*

Church, Leslie, *Oglethorpe.*

Coleman, Kenneth. *The American Revolution in Georgia.*

_____. *Colonial Georgia.*

Foster, William O. *James Jackson: Deulist and Military Statesman.*

Lanning, John Tate. *The Spanish Missions of Georgia.*

Lawrence, Alexander. *Storm Over Savannah.*

Luzekin, H. *From Savannah to Yorktown: The American Revolution in the South.*

Malone, H.T. *Cherokees of the Old South.*

Phillips, U.B. *Georgia and State Rights.*

Pound, Merritt. *Benjamin Hawkins, Indian Agent.*

Saye, Albert. *A Constitutional History of Georgia.*

EARLY NINETEENTH CENTURY GEORGIA
Social/Cultural/Economic/Political

	1800	'39	'50	'57	1860
Rise of Troup-Clark Parties	‒‒‒				
Cotton Booms	‒‒				
Gold		‒			
Indian Removal		‒‒‒			
Canal and R.R. Building		‒‒‒‒			
Ga. Historical Society Founded		‒			
Slavery Dominates			‒‒‒‒‒‒‒‒‒		
Georgia Prosperity			‒‒‒		
Slavery Expansion Crisis				‒‒‒‒‒‒‒‒‒‒	
Georgia Platform			‒		
Joe Brown				‒‒	

221

TOPICAL OUTLINE

I. **Social and Cultural Characteristics of the State (as of 1800-1860)**
    A. Major Cultural Groups
    B. Education
    C. Social Activities
    D. Architecture/Art

II. **Economic Development**
    A. Transportation
    B. Agriculture and Forestry
    C. Manufacturing
    D. The Discovery of Gold in Georgia

III. **Politics and Government**
    A. 1800-1820 — Organizing State Government
    B. 1820-1840 — Georgia Enters National Politics
    C. 1840-1860 — States Rights and Secession

OBJECTIVES

The student should demonstrate an understanding of:

1. The stratification of the class structures, methods of education, social activities, architecture and art and music of this period.

2. The development of the economic structures of agriculture, transportation and manufacturing which evolved during this time.

3. The political relationships in the national government of this time and the emerging system of state government in Georgia.

ACTIVITIES

1. Tapes, records, films, filmstrips, motion pictures, etc.: multisensory appeal makes the period seem more real.

2. Charts, tables, maps and graphs: makes numerical relationships and physical association more graphic, therefore easier for many to grasp.

3. Genealogy research: whether casual or in-depth, genealogical research gives the student a new pride and understanding of his background and the history of his local region.

4. Role-playing, drama, plays and slide presentations with scripts: permits the student to relate more easily to the customs and habits of the culture he is studying. Guarantees a greater interest. Can be of use in the study of clothing, architecture, weaponry, foods, etc., as a part of developing costumes and sets.

5. Researching of local history: Indians, settlers, industry, education — develops research skills, encourages interest in local background, may be of real historical and community interest.

EVALUATIONS

Oral Participation in Discussions

Completion of Graph/Map Blanks

Creative Writing

Art Work/Illustrations

SITES AND SOURCES

1. **Milledgeville**
   a. Governor's Mansion.
   b. Old State Capitol
   c. Tour of Homes

2. **Westville — 1850's Typical Georgia Community Exhibit**

3. **Dahlonega**
   a. First American Gold Rush
   b. Mint

4. **Indian Sites**
   a. New Echota
   b. Sequoyah Monument
   c. Indian Springs
   d. Vann House

5. **Textile Mill Sites**
   a. Columbus Iron Works
   b. Eagle and Phenix Mill Sites
   c. Fall Line

6. **Local Historic Districts**
   a. Restorations
   b. Museums
   c. Railroad and Riverboat Exhibits

BIBLIOGRAPHY

Bonner, James C. *A History of Georgia Agriculture, 1732-1860.*

Coulter, E.M. *Auraria: The Story of a Georgia Gold-Mining Town.*

_____. *College Life in the Old South.*

Flanders, Ralph B. *Plantation Slavery in Georgia.*

Kemble, Frances A. *A Journal of a Residence on a Georgia Plantation in 1838-1839.*

Longstreet, A.B. *Georgia Scenes.*

Lumpkin, Wilson. *The Removal of the Cherokee Indians from Georgia.*

Montgomery, Horace H. *Cracker Parties.*

Myers, Robert. *Children of Pride.*

Phillips, U.B. *Georgia and State Rights.*

Pound, Merritt B. *Benjamin Hawkins, Indian Agent.*

Shyock, Richard H. *Georgia and the Union in 1850.*

LATE NINETEENTH CENTURY GEORGIA

Social/Cultural/Economic/Political

Lincoln
Elected   —

Joe Brown   _____

Disruptions
Of War   _____

Wartime
Economics   _____

Reconstruction
1st Blacks In
Ga. Legislature   _____

Changing Agri. System
(Tenants & Sharecropping)   _____

Shifting Race
Relations   _____

Alliance/Independents
Populists   _____

Farm Depression   _____

Tom Watson
To Congress   —

Public Education
Advances   —

| 1860 | '66 | '68 | '70 | '90 | 1900 |

TOPICAL OUTLINE

I. **The Secession Crisis**
    A. Long-Range and Immediate Political Crises
    B. National Election of 1860
    C. Secession

II. **Civil War in Georgia**
    A. Military Actions
    B. Economic Changes
        1. Impact of the Railroads
        2. Changing Agriculture (Land and Capital)
        3. Problems in Labor and Industry
    C. Wartime Politics and Society

III. **Social and Political Relations in Postwar Georgia**
    A. Race Relations
    B. Role of Women
    C. Middle Class Emerges
    D. Political and Economic Reconstruction

IV. **Georgia in the New South**
    A. Politics
        1. Bourbonism
        2. Blacks in Georgia Politics
        3. Populism
    B. Economics, Rural and Urban Shift
    C. Social Changes

OBJECTIVES

Students should be able to:

1. Discuss fundamental (long-range) and immediate causes of the Civil War.

2. Summarize social, economic and political changes brought about by the Civil War and New South. Possibly the more advanced students could compare and contrast the two periods.

3. State in their own words or be able to write a brief summary identifying influential Georgians of the period (1860-1900).

4. Describe the cultural changes in Georgia after the Civil

War, especially in the area of race relations and public education.

ACTIVITIES

1. Films (State Library)
   a. True Story of the Civil War (No. 7061)
   b. Gone with the Wind Series
   c. Background of the Civil War (No. 4890)
   d. Civil War (No. 4816)

2. Filmstrips
   a. Civil Rights — the Legacy of the Civil War
   b. The Civil War and Reconstruction
   c. The Civil War Series by Singer
   d. Manufacturing in Georgia

3. Maps, Graphs and Charts
   a. Military Maps — Economic Growth Areas
   b. Graphs of Population Trends
   c. Charts of Economic Change

4. Field Trips (Recommended Sites Follow)

5. Civil War Newspapers (Have students make up their own.)

EVALUATIONS

Short Weekly Tests with Maps (Written)

Field Trip Evaluation by Students

Special Topic Reports (Written, Oral, Display)

Maps, Charts and Graphs Folder

SITES AND SOURCES

1. **Milledgeville (Old Governor's Mansion and Capitol)**
2. **Andersonville Prison and Cemetery**
3. **Macon (Hay House)**
4. **Chickamauga Battlefield**
5. **Cyclorama (Atlanta)**
6. **Fort Pulaski (Savannah)**

OTHER SOURCES

1. Georgia newspapers or microfilms are available through the University of Georgia library. These would be helpful in following the Civil War, Reconstruction and end of the century scene in Georgia. Papers are available from almost every Georgia community from the mid-1800's to the present.

2. Vanishing Georgia is a photographic collection at the Georgia Department of Archives and History. Consult the project for copies of local photos of your community in the late 19th century.

3. The Bicentennial publication, "Famous Georgians," is an excellent supplementary tool for teachers since it contains an introduction to Georgia history, biographical sketches of twenty-nine influential Georgians and bibliography for each Georgian. Order from:

    Georgia Department of Archives and History
    330 Capitol Avenue, S.E.
    Atlanta, Georgia 30334
    Send $2.50 check or money order

BIBLIOGRAPHY

Arnette, Alex M. *The Populist Movement in Georgia.*

Bonner, James C. *Milledgeville.*

Bryant, T. Conn. *Confederate Georgia.*

Conway, Alan. *The Reconstruction of Georgia.*

Futch, Ovid. *History of Andersonville Prison.*

Hill, Louise B. *Joseph E. Brown and the Confederacy.*

Leigh, Frances B. *Ten Years on a Georgia Plantation Since the War.*

Myers, Robert M. *The Children of Pride.*

Nixon, Raymond. *Henry Grady: Spokesman of the New South.*

Roberts, Derrell C. *Joseph E. Brown and the Politics of Reconstruction.*

Shadgett, Olive. *The Republican Party in Georgia.*

Woodward, C. Vann. *Tom Watson: Agrarian Rebel.*

Twentieth Century Georgia
Social/Cultural/Economic/Political

Event	1900	'08	'15	'17	'32	'36-40	'45	'48	'62	'67	'72	'76	1982
Grandfather Clause	—												
Leo Frank Lynched		—											
County Unit System			—										
Depression — New Deal					—								
E. Talmadge Governor				—									
Rivers' "Little New Deal"					—								
New Const.							—						
H. Talmadge Governor								—					
Urban Growth/ Industrialization									—				
Univ of Ga. Integrated								—					
C.U. System Outlawed									—				
Maddox Gov.									—				
A. Young Congress											—		
Carter Pres.												—	
New Const.													—

TOPICAL OUTLINE

I. **20th Century Politics to the 1920's**
   A. Woolhat Boys and Progressive Politics
   B. Race and Politics
   C. Rural Domination in Georgia and the Rise of Talmadge

II. **Economic Patterns in Early 20th Century Georgia**
   A. Farming in Georgia
   B. Natural Resources
   C. Georgia Manufacturers
   D. Urban Distribution

III. **Politics in the 1930's-'40's — the Talmadge Era**
   A. Richard Russell and Reform
   B. Talmadge, Georgians and the New Deal
   C. Arnall, Thompson and Talmadge
   D. Herman Talmadge and Rising Civil Rights Issues

IV. **Economic and Cultural Patterns to the Mid-Century**
   A. Population Shifts
   B. Growth in Public Education
   C. Georgia's Creative Heritage of the 20th Century

V. **Politics of Change: Georgia Since the 1950's**
   A. New Leaders: Maddox, King and Carter
   B. Integration in the Schools and Marketplace
   C. Two Party Politics Come to Georgia
   D. Today's Issues — Political, Economic and Social

OBJECTIVES

Students should be able to:

1. Identify major political personalities of the 20th century.

2. Explain the county unit system (1917-1962).

3. Illustrate the impact of the interstate highway system on Georgia population patterns.

4. Discuss the economic shift from rural agrarianism to urban industrialization.

5. Outline the Civil Rights movement for blacks in Georgia from 1948 to 1968.

6. Differentiate changes between the 1945 and 1983 state constitutions.

ACTIVITIES

1. Time line (1900-1983) unlabeled for students to fill in using their texts.

2. Map of Georgia counties: color your congressional district "yellow"; make a list of counties and county seats in your district; research U.S. congressmen from Georgia and write the names in their district; color all counties created after 1900 "red."

3. Field trips (suggestions follow).

4. Have state senator and/or representative visit class.

5. Research life of a leading 20th century Georgian.

6. Interviews with people directly involved in 20th century events.

EVALUATIONS

Written Quiz over Leading 20th Centuries Personalities

Economic Notebook Showing Change in Economy in 20th Century

Oral Reports on Biography

Room Display of Georgia Counties and Cities, with Historical Illustrations.

OTHER SOURCES

Institute of Government — University of Georgia

African-American Family History Association
2077 Bent Creek Way, S.W.
Atlanta, Georgia 30305

Rural Development Center
University of Georgia Extension Service
Tifton, Georgia

BIBLIOGRAPHY

Anderson, William. *The Wild Man From Sugar Creek: The Political Career of Eugene Talmadge.*

Arnall, Ellis. *The Shore Dimly Seen.*

Carter, Jimmy. *Why Not the Best?*

Felton, Rebecca. *Country Life in Georgia in the Days of My Youth.*

Golden, Harry. *A Little Girl Is Dead.*

Grantham, Dewey W. *Hoke Smith and the Politics of the New South.*

Orr, Dorothy. *A History of Education in Georgia.*

Range, Willard. *A Century of Agriculture in Georgia, 1850-1950.*

Raper, A.F. *Preface to Peasantry.*

Saye, A.B. *A Constitutional History of Georgia.*

Woodward, C. Vann. *The Strange Career of Jim Crow.*

_____. *Tom Watson, Agrarian Rebel.*

Favorite Ideas For The Georgia History Class

The Georgia Southwestern seminar participants had an opportunity to make suggestions about class activities, testing, textbooks, resources, teaching methods, etc. Lively exchanges, differences of opinion and sometimes very frank observations were shared to the benefit of all who were a part of the experience. Listed below are several "favorite tips" which may be of value to teachers of Georgia history.

1. Have your Georgia history students write "fan" letters or thank-you letters (individually) to some individual, corporation, site, etc., which is somehow related to a subject under consideration. Stress that this letter not be a "please send me all the information you have" type letter and NEVER have all your students write the same agency, individual, etc., requesting materials. The exercise involves many more significant skills and may be just the personal activity that all students need as individuals.

2. Before your Georgia history class begins, make a sturdy (metal or plastic) template of the outline of the map of Georgia. (The size should fit on standard 8½ x 11 paper.) Students should in turn make their own template from your pattern, and then have them use theirs each time you need to do work that requires the Georgia outline.

3. Students can construct wall hangings of fabric, paper, etc., which depict scenes from Georgia's history or symbols of events and/or persons from Georgia history.

4. Let students develop their own slide show or illustrated lecture for a Georgia history topic. (Instamatic cameras and color slides are almost foolproof.)

5.. Local resources or nearby sites are vital links to Georgia history; have your students help you "inventory" local places to visit, work with you to have good pre-orientation for field trips and significant follow-up to field trips. (You might have them develop "rating scales.")

6. Do not leave music and art out of the story of Georgia's past.

7. Involve students in looking at original "research materials." A newspaper of just 20 years ago is "research

material"; old photos are; old local buildings are. Follow up by having students "write it up"; construct a newspaper of 20-50 or 100 years ago, FOR YOUR LOCAL COMMUNITY, using topics, people, events, places, etc., familiar to the local student.

8. Discuss with your class the issues before Georgia's General Assembly prior to its sessions and do follow-up reading and discussions as actions are taken.

9. Making reports or writing "term papers" can be a waste of time but following good and well-understood guidelines can make these worthwhile.

10. Students can construct a class time line that is maintained as you cover the course. Let them decide where and how it should be displayed and maintained.

11. Have each student develop his/her own time line of his/her life, marking major events in Georgia, U.S. and world history, alongside the birth of his/her own brothers or sisters, moves, etc.

12. In conjunction with field trips or individual student trips to significant sites, let students design and produce travel brochures or information brochures. (Involve artists, idea folk and writers among your students as seems natural.) You should be able to stockpile easily dozens of commercially produced brochures. (Check with Georgia Welcome Centers.) Have these brochures available to students to get ideas and then have them give it a try. Sites may be interested in receiving copies of what your students come up with.

13. MAKE SURE THAT, AT THE END OF THE DAY, THE STUDENTS GO HOME AT LEAST AS TIRED AS YOU ARE!

Resource People and Places For Georgia History

The list that follows is an introduction to a world of good help and ideas for teaching and researching history and culture for Georgia and your community. Please have your students keep in mind that requests for information should be specific and brief and that they should not expect an unlimited amount of time to be devoted by the agency or individual. It is not considered good practice to have *all* your students write the same individual or agency. You can imagine the volume of requests that such practices would produce. In many cases, it is a good idea for you, as the teacher, to make initial contacts in order to evaluate the relative value of your students' writing. When at all possible, it is a nice gesture to enclose a self-addressed, stamped envelope for replies.

An additional note: Some of these agencies and/or individuals might provide good visiting resources for your classes. Be aware, however, that some are paid by their own institutions for such efforts, while others routinely are paid by those who invite them. Many, fortunately, are willing to make visits and offer other services as their contribution to your efforts.

American Association for State
and Local History
708 Berry Road
Nashville, Tennessee 37204

If you teach any state or local history, you need to contact them.

Georgia Historical Society
501 Whitaker Street
Savannah, Georgia 31499

Student memberships are available.

Ga. Dept. of Archives & History
330 Capitol Ave., S.E.
Atlanta, Georgia 30334

Guardians of Georgia's historic records and "Vanishing Georgia" photo collection.

Dept. of Natural Resources
Historic Preservation Section
270 Washington Street, S.E.
Atlanta, Georgia 30334.

Ken Thomas (listed elsewhere) is an excellent contact to help with historic sites and sources.

Ga. Trust for Historic
Preservation
1516 Peachtree St., N.W.
Atlanta, Georgia 30309

Promotes historic preservation in Georgia.

The Martin Luther King, Jr. Center for Non-Violent Social Change, Inc. 449 Auburn Ave., N.E. Atlanta, Georgia 30312	Houses archives, museum of Dr. King and the movement.
Atlanta Historical Society 3101 Andrews Drive, N.W. Atlanta, Georgia 30305	One of the nation's great local historical societies. Beautiful exhibits.
Institute of Government Terrell Hall The University of Georgia Athens, Georgia 30602	Write them for a list of their publications.
Ga. Endowment for the Humanities 1589 Clifton Road, N.E. Emory University Atlanta, Georgia 30322	Always interested in advancing history in Georgia as part of the humanities.
African-American Family History Association c/o Carole Merritt 2077 Bent Creek Way, S.W. Atlanta, Georgia 30305	(See elsewhere.)
Rural Development Center Cooperative Extension Service University of Georgia Tifton, Georgia	Contact them for their publications related especially to statistics of historic importance in Georgia.
Mid-South Humanities Project P.O. Box 23 Middle Tennessee State University Murfreesboro, Tennessee 31732	This group has been very active in projects in state and local history research and teaching throughout the South.
Alice Knierim Ga. Dept. of Archives & History 330 Capitol Avenue, S.E. Atlanta, Georgia 30334	Educational programs leader with Ga. Dept. of Archives.
Virginia Shadron Ga. Dept. of Archives & History 330 Capitol Avenue, S.E. Atlanta, Georgia 30334	A most helpful guide to archives research.
Ken Thomas Ga. Dept of Natural Resources Historic Preservation Section 270 Washington Street, S.E. Atlanta, Georgia 30334	Top genealogist.
Carol Merritt African-American Family History Association 2077 Bent Creek Way, S.W. Atlanta, Georgia 30305	A major Georgia resource for black history information.

The Ga. Directory of Humanities
Scholars
The Ga. Endowment for the
the Humanities
1589 Clifton Road, N.E.
Emory University
Atlanta, Georgia 30322
(404) 329-7500

Lists over 500
humanities scholars who are
interested in assisting humanities
projects, many of which may be
related to Georgia history.

Most of Georgia's college campuses have faculty who are involved in Georgia history to some degree. The following, by no means an inclusive list, is a sampling:

Albany State College..Dr. Lee Formwalt
Armstrong College..Dr. Roger Warlick
Augusta College..Dr. Edward Cashin
Columbus College...Dr. John Lupold
Fort Valley State College............................Dr. Lee Pendergrass
Gainesville Junior College................................Dr. Steve Gurr
Georgia College...Dr. Frank Vinson
Georgia Southern College...........................Dr. Frank Saunders
                                                                     Dr. Ray Shurbutt
Georgia Southwestern College......................Dr. James Bagwell
North Georgia College...Dr. Ray Rensi
University of Georgia...............................Dr. Phinizy Spalding
                                                                 Dr. Kenneth Coleman
Waycross Junior College......................................Dr. Ted Harris

Local History

Using Local History In The Classroom

Teachers are already familiar with the advantages of using local history in the classroom: the availability of sources, the opportunity to develop new skills and the relevancy, and therefore, the popularity of such endeavors with students. In using local history, teachers should relate it to the national and state developments rather than treating it as a separate unit. Additionally, they should try to compare the evolution of a particular town or county to other locations which have had a different history and try to have students understand *why* an area grew in a particular way, not just learn the dates of its development.

The three major sources for researching local history are: (1) published accounts, newspapers and public records; (2) people who lived through a particular experience (subjects for oral history); and (3) the community's built-environment. Published or unpublished accounts are readily available, and different types of documents might be introduced into a classroom in order to familiarize students with the interpretation of historical sources. Oral histories can be a useful source of information, but students should be well-versed in their subject before they approach a potential interviewee. Students should also concentrate on a particular topic rather than merely asking what the "good old days" were like. Teaching the community's history through its buildings can also be extremely rewarding for both teachers and students, but instructors need to do a great deal of preparation. In some locations, the preservation planners attached to the Area Planning and Development Commission will assist teachers in presenting architectural material.

Local History Topics

Teachers can collect their own local history or they can have their students research topics to use in class. In the Columbus College summer seminar, the participants were asked to prepare a project, based on primary sources, which they could use in their classes and which related to the seminar's theme — "Change or Modernization in Twentieth Century Georgia." Given those parameters, most teachers pursued topics dealing with local history. The following excerpts from some of the GEH summer seminar projects are meant to give teachers ideas about topics they and their students can investigate. These projects explored a wide range of topics from farms and mill villages to religion and recreation: their common thread is that they all investigated a limited area and are based on the typical sources available for local history. Further examples, including sources, methodology and application, may be found in *Local History Resources at Your Doorstep, A Manual for Teachers* produced by the Atlanta Historical Society and the Georgia Department of Archives and History.

County Studies

A county represents an excellent unit for study since state and federal governments collect and compile statistics at the county level. A wealth of local data, both historical and contemporary, can be found in any public library or county courthouse. Teachers can have students obtain specific information from the federal census or from publications of state agencies. Then, by using graphs and charts, the students can plot this data over time. These graphs, however, are not the end product. They are meant to raise questions about *why* and *how* changes occurred — questions that can be addressed in class discussions, and in some cases, answered only after further research. As with other local topics, a county should not be studied in isolation but should be compared with surroundings, especially dissimilar counties.

Example 1: Disappearing Farms

One type of county study might measure urbanization by charting social or economic change in a spatial context, i.e., the decline of farms in a county. Such a study should be interesting and relevant to students in the Georgia history class. The students can recognize particular areas of a county, and by visualizing these areas as farms in the recent past, they can appreciate the impact of modernization or urbanization. In conjunction with this study unit, the students might examine what life was like on those farms. Every student may select a particular farm location and investigate that site using a camera and interviews with "old timers." In collecting the data, the students may use state and federal censuses, old county maps, oral history interviews with former farmers, historic photographs of farms and slides of the present condition of the old farm sites.

EXAMPLE 2: SINGLE AGENTS OF MODERNIZATION

In some counties, it is possible to identify a single agent of modernization such as a new large-scale industry or a major highway and to determine its impact. Other topics might include population shifts and developing patterns of home building. In such class projects, students may use population and agricultural statistics, building permits and maps to document the impact of the agent of modernization being studied.

EXAMPLE 3: EVOLUTION OF PUBLIC PARKS

The increase in suburbs has been paralleled by the growth of public parks and recreational facilities. Thus, a Georgia history class may trace the development of public parks in a county. Such types of studies have become more popular among historians as the general public has become more involved in recreational pursuits. In addition to showing students when, where and why their parks were created, this study could also introduce a class to questions involving the growth pattern of a city and the depth and dimensions of segregation. In presenting this material, students may utilize color-coded maps indicating when facilities were built and slides of historic and contemporary views of these sites.

NEIGHBORHOOD STUDIES

Neighborhoods represent excellent laboratories for studying local history. They can be used to introduce students to architectural details, to explain social history in terms of housing patterns and family structure and to illustrate how physical changes have occurred within a community. In selecting a neighborhood to investigate, however, one should not just consider the "historic district" or the row of Victorian and Neo-Classical houses found in most Georgia towns. Do not neglect mill villages, black residential areas and roads that include "strip-development." If possible select an area that incorporates many different types of structures.

Begin by familiarizing the students with the area and its architecture through slide lectures and field trips. Use manuscript censuses and city directories to identify the occupations and the number of people who lived in each house. If available, a Sanborn insurance map could be utilized in conjunction with a manuscript census to correlate the number of occupants to the size of the house. Students may be surprised to learn how many people shared a limited number of rooms. Also, family structure is reflected in the census data. Changes in occupation and family size between census years can pinpoint when a neighborhood entered a transitional period.

When viewing a neighborhood, do not just look at houses. Note the plantings, the trees and the entire streetscape; discuss how these aspects reflect the period when the neighborhood was established. Also investigate the institutions which originally served the neighborhoods — schools, churches, fire stations, etc. — and note how they evolved over time.

EXAMPLE 1: THE TRADITIONAL NEIGHBORHOOD

In studying the traditional neighborhood, the Georgia history class may pose several important questions to guide its research and then seek information to document its answers. The questions may include but not be limited to the following: what happened in the neighborhood, why did it happen, what have been the consequences and what patterns appear likely in the future? Such a study will allow students an opportunity to research the origins of a particular neighborhood, noting its specific social, economic and physical characteristics, and to determine the nature and extent of change which has occurred. Additionally, this type of project can allow a teacher to discuss a wide range of topics.

EXAMPLE 2: MILL VILLAGES

Mill villages, usually associated with the textile industry, were built throughout Georgia in the late 19th and early 20th centuries. Investigation of this type housing incorporates features of traditional neighborhood studies, and such studies can also raise questions about paternalism and the relationship between labor and management in the state's most prevalent industry.

Oral history can be used in studying any neighborhood, but it is especially relevant to mill villages since the experiences of all the workers were so similar. Teachers who use mill villages as a study unit can raise questions about the living conditions of workers. How did their lives compare with those of tenant farmers? What freedoms did the workers surrender in order to live in the company's houses?

EXAMPLE 3: SEGREGATED NEIGHBORHOODS

In most urban areas and even in smaller towns, the racial or ethnic composition of neighborhoods has shifted over time. Those changes can be studied and plotted using maps and publications of city planning departments along with city directories that indicate race. Using these types of sources, the teacher or students of a Georgia history class may study the patterns of segregated housing in white and black neighborhoods, comparing them with contemporary housing patterns. Other topics for study may include schools, land ownership, population density and recreational and social facilities.

RELIGIOUS STUDIES

Analytical investigations of local religious institutions can reveal significant social changes. Using primary materials, including oral histories, the Georgia history teacher or class can determine the social contexts of the origins of religious denominations in a community. Even more specifically, a class project might focus on the growth or decline of religious denominations by charting statistics on church attendance and membership and doing interviews with the ministers of the various denominations.

AASLH How To Guides for Local History

The following is a list of "how to" guides that are available from the American Association for State and Local History:

1. Writing Local History: The Use of Social Statistics.

2. Designing Your Exhibits: Seven Ways to Look at an Artifact.

3. Methods of Research for the Amateur Historian

4. Tape-Recording Local History

5. The History of a House: How to Trace It

6. Ethnic Groups: Research for the Local Society

7. From Memory to History: Using Oral Sources for Historical Research.

8. Preparing Exhibits: Methods, Materials, and Bibliography

9. Videotaping Local History

10. Old Movies: A Source of Local History Programs

11. Historic Houses as Learning Laboratories: Seven Teaching Strategies

12. Compiling Local History Bibliographies

13. Local History Manuscripts: Sources, Uses, and Preservation

14. Historical Markers: Planning Local Programs

15. History for Young People: Projects and Activities

16. Black Genealogy: Basic Steps to Research

17. Using Memoirs to Write Local History

18. Collecting Historical Artifacts: An Aid for Small Museums

19. Planning Exhibits: From Concept to Opening

20. Planning Museum Tours: For School Groups

BLACK HISTORY

BLACK HISTORY IN THE GEORGIA HISTORY CLASS

Increasingly, the curriculum of Georgia history in our schools is becoming more accurately reflective of the *total* story of Georgia's past as more frequent and worthwhile efforts are made to enhance the study and teaching of such elements of Georgia history as the history of black Georgians. During the seminars at Columbus, Georgia Southern and Georgia Southwestern Colleges, considerable attention was given to the urgency of moving toward a more cross-cultural and ethnically-balanced approach to Georgia history. The seminars devoted several sessions to frank discussions of race as an historic and classroom issue in Georgia history, and in the process, many of the participants gained new insights which may further facilitate progress in what is sometimes a troubled area for classroom teachers of Georgia history. One of the best ways to incorporate black history, and in the process educate all of your students to appreciation for the multi-ethnic nature of our state's history, is to have students do research and write about ethnically-based subjects. While many see the history of any particular ethnic group as simply a thread in the wider tapestry of history, it sometimes gives better focus and understanding to single out a distinctly ethnic element, examine it on its own and *then* examine it in the context of the wider culture.

RESEARCHING BLACK HISTORY

Georgia history students will seldom produce research that breaks new grounds, but a vital part of the exercise in teaching Georgia history is to provide exposure for your students to the historic resources of their community. The nature of record keeping in the American South up until the very recent past has been such as to provide an unusually rich mine for investigations of black history. An exercise that could possibly be of value for your students would be that of having them locate official records in their community which identified citizens by race. Based on this very elementary research (a visit to the Clerk of the Probate Court), students may be led to ask questions about how and why particular records were maintained by county government and what are the implications for politics, society and race in their community's past.

Example 1: Black Politics During Reconstruction

In one of the Georgia Southern seminar projects, a participant examined black politics during Reconstruction, focusing on three of Georgia's most famous black political figures of the late 19th century: Henry McNeal Turner, Aaron A. Bradley and Tunis G. Campbell. A comparative study of the various historical accounts of these or other black politicians would make an interesting project in a Georgia history class. Perhaps your students could examine the first historical accounts of black political figures, ask themselves if they see bias, compare the first accounts with more recent views and again look for bias, making comparisons that might bring a sense of balance and appreciation for the changing nature of history.

Example 2: The Black Church

Churches are an important part of all Georgia communities, and they have been especially central in the development of black communities. Students traditionally lack information about the history of even their own churches, let alone those of others. A research project for students, perhaps in groups, might involve a combination of interviews, talks by local communicants in various churches and traditional library-based research of secondary sources. The process might be most worthwhile if students researched churches other than their own. In this kind of class activity, both students and teachers begin to deal with history in its most vital manifestations.

Example 3: Black Education in Georgia

The subject of education for both white and black Georgians is a good one for students to investigate, and it is another one of those topics in which localism is an important possibility. Changes in education, physical as well as philosophical and racial, are obvious topics to which many local residents are able to speak in interviews, for virtually no one in a community can remain unaffected by local education. Students might benefit from research about education in their community. If and when the history of local education involves the issue of race, the students will, of necessity, be drawn into that topic. In the process and with careful direction, better understanding of the local community (a noble educational goal it would seem) is a likely by-product.

EXAMPLE 4: DISFRANCHISEMENT OF BLACKS

In the Columbus College seminar, one of the participants examined tax and voting records to research the disfranchisement of blacks in Liberty, McIntosh, Tattnall and Toombs Counties. Students in the Georgia history class could undertake a similar project about their own county. One of the most valuable benefits in having students look for political statistics may be that of having them understand the scope and content of public records in a given community or related to a given topic. The city hall, county courthouse, school superintendent's office, etc., provide excellent opportunities for students to see the raw materials from which history is made.

EXAMPLE 5: RESIDENTIAL DISTRIBUTION OF BLACKS

In larger communities, one of the possibilities for studying race relations and the process of integration in modern Georgia is that of examining neighborhood residence patterns and their changes in racial composition. Using the city directory and the city's Comprehensive Development Plan, for example, a Columbus College seminar participant graphically identified areas predominantly occupied by whites and blacks in Columbus for the periods 1900, 1950 and 1980. In addition to leading students to new research and resource possibilities, studies like this one are excellent for development and interpretation of maps, charts and related illustrations. While race may be the primary focus of such a study, the approach may also be applied to such topics as declining downtown commercial centers, mall development and its impact and the influence of highways or other public facilities on community development, economic growth and social change.

BIOGRAPHY

The Biographical Approach to Georgia History

Much of the teaching of Georgia history over the years has been based on the study of the lives of famous Georgians. The biographic approach to history is almost as old as history itself and may be found in the study of U.S., European or any other history. The "Great Man Theory" of history has been expoused and criticized by generations of students and teachers, but despite its obvious limitations, the study of human lives remains a favorite tool for understanding the past.

Biographical Research in the Georgia History Class

Georgia is fortunate to have a flavorful array of personalities throughout its history, and any teacher of Georgia history is familiar with the political, social and cultural leaders from Oglethorpe and Tomo-chi-chi to Rebecca Felton, Tom Watson and Eugene Talmadge to Andrew Young and Martin Luther King, Jr. Students frequently are more comfortable doing papers and projects on the lives of famous people than on other topics. Organization may seem easier, materials may be more readily available, and personal identification with or admiration for an individual may make the effort more pleasant and meaningful for the student. All too often, however, students do little more than "cut and paste" a biographical sketch together, without much digesting, analysis or fitting their hero or heroine into the wider tapestry of Georgia history or local history. The following ideas from summer seminar participants may be helpful as teachers and students turn to biography as a means to understanding Georgia's history.

Example 1: Famous Georgians

Teachers who would like their students to have experience with writing research papers might well consider the biographical paper as a good beginning point, but there are distinct advantages to giving a biographical paper some special focal point, i.e., answering a specific question or tracing the development of an idea. All too frequently, biographical papers follow a standard pattern of relating birth, youth, education, early years, career, family and death. To have your students get to know that their subject's life was not just cut and dry and that virtually all important historical figures are the subject of interpretation and debate is a commendable objective. Once the element of questioning has been established, then the student might do a paper based on his own efforts to answer the question(s). He can find sources, look for conflicting views, try to understand the bases of these views and make judgments about the relative importance or credibility of these views based, among other things, on such considerations as the backgrounds of those who put them forward, the time they were presented, etc. It is not too much to ask an eighth grade student to draw some conclusions once the research has been done, for the end product of such a study would be considerably more valuable than just another paraphrasing of standard biographical data.

Example 2: Group Biography Projects

Another possibly meaningful approach to having students do biographical papers is illustrated by two Georgia Southern seminar participants who studied a group of Georgians — United States Senators. The group biography is an established method of examining the composition and nature of specific groups. Reformers, political figures, religious figures and cultural leaders have been considered in such research and publication. Some of these studies make considerable use of comparative data while others stick to traditional narrative or descriptive treatments. In either case, conclusions are the end product which makes the undertaking worthwhile. Further, in recent years, very sophisticated computer-based analyses of political behavior among given groups have enjoyed considerable attention in the historical profession. Controversial issues such as the profitability of slavery and the destiny of the Old Whig party have enjoyed renewed investigation, in part, based on group biographical investigations. While your Georgia history students might not be inclined to reach for that level of sophistication, there is the basis here for making some important points about the nature of research and historical evidence, subjects perhaps too frequently shortchanged in the teaching of history at every level.

A common complaint from teachers in middle grades and secondary schools as well as in colleges and universities is that student papers are more often than not disappointing excursions into "copying information." The old "stack of encyclopedias" approach to research is nothing new to any of us. Group biography, however, may be a means by which the teacher can convert the "copy syndrome" into worthwhile research, at least at the very basic level.

Once you or your students have determined an identifiable group (writers, governors, sports figures, etc.) of Georgians to research, have the students research comparative data, record the information in a graphic way and then have them attempt to convert this raw data into some conclusions. On what data do they base these? Rather than having students copy the narrative description of the life of someone, therefore, the students have the assignment of locating (perhaps within some fairly simple and commonplace narrative source) basic data about not just one figure but a number of individuals with some common thread. It is likely in this kind of assignment that your students will discover a great truism in the process: "facts" are not always commonly accepted. There is nothing like finding a conflict in the dates, times, ages or other quantitative data and facing the question of determining which one is right.

Group biography may be pursued in other ways. Let students identify groups of individual Georgians with some common tie (religion, race, chronology, etc.), chiefly based on the people referred to in their textbook, and then have the students do brief sketches, looking for common factors between and among individuals.

EXAMPLE 3: BIOGRAPHY OF GEORGIANS IN PERIODS/EVENTS

Georgia's history is largely the story of the lives of its outstanding citizens. During the 18th century, the focus of much of this history is to be found on those individuals who played significant parts in the establishment of independence from England. During the mid-19th century, Georgia's history is in no small part the story of the War Between the States, its civilization and military leadership and the postwar roles for those leaders. Turn-of-the-century Georgia history is often seen in the lives and careers of Georgians who represented a transitional generation. During the summer of 1983, participants in the three seminars produced a number of papers which focused on Georgians who fit into these general patterns.

Most students around Georgia will have little access to original 18th century sources, but working with a figure from this period might be helpful to them in understanding the changing availability of materials as one moves through time. Having a student or several students choose to work on an 18th century topic, others on the 19th century and still others on 20th century subjects might be most valuable for what the experience can teach about where history comes from. Traditional straightforward biographical studies become more meaningful as students consider how we get to know people who were important to Georgia generations ago.

Nineteenth century Georgia biography offers a richer variety of possible sources, and throughout that part of Georgia which was settled prior to 1850, there are usually some interesting sources, chiefly newspapers, which can give the students some research experience. Also, the popularity of some individuals usually results in a considerable volume of publications and provides possibilities for a wider variety of interpretations of their lives. When autobiographical or other writings by the subject are available, it is important to have students consider these as primary sources; for having available something of the persons themselves in the form of their own writings is an excellent source even for the novice writer of a biographical sketch.

When working on a 20th century figure, the researcher-writer is fortunate to have available a vast collection of Georgia newspapers. The University of Georgia Library Newspaper Collection is readily available in microfilm, and your local or regional library or certainly area college libraries can provide a computer print-out of availability of particular newspapers. Virtually every county, if not every town, has some nearby newspaper at intervals in the 20th century. While biographical studies are tremendously enhanced by the availability of these papers, it is reasonable to expect and hope that students, once they turn to newspapers for research, will be lured into any number of possible research topics, discovering that biography, for instance, does not have to be simply the rehashing of a life of some well-known Georgian. It might well reveal more about the life of some more obscure local but certainly significant figure from Georgia's past. The vast majority of Georgians have not been the subject of even a biographical sketch, let alone a full-fledged biography. Perhaps the greatest value of having students even consider biography research is for them to see how it's been done in order that they attempt to do one from scratch.

EXAMPLE 4: CREATIVE BIOGRAPHICAL RESEARCH — DRAMATIZING GEORGIA'S COLONIAL HISTORY AT A "TOWN MEETING" ASSEMBLY

During Georgia's semiquincentenary, famous Georgians were the subjects of speeches, articles, books and a variety of special dramatic programs. When all is said and done, Georgia's 250 years of history is largely the story of the lives of Georgians, and it is neither unusual nor inappropriate that we turn to individuals in celebration of the state's history. Students across Georgia got involved in the celebration in a number of ways. Probably thousands of term papers about famous Georgians or book reports on the biographies and autobiographies of notable Georgias were produced. No doubt many of these were well done, exciting for the students, pleasant for the teachers and generally worthwhile as exercises in basic research and writing. In some instances, however, efforts were made to go a step beyond the traditional study and reporting on Georgia biography. While there were no doubt a great many similar projects, one of the outstanding efforts in creative biography took place in Georgia's colonial capital, Savannah. Thanks to the generosity of Mrs. Frank A. Hollowbush, The Georgia Semiquincentenary Commission, Mr. and Mrs. Leopold Adler, II, and the Savannah College of Art and design, students and teachers of Georgia history can share in this very special project, a series of "living history lessons developed by the Heritage Classroom Program at The Massie Heritage Interpretation Center" in Savannah.

The fundamental concept of this project is the teaching of history by way of "Town Meetings" in which historic figures come to life. The following from the "Description of a Town Meeting" outlines the idea:

> *A town meeting is an assembly with a program which has been carefully planned and researched. The central figure at the meeting is a person who influenced the Georgia Colony in its early years. The meeting takes place at a definite time in colonial history. Teachers and students must study the period and the colonial character who will be featured at the meeting.*

....The assembly may include appropriate musical selections, songs, poems and skits by students as well as the featured attraction: an address by the colonial character, which is followed by an information question and answer period.

In carrying out the project in Savannah, the Massie Center participants focused on colonial figures important to the immediate area; obviously, other areas of the state and other periods of time would easily fit the scheme. In the Savannah program, James Oglethorpe, Tomo-chi-chi, Mary Musgrove, Paul Amatis, Dr. Samuel Nunes, the Reverend Andrew Bryan and the Reverend Martin Boltzium were the characters.

While the Savannah program involved the general public as well as students and included a variety of activities, the idea may be reduced in scope and content to the basically biographical research and application elements. At the Massie Center, students developed the program and the materials related to the colonial characters, and for each character, a three-part, brief collection was developed: a biographical sketch, a fact sheet and a bibliography. The purpose of the development of this material was in part to expose students to the basic notions and facts about the character and to have the students get a "feel" for the character's style, ideas and role in early Georgia. This use of biographical research to the end of appreciating a characterization in a dramatic reenactment setting may be considered an adjunct to an elaborate "role-play" approach to the study of history. In this process, the end product is not simply a neat but probably unimaginative biographical sketch but a "store of information" on which the student may draw in the context of dramatic characterization.

Perhaps too frequently, we have students produce a written product, and even if we ask them to read the product to their classmates, we have not really called on them to "use" the material they have gathered, the information they have collected or the ideas they have gained in the process. The coupling of traditional library research, calling in the process of good solid reading and writing skills, with spontaneous interpretations and utilization of newly acquired information and ideas injects a potentially significant element into the biographical process.

RESOURCE BIBLIOGRAPHY

Following each of the articles in Part I and the chronological topical outlines in Part II of the sourcebook is a brief bibliography on Georgia history. This general bibliography, therefore, is designed to provide additional basic sources that may be helpful in planning any or all parts of courses and/or projects related to Georgia history. These bibliographic sources are subdivided into several categories, and taken as a whole, they are in no way intended to represent an exhaustive list.

GEORGIA HISTORY TEXTS

Bonner, James C. *The Georgia Story*. Oklahoma City: Harlow Publishing Corporation, 1961.

Coleman, Kenneth. *Georgia History in Outline*. 3rd ed. Athens, Ga.: University of Georgia Press, 1978.

———————————. *A History of Georgia*. Athens, Ga.: University of Georgia Press, 1977. (Newest College Level Text).

Hepburn, Lawrence R. *The Georgia History Book*. Athens, Ga.: University of Georgia Press, 1982. (Newest Middle Grades Text).

McCullar, Bernice. *This Is Your Georgia*. Rev. ed. Montgomery, Ala.: Viewpoints Publications, 1972.

GENERAL HISTORIES OF GEORGIA

Bartley, Numan V. *The Creation of Modern Georgia*. Athens, Ga.: University of Georgia Press, 1983.

Bonner, James C. *A History of Georgia Agriculture, 1732-1860*. Athens, Ga.: University of Georgia Press, 1964.

Coulter, E. Merton. *Georgia: A Short History*. 2nd ed. Chapel Hill: University of North Carolina Press, 1960.

Johnson, Amanda. *Georgia as Colony and State*. Atlanta: Cherokee Publishing Co., 1960.

Joiner, Oscar, et al. *A History of Public Education in Georgia, 1734-1976*. Columbia, S.C.: R.L. Bryan, 1979.

King, Spencer B. *Georgia Voices: A Documentary History to 1872.* Athens, Ga.: University of Georgia Press, 1966.

Konter, Sherry. *Vanishing Georgia.* Athens, Ga.: University of Georgia Press, 1982.

Orr, Dorothy. *A History of Education in Georgia.* Chapel Hill: University of North Carolina Press, 1950.

Range, Willard. *A Century of Georgia Agriculture, 1850-1950.* Athens, Ga.: University of Georgia Press, 1954.

Saye, Albert B. *A Constitutional History of Georgia, 1832-1945.* Athens, Ga.: University of Georgia Press, 1948.

Stevens, William B. *A History of Georgia from Its Discovery by Europeans to the Adoption of the Present Constitution in MDCCXCVIII.* Savannah, Ga.: Beehive Press, 1972.

Topical/Period Histories

Abbot, Belle K. *The Cherokee Indians in Georgia.* University, Ala.: Confederate Publishing Co., 1980.

Bryan, Thomas Conn. *Confederate Georgia.* Athens, Ga.: University of Georgia Press, 1953.

Coleman, Kenneth. *The American Revolution in Georgia, 1763-1789.* Athens, Ga.: University of Georgia Press, 1958.

_____. *Colonial Georgia: A History.* New York: Scribner, 1976.

Coulter, E. Merton. *Negro Legislators in Georgia During Reconstruction.* Athens, Ga.: Georgia Historical Society, 1968.

Dittmer, John. *Black Georgia in the Progressive Era, 1900-1920.* Urbana, Illinois: University of Illinois Press, 1977.

Drago, Edmund L. *Black Politicians and Reconstruction in Georgia: A Splendid Failure.* Baton Rouge: Louisiana State University Press, 1982.

Gordon, Asa H. *The Georgia Negro: A History.* Reprint ed. Spartanburg, S.C.: Reprint Co., 1972.

Hornsby, Alton. *The Negro in Revolutionary Georgia.* Atlanta: Georgia Commission for the National Bicentennial Celebration and Georgia Department of Education, 1977.

Jones, Jacqueline. *Soldiers of Light and Love: Northern Teachers and Georgia Blacks, 1865-1873.* Chapel Hill: University of North Carolina Press, 1980.

Killion, Ronald G. *Georgia and the Revolution.* Atlanta: Cherokee Publishing Co., 1975.

Strickland, Reba C. *Religion and the State in Georgia in the Eighteenth Century.* New York: AMS Press, Inc., 1967.

Sweat, Edward F. *Economic Status of Free Blacks in Antebellum Georgia.* Atlanta: Southern Center for Studies in Public Policy, 1974.

Wood, Betty. *Slavery in Colonial Georgia.* Athens, Ga.: University of Georgia Press, 1984.

LOCAL HISTORY TEACHING AND PROJECTS

America the Beautiful Fund. *Old Glory: A Pictorial Report on the Grass Roots History Movement and the First Hometown History Primer.* New York: Warner Paperback Library, 1973.

Bonner, James C. *A Student's Guide to Localized History.* New York: Teachers College Press of Columbia University, 1965.

Kyvig, David E. and Marty, Myron A. *Nearby History: Exploring the Past Around You.* Nashville, Tenn.: American Association for the State and Local History, 1982.

Merritt, Carole. *Homecoming: African-American Family History in Georgia.* Atlanta: African-American Family History Association, 1982.

Metcalf, Fay D. and Downer, Matthew T. *Using Local History in the Classroom.* Nashville, Tenn.: American Association for State and Local History, 1982.

_____. *Teaching Local History: Trends, Tips and Resources.* Boulder, Colo.: Social Science Education Consortium, Inc., 1977.

Northrup, Terry and Crawley, Nora S., eds. *Crackers and Red Suspenders: Teaching Local History and Government in Georgia.* Atlanta, Ga.: Georgia Council for the Social Sciences, 1976.

Weitzman, David. *My Backyard History Book*. Boston: Little, Brown and Co., 1975.

_____. *Underfoot: An Everyday Guide to Exploring the American Past.* New York: Charles Scribner's Sons, 1976.

BIBLIOGRAPHIES AND RESEARCH GUIDES

Bonner, John Wyatt. *Bibliography of Georgia Authors. 1949-1965.* Athens, Ga.: University of Georgia Press, 1966.

Davis, Robert S. *Research in Georgia.* Easley, S.C.: Southern Historical Press, 1981.

Dorsey, James E. and Rowland, Arthur Ray. *A Bibliography of the Writings on Georgia History, 1900-1970.* Rev. ed. Spartanburg, S.C.: Reprint Co., 1978.

Dorsey, James E. *Bibliography of the Writings on Georgia History: A Supplement.* Swainsboro, Ga.: Magnolia Press, 1983.

_____. *Georgia Genealogy and Local History: A Bibliography.* Spartanburg, S.C.: Reprint Co., 1983.

Merritt, Carole. *Historic Black Resources.* Atlanta: Georgia Department of Natural Resources, 1985.

Purdie, Helen, comp. *Georgia Bibliography: County History.* Atlanta: Georgia Department of Education, 1979.

Simpson, John E. *Georgia History: A Bibliography.* Metuchen, N.J.: Scarecrow Press, 1976.

PERIODICALS

Annals of Georgia

Atlanta

Atlanta Historical Bulletin

Atlanta Historical Journal

Atlanta Journal-Constitution Magazine

Atlanta Journal Magazine

Augusta Magazine

Brown's Guide to Georgia

Georgia Historical Quarterly

Georgia Journal

Georgia Life

Georgia Magazine

Georgia Pioneers

Georgia Review

Georgia Social Science Journal

Journal of Southern History

Journal of Southwest Georgia History

Richmond County History

West Georgia Studies in the Social Sciences

APPENDIX

CONTRIBUTORS

ROGER G. BRANCH, SR. is Professor and Chairman of the Department of Sociology and Anthropology at Georgia Southern College in Statesboro, Georgia. He received the A.B. degree in Journalism and the M.A. and Ph.D. degrees in Sociology from the University of Georgia, and he holds the B.D. and Th.M. degrees in Religion from the Southeastern Baptist Theological Seminary. His publications include two books and eleven articles. A major area of his scholarly interests is the rural South, its social history and lifeways, with particular emphasis on Southern Georgia. A frequent resource scholar for GEH programs, he also directed the acclaimed "Catface Country: The World of the Turpentiner," a GEH project.

HOLLIS L. CATE, Professor of English at Georgia Southern College in Statesboro, Georgia, holds the A.B. degree from Presbyterian College and the M.A. and Ph.D. degrees from the University of Georgia. He has published over a dozen notes and articles in scholarly journals, including the *Markham Review, College Literature* and *Hartford Studies in Literature*. Professor Cate's areas of specialization are American Literature and Modern Drama.

KENNETH COLEMAN, Professor Emeritus of History at the University of Georgia, is a native of Decatur, Georgia. He received the A.B. and M.A. degrees from the University of Georgia and the Ph.D. degree from the University of Wisconsin in 1953. The "Dean of Georgia Historians," Professor Coleman was on the faculty of the University of Georgia from 1949-1976 and specialized in Georgia History. Most of his publications focus on eighteenth century Georgia, and among his books, published alone or in conjunction with others, are: *A History of Georgia, Georgia History in Outline, Colonial Georgia: A History, The American Revolution in Georgia, 1763-1789, The Colonial Records of the State of Georgia* (7 vols, edited) *and The Dictionary of Georgia Biography.*

GILBERT C. FITE is the Richard B. Russell Professor of History at the University of Georgia. A native of South Dakota, he received his B.A. and M.A. degrees from the University of South Dakota and his Ph.D. degree from the University of Missouri. He has authored or co-authored 16 books and some 50 articles, including his two latest books: *American Farmers: The New Minority* (1981) and *Cotton Fields No More: Georgia Agriculture, 1865-1980* (1984). In 1974, he served as President of the Southern Historical Association, and he is currently writing a biography of Senator Richard B. Russell of Georgia.

WAYNE FLYNT is Hollifield Professor of Southern History at Auburn University. He received his A.B. degree from Samford University in 1961 and his M.S. and Ph.D. degrees from Florida State University in 1962 and 1965 respectively. He is the author of five books, including *Dixie's Forgotten People: The South's Poor Whites*, and his books have won a number of awards, including the Rembert Patrick Award for the Best Book on Florida History, the Award of Merit from the American Association for State and Local History and the Book of the Year Award from the Mississippi Council for Christian Social Action. In 1983, he was inducted into the Alabama Academy of Distinguished Authors.

CHARLOTTE A. FORD, Associate Professor of History at Georgia Southern College in Statesboro, Georgia, holds the A.B.J. degree from the University of Georgia and the M.A. degree in History from Georgia Southern College. Her areas of specialization are Georgia, women and the South. The author of "Tomlinson Fort" in *The Dictionary of Georgia Biography* and "Eliza Frances Andrews (1840-1931), Practical Botanist" in the *Georgia Historical Quarterly*, Spring, 1976, she has also given papers at local, state and regional professional meetings.

WALTER J. FRASER, JR. is Professor and Chairman of the Department of History at Georgia Southern College in Statesboro, Georgia. He holds the B.A. degree from the University of Virginia, the M.A. from East Carolina University and the Ph.D. from the University of Tennessee. Prior to joining the Georgia Southern College faculty, he taught at The Citadel for 13 years. Professor Fraser is the author of over two dozen articles and reviews which have appeared in such journals as the *Virginia Magazine of History and Biography, Journal of Southern History* and *Journal of American History*. He is coeditor of *From the Old South to the New: Essays on the*

Transitional South (1981), *The Southern Enigma: Essays on Race, Class, and Folk Culture* (1983) and *The Web of Southern Social Relations: Women, Family, and Education* (1985).

CHARLES STEPHEN GURR, an Ellaville, Georgia native, is a graduate of Georgia Southwestern Junior College, Peabody Teachers College of Vanderbilt University and the University of Georgia where he received the Ph.D. degree in History in 1973. Formerly Professor of History and Chairman of the Department of History and Division of Arts and Sciences at Georgia Southwestern College where he taught for eighteen years, Dr. Gurr has served as a consultant or board member for a number of regional and state historical boards and agencies and is currently associated with the Georgia Historical Society and the Georgia Trust for Historic Preservation. He is coeditor with Kenneth Coleman of the two-volume *Dictionary of Georgia Biography* and has published in the *Journal of Southern History, American Historical Review* and *Journal of American History.*

LESLIE S. HOUGH is Director of the Special Collections Department (Southern Labor Archives, University Archives, Popular Music Collection and Rare Book Collection) at Georgia State University. He received his B.A. degree from Olivet Nazarene College and his M.A. and Ph.D. degrees in History from the University of Virginia. An Associate Professor at Georgia State University, Dr. Hough teaches in the Labor Studies Program and the Colleges of Arts and Sciences and Public and Urban Affairs. Among his many professional activities, he has held several leadership positions in the Society of Georgia Archivists, co-directed the Ohio Labor History Project (1975-1977) and served as a consultant for the Center for the Study of Southern Culture. He is the author of biographical sketches in *The Dictionary of Georgia Biography,* coeditor of *Southern Workers and Their Unions (1982)* and co-author of articles which have appeared in *Georgia Archive, Manuscript* and *Labor History.*

JOHN S. LUPOLD, Professor of History at Columbus College, received his B.A. degree from Wofford College and his M.A. and Ph.D. from the University of South Carolina. Since his arrival in Columbus in 1970, he has focused his research on the city's industrial development. Co-founder of the Columbus College Archives and involved in historic preservation at the local and state levels, Dr. Lupold wrote a brief history, *Columbus 1825-1978,* for the city's sesquincentennial celebration and prepared the National Historic Landmark nomination for the Columbus Riverfront Industrial District. His publications have appeared in the *Georgia Historical Quarterly, Provenance, Urban Georgia, The Dictionary of Georgia Biography* and *The Encyclopedia of Southern Culture.*

CHARLTON MOSELEY is Professor of History at Georgia Southern College in Statesboro, Georgia. An alumnus of Georgia Southern where he earned both his B.S. and M.A. degrees, Professor Moseley received his Ph.D. in American History from the University of Georgia in 1968. He has published a number of articles in the *Georgia Historical Quarterly,* most of them on such topics as the Ku Klux Klan and lynching in Georgia in the early twentieth century. Additionally, he has contributed numerous biographical sketches to the *Encyclopedia of Southern History* and *The Dictionary of Georgia Biography.*

V. RICHARD PERSICO, JR. is Assistant Professor in the Department of Sociology and Anthropology at Georgia Southern College in Statesboro, Georgia. He holds the B.A. degree in Anthropology from Rhodes College and the M.A. and Ph.D. degrees in Social Anthropology from the University of Georgia. His areas of special interest include the ethnohistory of the Southeastern Indians, ethnology of the American South and modernization and change among rural peoples. Dr. Persico has served as a Humanities scholar for numerous projects supported by the Georgia Endowment for the Humanities.

DELMA E. PRESLEY is Director of the Georgia Southern Museum and Professor of English at Georgia Southern College in Statesboro, Georgia. The Toccoa, Georgia native has been on the faculty of Georgia Southern College since 1969, the year he received his Ph.D. from the Graduate Institute of the Liberal Arts of Emory University. His publications include *Dr. Bullie's Notes* (1976), *Okefenokee Album* (1981) and numerous articles and essays in anthologies and journals of history and literary criticism. Since 1971, he has directed seven projects funded by the Georgia Endowment for the Humanities, and in 1982, he directed "Project RAFT: Restoring Altamaha Folklife Traditions," funded by a major grant from the National Endowment for the Humanities.

R. FRANK SAUNDERS, JR., Professor of History at Georgia Southern College in Statesboro, Georgia, holds the Ph.D. degree from the University of Georgia. Besides Georgia History, his specializations include U.S. Colonial, Afro-

American and Southern History. He is the co-author of *Swamp Water* and *Wiregrass* (1984), coeditor of *The Web of Southern Social Relations* (1985) and author of numerous articles and reviews which have appeared in publications such as *The Dictionary of Georgia Biography, Georgia Historical Quarterly* and *Atlanta Historical Journal.*

A. ELIZABETH TAYLOR, now retired and living in Columbus, Georgia, received her B.A. degree from the University of Georgia, her M.A. from the University of North Carolina (Chapel Hill) and her Ph.D. from Vanderbilt University. From 1943-1981, she taught history at Texas Women's University (formerly Texas State College for Women) in Denton. She is the author of *The Woman Suffrage Movement in Tennessee* and has contributed articles to many journals, including the *Journal of Southern History, North Carolina Historical Review, The Dictionary of Georgia Biography* and *Arkansas Historical Quarterly.* Currently, she is completing an article on woman suffrage for the forthcoming *Handbook of Texas History.*

1983 Summer Seminar Participants
GEH Seminars on Georgia History
Columbus College

Barron, Ernestine W.
Columbus

Bohannon, Linda
Columbus

Creek, James H.
Columbus

Fineran, Kathleen T.
Columbus

Harrison, William G.
St. Simons Island

Hooks, Christine
Tennille

Kimbro, Barbara G.
Columbus

Madray, C. Ashley
Jesup

Matthews, Becky
Junction City

Myers, Whitney L.
Griffin

Nash, Gene A.
Vidalia

Parrish, Delayne LaRee
Funstion

Robinson, Harriet Ann
Columbus

Scarbrough, Robert G. Jr.
Columbus

Steadham, Zan S.
Temple

Swann, James Rocky
Butler

Taylor, Pamela S.
Columbus

White, Walter G.
Columbus

Wojciechowski, Kenneth R.
Columbus

Georgia Southern College

Boatright, Jerry
Alma

Childers, Martha Dean
Statesboro

Cook, Jan S.
Statesboro

Edgy, David Lyman
Baxley

Futch, Caroline E.
Statesboro

Gilmer, Uretha
Columbus

Harrison, Robert Louis
Statesboro

Lewis, Jeffrey Daryl
Reidsville

Love, Lynn
Dublin

Sanders, Gary
Statesboro

Smalls, Mary L.
Savannah

Tomblin, Doris
Hagan

Welden, Charles M.
Dudley

Whitaker, Regina Evelyn
McIntyre

Winsell, Keith A.
Atlanta

Braxton, Verdel Miller
Savannah

Hurt, Gloria W.
Savannah

Wall, Marilyn J.
Statesboro

Willingham, T.A.
Rockmart

Pollard, Carolyn T.
Alamo

GEORGIA SOUTHWESTERN COLLEGE

Anderson, Alan
Americus

Anderson, Emily
Valdosta

Barbree, Carolyn B.
Albany

Crockett, Winnie
Columbus

Douglas, Melvin Lonnie
Columbus

Fort, Allen B.
Valdosta

Harris, Thomas
Albany

Holton, William Patrick
Leesburg

Hudson, Gordon Bradley
Juniper

Jordan, Darryl
McDonough

Lavender, Doris D.
Fort Valley

Lloyd, William L.
Woodland

Robinson, Evelyn
Fort Valley

Rowland, Douglas Fairbanks
Columbus

Rush, Randy
Perry

Shadrick, Charles Harold
Morris

Wade, Roslyn F.
Buena Vista

Welch, Susan Parker
Americus

Whitson, Edwin
Albany

About the Editor

James L. Hill, a native of Meigs, Georgia (Thomas County), is a graduate of Fort Valley State College, Atlanta University and the University of Iowa where he received the Ph.D. in American Civilization in 1976. From 1964-68, he taught English and French in the public schools of Winder, Georgia and Sparta, Georgia. Subsequently, he taught at Paine College and Benedict College, where he also served as Chairman of the Department of English; and since 1977, he has been employed at Albany State College where he is Professor of English and currently serves both as Chairman of the Department of English and as Dean of the School of Arts and Sciences.

Professor Hill's affiliation with the Georgia Endowment for the Humanities (GEH) began in 1977 after he joined the Albany State College faculty. That same school year, he directed a GEH project entitled "The Literacy Crisis in the Schools," which was a state-wide series of one-day workshops on public school education. In 1980, he was appointed to a four-year term on the GEH Board of Directors, and in 1982 and 1983, he served respectively as Vice-Chairman and Chairman of GEH. At the end of his four-year term with GEH, he was elected to a three-year term on the board of the National Federation of State Humanities Councils and is currently liaison between GEH and the Federation. The summer seminars which resulted in *A Sourcebook for Teachers of Georgia History* were initiated during his tenure as GEH Chairman.

His contributions to the Humanities extend beyond his work with state councils. A former member of the Executive Committees of the National Council of Teachers of English (NCTE) and the Conference on College Composition and Communication (CCCC), Professor Hill also served as Chair of CCCC in 1982. Currently, he is a member of the NCTE College Section Committee and President of the South Atlantic Association of Departments of English (SAADE). During the past two summers, he directed NEH-funded Humanities institutes for academically talented high school students from across Georgia.

Professor Hill has published articles in several professional journals, including the *Journal of Negro History, Black Books Bulletin, Arizona English Bulletin* and *Umoja.* He is a contributor to *Blacks and Native American in South Carolina* (1976), founder and editor of the Albany State College *Journal of Arts and Sciences* and a contributing editor to *Contributions of Black Women to America* (1982).